Art and Psychoanalysis

Peter Fuller was born in 1947 in Damascus. He was educated at Epsom College and Peterhouse, Cambridge, where he read English. Since 1969, he has worked as an art critic and writer and contributed frequently to *New Society*, *The Guardian*, *Arts Review*, *Art Forum* and *Art Monthly*.

His books include *The Psychology of Gambling* (with Jon Halliday), *The Champions*, *Robert Natkin*, *Beyond the Crisis in Art*, *Aesthetics after Modernism* and most recently *The Naked Artist*. He has also published a number of short stories.

Art and Psychoanalysis

Peter Fuller

Writers and Readers

Writers and Readers Publishing Cooperative

Published 1980 by
Writers and Readers Publishing Cooperative Ltd.,
144 Camden High Street · London NW1 0NE

Copyright © Peter Fuller 1980

Reprinted 1981, 1983

Designed by Malcolm Smythe

Typeset by
Malvern Typesetting Services Limited in Garamond

Printed and Bound in Great Britain by
Biddles Limited, Guildford, Surrey

Writers and Readers gratefully acknowledge the assistance of the Arts Council
of Great Britain *in the publication of this book.*

ISBN 0 906495 24 5 case
ISBN 0 906495 32 6 paper

To
Charles Rycroft
and
Kenneth Wright
with respect and gratitude

CONTENTS

Acknowledgements

This book is based on a series of four seminars which I gave for the Goldsmith's M.A. Course in Fine Art during the summer of 1979. I am very grateful indeed to Michael Williams who organised the course for inviting me to do this work. I also wish to thank both him, his colleague Richard Wentworth, and my students for their numerous contributions to the lively discussions we had after each paper. These led to many of the revisions and expansions which I have made for this published version.

John Berger read the MS. and made many helpful suggestions. But my debt to him is much greater than that. He once described Frederick Antal as 'the art historian who, more than any other man, taught me how to write about art.' What he said of Antal, I can say of Berger himself. This book also owes a particular debt to Charles Rycroft: some years ago, he urged me to study the work of the British 'object relations' school of psycho-analysis. Thus I became acquainted not just with Dr. Rycroft's own writings, but also with those of Marjorie Brierley, Harry Guntrip, Masud Khan, Marion Milner, and D. W. Winnicott. This book is pervaded by the influence which they have had upon me.

I am also especially grateful to my friends, Anthony Barnett and Andrew Brighton from whom I am continuously learning, and to Kenneth Wright with whom I went through what is one necessary qualification for writing anything worthwhile about psychoanalysis

I also wish to thank Colette, my wife, who read the MS. and detected many of its flaws and who further endured all the narcissistic self-preoccupations involved in my preparation of the text for the press. My editor at Writers and Readers, Lisa Appignanesi also made numerous constructive suggestions, almost all of which I have incorporated; I would like to thank her not only for these, but also for her sustaining enthusiasm for this project.

It is customary to exculpate those acknowledged from any blame; in this case it is necessary to do this firmly rather than formally. This book is, by its very nature, speculative and ex-ploratory. I alone am responsible for any errors it may contain.

Preface

These lectures were originally given at Goldsmith's College under the rubric 'Post-Freudian Developments in Psycho-Analysis and their Relevance to Aesthetics'. They arose out of my growing dissatisfaction with the aridity of much of the current left debate about the visual arts. Here, with a few notable exceptions, the choice offered is that between a crude populism (of the 'Art for Whom?' variety) and structuralism or one of its derivatives. All such positions share a rejection of the category of the aesthetic, *tout court*, or a denigration of it as a manifestation of ideology.

Instead of merely denouncing aesthetic judgements, criteria and experience, I have attempted to ask whether it is not possible to begin to de-mystify them and to reveal their material bases, which lie not only within ideology, but also in the affective potentialities of the human subject, and the material processes in which he or she engages when making a work of art. This mode of inquiry relates to a recent emphasis in Marxism which seeks to stress that even in the midst of their social life, men and women are biological beings, subject to specific limitations, possibilities, and conditions of life which nature imposes upon them, and which are not readily trans-formable through history. Although I do not think that aesthetics are reducible to psychoanalysis, I do feel that it can serve to illuminate significant elements which are not readily reachable through any other discipline.

Psychoanalysis, of course, has many tendencies. The work which has had the strongest influence upon me is that which has been carried out in Britain since the Second World War. I have tried to give at least some indication of the history and development of this school. I consider British 'object relations' theory to have much more to contribute to the study of visual aesthetics than, say, the structural-linguistic models for psycho-analysis proposed in Paris by Lacan and his followers, which are so influential in certain quarters of the art world today. In part, this book is an attempt to insert the theories and insights of the British school into a cultural debate for which they seem to have considerable importance, but in which they have hitherto been largely neglected.

In my first lecture, I attempt to explain the inadequacies of traditional Marxist aesthetics, and their derivatives, and then I elaborate a critique of classical, Freudian, psychoanalytic theory in the light of Freud's study of the Moses of Michelangelo. In the second lecture, I begin by recounting the story of the re-discovery of the Venus de Milo in the early 19th century, and examine some of the many reconstructions of it. I then trace its complex cultural trajectory, but demonstrate that my own earlier attempts to do this in purely sociological terms were inadequate. Kleinian aesthetics enable me to move towards a fuller account of both the aesthetic experience derivable from the Venus, and its exceptional endurance as a cultural phenomenon. In the third lecture, I look at an account which Marion Milner, an object-relations analyst, wrote about lear-ning to draw and paint. I relate her difficulties with perspective to the development of my own 'taste'; Clive Bell's aesthetic theories; the emergence of modernism, and work in object-relations theory on the nature of the infant's experience in the mother-child relationship. In the final lecture, I use the ideas of Winnicott and Bion, respectively, to illuminate the nature of the spatial structures, chromatic effects, and emotional meanings of certain recent American 'Colour Field' paintings—especially those of Mark Rothko and Robert Natkin.

I do not claim to have arrived at answers so much as to have raised questions. This book is exploratory and speculative rather than definitive. My intention has been to open up an area of discussion: I find it necessary to insist upon the 'scientific' character of neither my methods nor my insights.

TWO PRELUDES

Before the hermeneutics, on Freud's 'The Moses of Michelangelo', I wish to make two relatively lengthy statements of a general character. These both have something of an autobiographical complexion, but, as I hope you will soon realise, they are both essential to the argument I wish to put forward. My first prelude is an explanation of why I decided on this particular theme, 'Developments in post-Freudian Psychoanalytic Theory and their Relevance to Aesthetics.' My second is a short account of my own relationship to psychoanalysis.

Let me first explain why I chose this subject rather than, say, 'Art and Politics'. In a recent issue of *London Magazine*, Timothy Hyman categorised me as one of the 'social critics' and claimed that I was demanding 'the politicisation of art'.[1] Now it is true that much of my writing about recent British and American art has stressed political, social, and economic aspects of art production and the way in which such factors are involved in the determination of the character of a work of art and also mediate works of art to their publics. But I do not see how such an emphasis can come to be read as a demand for 'the politicisation of art'.

Indeed, I find it ironic that I should be accused of wanting to 'politicise' art when, under the influence of that provocative Italian Marxist, Sebastiano Timpanaro, I have recently found myself looking very closely indeed at what one of his commentators has called 'the relatively stable biological conditions which are at least elements of much human cultural activity'.[2]

Those who know anything about my work will not need to be reminded of the influence which Karl Marx has had upon me. But one of the problems which he hardly begins to help me with is that implied in the question, 'How can a work of art outlive its origins?' To put it bluntly, if the ideological, political, social and economic mediations of a work are *so* important, how is it that I can walk into the Victoria and Albert Museum, look at a piece of sculpture from an ancient Indian civilisation of which I know next to nothing, and still enjoy it.

Marx was not entirely untroubled by this problem. He devoted some five enigmatic and ultimately unsatisfactory paragraphs to it in his 'introduction' to *A Contribution to the Critique of Political Economy*, written in 1857, but not published during his life-time. He noted that 'In the case of the arts, it is well known that certain periods of their flowering are out of all proportion to the general development of society, hence also to the material foundation, the skeletal structure as it were, of its organization.' Marx then points out that the mythology on which Greek art depends *is* linked to the society which gave rise to them both, so that it would not be possible to produce Greek art in the age of industrialisation, 'self-acting mule spindles and railways and locomotives and electrical telegraphs.' He asks, 'What chance has Vulcan against Roberts & Co., Jupiter against the lightning-rod and Hermes against the Credit Mobilier?' But, he adds, 'the difficulty lies not in understanding that the Greek arts and epic are bound up with certain forms of social development. The difficulty is that they still afford us artistic pleasure and that in a certain respect they count as a norm and as an unattainable model.'[3]

Marx's solution to this problem is hardly convincing; he suggests that just as a man finds joy in the naïveté of a child, the charm of Greek art lies in the fact that it belongs to 'the historic childhood of humanity, its most beautiful unfolding.' He adds:

'The Greeks were normal children. The charm of their art for us is not in contradiction to the undeveloped stage of society on which it grew. (It) is its result, rather, and is inextricably bound up with the fact that the unripe social conditions under which it arose, and could alone arise, can never return.'[4]

This explanation will not do. Admittedly, Marx's primary personal interest was in literature rather than the plastic arts. But one only has to ask whether the pleasure one derives from looking at the Hermes of Praxiteles, or the Venus de Milo, can really have much to do with the perception through them of 'unripe social conditions' to realise the inadequacy of Marx's thesis. Marx's idealisation of Greek civilisation and his characterisation of Greek art as 'an unattainable model' were themselves historically determined: the views he expresses here on these matters were part of the ideological luggage of many 19th century intellectuals. Ernst Fischer has pointed out:

'Today we may doubt whether, compared to other nations, the ancient Greeks were "normal children". Indeed, in another connection Marx and Engels themselves drew attention to the problematic aspects of the Greek world with its contempt for work, its degradation of women, its eroticism reserved solely for courtesans and boys.'[5]

Marx may well have realised that his thoughts on this question did not amount to more than a hopeless aside: after all they are really no more than jottings about a matter which he knew he had failed to resolve, tagged on at the end of an unfinished draft. But the following year Marx wrote the version of the 'preface' to *A Contribution to the Critique of Political Economy* which he did publish. In this text, insofar as they were mentioned at all, 'artistic forms' were listed together with legal, political, religious, philosophic, in short, 'ideological' forms which Marx conceived of as constituting the 'superstructure' which was ultimately determined by 'the mode of production of material life', the economic base, or 'structure'.[6]

I am not about to reject Marx's distinction between 'structure' and 'superstructure'. Certainly, we can now advance a more nuanced account of the relations between the two, of the relative autonomy of components of the latter, of the inter-action of these components one upon another, and upon the structure itself. We can also identify significant elements of social reality which, as we shall see, belong to neither. Nonetheless Marx's differentiation remains useful. But aesthetics were never more than an incidental side-line for Marx. I am convinced that his later formulation on art was retrogressive. For however inadequate the *solutions* in the unpublished version, at least Marx recognised the problem there. In the later text, however, the issues of aesthetic pleasure and of the social and cultural transcendence of certain works of art are simply suppressed: 'artistic forms' become the ideological products of specific structures.

You could, if you wished, exculpate Marx on the grounds that he had more important *political* and *economic* tasks to attend to—and, *up to a point*, you would be right. But my own view is that this lacuna in Marx's thinking was symptomatic of a deeper and more significant evasion, one which was to become exaggerated within most branches of the Marxist tradition, and is today associated with the tragic assault upon the concept of the human subject in Marx's name.

Of course, idealist thinkers among the 19th century bourgeoisie encountered none of the difficulties which Marx and socialist theorists met with in accounting for the pleasure which they derived from the art of the past. For them, great art was great art because it somehow embodied timeless, universal, spiritual truths which remained eternally manifest precisely because they were somehow *above* the vicissitudes of history, where they hovered as spectral incarnations of aspects of some idealised human essence. Thus Walter Copland Perry, a 19th century specialist in Greek and Roman sculpture, once wrote of the Venus de Milo, 'The figure is ideal in the highest sense of the word: it is a form which transcends all our experience, which has no prototype or equal in the actual world, and beyond which no effort of the imagination can rise.'[7] This sort of view could be summed up in the slogan which still sells newspapers for the *Daily Telegraph* today: 'Times change: values don't.'

Left critics have, quite rightly, shown little patience with such arguments. We have seen it as just one more attempt by the bourgeoisie to 'universalise' their own, particular ideology, to turn that which is historically specific into something apparently eternal. It was no accident that Walter Copland Perry produced his eulogy of the Venus in the midst of a *Victorian* neo-classical revival. In his great novel, *A Painter of Our Time*, John Berger makes his hero, a Socialist artist called Janos, write, 'Those who think that art is transportable, timeless, universal, understand it least of all. They put a Hindu sculpture next to a Michelangelo and marvel at the fact that in both cases the woman has two breasts.'[8]

This is all very well, but is it necessarily more foolish in aesthetics to begin from the relative constancy of the human body rather than from the allegedly determinative effects of the 'structure' (in the Marxist sense) on works of art? Have we on the left produced a more adequate account of how a work of art outlives its origins than the 'spiritualist' approach? Interestingly, one of the weaknesses of what is in so many ways such a valuable book—Berger's *Ways of Seeing*—is that it lacks any satisfactory answer to the latter question. In a review of the book, Daniel Read perceptively pointed out that one of Berger's main theses 'challenges the right of established criticism to preserve oil painting for the bourgeoisie' while another of his arguments 'insists that oil painting is the bourgeois art form, bar none.' In other words, Berger posits the European tradition of oil painting as 'the art form par excellence of the social power of the private control of capital', but he does not establish how, if this is so, a socialist can possibly take pleasure in it or why he should worry about the fact that the bourgeoisie has, through its institutions and art writing, effectively sequestered that tradition unto itself.

The problem, Daniel Read suggests, is more apparent than real because Berger does distinguish between 'masterpieces' and the tradition, and, as Read puts it, 'it is only, and exactly, the masterpieces, the works which negate the market of their origin, which can come to life again for a new class through new means of reproduction.' This, he suggests, 'is possible precisely because they are not entirely limited by the social relations that produced them.'[9] But in fact Read's point amounts to a tautology: works of art which transcend the social relations which produced them are masterpieces; masterpieces are works of art which transcend the social relations that produce them. Berger himself accepts that the question remains unresolved. In 1978, he wrote, 'The immense theoretical weakness of my own book is that I do not make clear what relation exists between what I call "the exception" (the genius) and the normative tradition.'[10]

Of course, the terms of this debate have changed considerably since Marx's day. In Britain for most of this century the 'spiritualist' approach has progressively and since the Second World War decisively given way to a 'formalist' viewpoint. This involves the assertion that the aspect of a great work of art which is above history resides not so much in the spiritual values it represents, as in its formal characteristics which belong to a similarly inviolable and transcendent realm of eternal 'quality'. Thus for Roger Fry, the most perceptive of the formalist writers, the 'accumulated and inherited artistic treasure of mankind' was made up almost entirely of those works in which 'formal design is the predominant consideration.' For Fry: 'The esthetic emotion is an emotion about form. . . . The form of a work of art has a meaning of its own and the contemplation of the form in and for itself gives rise in some people to a special emotion which does not depend upon the association of the form with anything else what ever.'[11] Or, as Clive Bell subsequently put it: 'The artist . . . is concerned with a problem which is quite outside normal experience.'[12] Post Second World War formalist criticism in Britain and America was destined to re-state the arguments which Fry had already put more eloquently half a century before.

But the ground of the 'left' analysis has shifted, too. I do not think that anyone is still arguing that the pleasure to be derived from Greek art is explicable along 'historic childhood of humanity' lines. We are much more likely to read that the reason a work of art can be transposed from the social formation of its origins has to do with the fact that it is somehow 'soluble' within our own culture. According to this argument, *Greek* art, and, more especially, Greek sculpture, has not really survived at all. The fragments which still exist physically have been entirely reconstituted and quite literally re-*produced* within the host culture within which they are resurrected. My response to a Greek sculpture has nothing essential in common with that of, say, a 5th century B.C. Athenian.

According to this account, the surviving work is passive and inert. Though malleable within changing historical modes of perception and appreciation, it cannot speak to us. This argument actually has considerable force. The experience of bits and pieces of the Parthenon frieze inside a modern British Museum seems to have precious little in common with the experience of the intact work on the outside of a temple on the summit of the Acropolis at the height of Greek civilisation. Indeed, I have myself elaborated the *relativity* of responses to two notoriously versatile survivors, the Mona Lisa and the Venus de Milo. But I found that there came a point at which this sort of study, though deeply illuminating, also turned out to be highly unsatisfactory because one was left with exactly the same problem one set out with. It was relatively easy to establish that these works had been uprooted from their original contexts, mutilated at the level of signifier and of signified, and used in many different ways as they passed through successive cultures. But why were these specific works (rather than their rivals) able to re-incarnate themselves within one set of mediations after another? I must admit that I was stuck on this problem for a long time. I abandoned the work I had begun on the Venus de Milo because of it. Although I recognised the 'iconic' status these works had achieved as trademarks or tokens for art itself, I nonetheless came to feel that one reason they survived from one culture to another had to do with a residue within them—and a rather plenitudinous residue at that—which did evoke a relatively constant response. Moreover, it did so despite shifts and gyrations in the ideology of successive viewers and variations in the channels through which the works were mediated to their changing publics. Interestingly, this could be identified neither with Berger's transcendent masterpieces, nor with Fry's allegedly culturally resilient 'pure form'. The Mona Lisa, for example, was a formally mediocre work, anything but a masterpiece.

Several factors helped to 'unstick' my thinking on this point. One of them was my encounter with Sebastiano Timpanaro's writing, and later also with Raymond Williams' brilliant critical exegesis of it. Timpanaro is a little known Italian Marxist, a philologist by profession. His work emphasises that Marxism is, first and foremost, a *materialism*. Uncontroversially, he stresses that Marxism was born as an affirmation of the decisive primacy of the socio-economic level over juridical, political and cultural phenomena, and as an affirmation of the historicity of the economy. But he argues that in Marxism in general, and in the Western Marxist tradition in particular, the very strength with which this affirmation was originally made tended to eclipse other crucial components of materialism. He writes:

> 'By materialism we understand above all acknowledgement of the priority of nature over "mind", or, if you like, of the physical level over the biological level, and of the biological level over the socio-economic and cultural level; both in the sense of chronological priority (the very long time which supervened before life appeared on earth, and between the origin of life and the origin of man), and in the sense of the conditioning which nature *still* exercises on man and will continue to exercise at least for the forseeable future.'[13]

Timpanaro criticises recent tendencies in Marxism for evading the issues of man's relatively constant biological condition and of his dependence on nature. He is not a humanist: he rejects anthropocentrism and sees man's relationship to nature to be characterised by elements of passivity, and a cause for pessimism. In any forseeable future, men and women will grow old and die. Timpanaro also envisages an ultimate, if remote, 'natural' end to the human species and the world which it inhabits. It seems, at best, very, very improbable that such things could be superseded even under communism.

(Politically, too, Timpanaro recognises that 'tranquil faith in historical progress as a certain bearer of communism has vanished.')

Now Timpanaro's position seems to have very great relevance in the terrain of aesthetics, and he throws out numerous hints and leads in this direction. He points out that one of the factors that has rendered cultural continuity possible is the fact that 'man as a biological being has remained essentially unchanged from the beginnings of civilization to the present,' and he has no hesitation in referring to certain kinds of art which 'clearly relate to elements of our biological condition, often much more strongly than to elements of our socio-historic experience.' Although of course he admits that the underlying biological condition is mediated by socio-historical experience and its cultural forms, he also—in my view quite rightly—maintains that 'this mediation provides no basis for that still common kind of reduction in which the biological is a mere datum and all effective working social and historical.'

Timpanaro strongly re-affirms the validity of Marx's distinction between structure and superstructure, but he also maintains: 'One cannot help but recognise also that there are *non-superstructural* elements in cultural activities and institutions.' Thus the structure-superstructure distinction, for all its importance, 'becomes inadequate . . . when it is taken as an exhaustive classification of reality, as if there were nothing that existed which was not either structure or superstructure.' Thus Timpanaro writes:

> 'To give a banal example: love, the brevity and frailty of human existence, the contrast between the smallness and weakness of man and the infinity of the cosmos, are expressed in literary works in very different ways in various historically determinate societies, but still not in such different ways that all reference to such constant experiences of the human condition as the sexual instinct, the debility produced by age (with its psychological repercussions), the fear of one's own death and sorrow at the death of others, is lost.'[14]

To put this extremely crudely, one reason why I can spontaneously enjoy Indian temple sculpture, why it can communicate to me actively, and not just as a historical document, despite the vast differences between my religious, social, political and economic circumstances and those of the artists who made it, is that this sculpture vividly and forcefully

celebrates sexual experience which—despite all the manifold
shifts in its cultural mediations—remains very much the same.
Furthermore, to dismiss that experience as a secondary or
contingent aspect of the 'real' religious meaning of the work is
quite plainly to tumble into the notorious idealism of Jung
epitomised in the question perhaps erroneously attributed to
him, 'What is the penis but a phallic symbol?'

Raymond Williams is prepared to go even further than
Timpanaro. In his commentary on the latter, Williams identifies a 'biological' element within the signifiers of art, as well as
within the signified.

> 'The deepest significance of a relatively unchanging biological
> human condition is probably to be found in some of the basic
> material processes of the making of art: in the significance of
> rhythms in music and dance and language, or of shapes and
> colours in sculpture and painting. Because art is always *made*,
> there can of course be no reduction of works of this kind to
> biological conditions. But equally, where these fundamental
> physical conditions and processes are in question, there can be no
> reduction either to simple social and historical circumstances.
> What matters here—and it is a very significant amendment of
> orthodox Marxist thinking about art—is that art work is itself,
> before everything, a material process; and that, although dif-
> ferentially, the material process of the production of art includes
> certain biological processes, especially those relating to body
> movements and to the voice, which are not a mere substratum
> but are at times the most powerful elements of the work.'[15]

It is in this sense, that I am now prepared to concede to the
formalists that—since men and women at all times and in all
places are subject to, say, the same laws of gravity, and possess
roughly the same physical and sensory potentialities—it may be
possible to identify a necessary (though not a sufficient)
component common to all 'good' sculpture which is not subject
to significant historical determination or cultural variation. Art
after all has not shown itself to be subject to progress or to
consistent developmental improvement. It would be merely
foolish to assert that 20th century sculpture was 'better' than,
say, the sculpture of the earliest known civilisation, that of
Sumeria. Even when art *does* seem to have been driven along by
its own autonomous historicism (i.e. in Greek sculpture between the 7th and the 4th centuries B.C. or in American art
between 1945 and 1970), it can often be seen retrospectively

that the impression of progress was illusory. Consistent stylistic innovation does not always correlate with an equally consistent accretion of 'quality'. The best works often come early in such sequences. From all this, I am tempted to conclude that a very important part in what gives a work of art enduring value concerns the nature of its relationship to elements of experience which do not change, or rather which change at a very slow rate indeed and, for our purposes, may effectively be regarded as constants.

It may seem strange that I have begun a discussion of art and psychoanalysis by laying such a heavy emphasis on Timpanaro's contribution. Those who know anything about Timpanaro tend to remember him for his notorious polemic against Freud, *The Freudian Slip*.[16] Timpanaro is no friend of psychoanalysis. Indeed, he attacks it because he believes—quite erroneously as I shall soon demonstrate—that it arose 'in polemical opposition to materialist psychology, and sought to render psychic phenomena independent of anatomical and physiological data.' Timpanaro thinks that psychoanalysis has been 'too concerned to detach psychology from neuro-physiology', and that it is therefore 'permeated with anti-materialist ideology'. He even goes so far as to say: 'It may be that Pavlov will have more to tell us than Freud.'[17] And he perceives a need for psychoanalysis to submit itself to the inductive method and Popperian criteria before it can be accepted as 'scientific'.

In adopting this position, Timpanaro is making the same mistake as Freud—or rather he has accepted too uncritically Freud's own characterisation of the discipline which he founded. Timpanaro designates psychoanalysis as a natural science and then castigates it for not being like one. But what if, in fact, psychoanalysis were a discipline much closer to say philology, of which Timpanaro himself is an expert professional practitioner? I must disclaim any originality in asking this question. The idea that, Freud's own views notwithstanding, 'psychoanalysis is not a causal theory but a semantic one' was forcefully brought home to me by Dr. Charles Rycroft who, a few years ago, pointed me in the direction of so much of what I now think on the theoretical level at least about psychoanalysis. But it is surprising that Timpanaro nowhere shows any sign of having considered this possibility himself. After all, his own work draws attention to representations—e.g. those arising from the sexual instincts, fear of death, mourning, etc.—which, precisely because of our relatively constant underlying biological condition, themselves remain relatively constant, though subject to all manner of particular mediations and vicissitudes. Those representations—or more exactly the ways in which the individual self experiences, organises and sometimes distorts them—are among the objects of psychoanalytic inquiry. With Rycroft, I maintain that such inquiry is pursued within the territory of meaning rather than that of physical causes. Quantities, Popperian criteria, not to mention neurophysiology may be as irrelevant to psychoanalysis as they are to linguistics.

There is however an important qualification to add to this. In his stimulating introduction to *Psychoanalysis Observed*, Rycroft writes:

'The statement that psychoanalysis is a theory of meaning is incomplete and misleading unless one qualifies it by saying that it is a *biological* theory of meaning. By this I mean that psychoanalysis interprets human behaviour in terms of the self that experiences it and not in terms of entities external to it, such as other-wordly deities or political parties and leaders, and that it regards the self as a psychobiological entity which is always striving for self-realization and self-fulfilment.'[18]

This qualification is of very great importance: it indicates why, throughout our discussion, we need have no truck with the Althusserian-Lacanian gnosis which presents itself as a variant of Freudian psychoanalysis, and which is regrettably so prevalent in certain sectors of the art community today. Althusser himself has described Lacan as dispersing 'the temporary opacity of the shadow cast on Freudian theory by the model of Helmholtz and Maxwell's thermodynamic physics' with 'the light that structural linguistics throws on its object.'[19] Althusser is quite right about the need to purge psychoanalysis of its mechanistic legacy. But, as Timpanaro has pointed out, 'Althusser's anti-humanism . . . arrives at a denial of the individual as a *relatively* independent psycho-physical entity—which is no better, despite the scientistic pomposity with which it is declaimed, than the old denial of the empirical ego on the part of idealism.'[20] To believe that there can be a reconciliation between a position of this kind and psychoanalysis is as foolish as to preach 'Christian Atheism'. In my view, the pursuit on which Lacan is engaged has little to do with psychoanalytic inquiry properly understood.

To Rycroft's description of psychoanalysis I only wish to add that the fact that it is a discipline which takes subjectivity, or rather an infinite range of particular subjectivities, as its object evidently means that it is subject to peculiar epistemological problems which do not arise in any other discipline. Nonetheless, the sort of knowledge to which it gives rise could *not* be arrived at say through behavioural observation, investigation of neurones, or exploration of ideology. It may well be that its 'special conditions' preclude it from ever being categorised as one of the natural sciences. Nonetheless, psychoanalysis recognises, indeed constantly emphasises, that the character and limitations of those subjective worlds which it studies and in therapy affects, however varied and diverse they may be, are intimately related to the biology of the human condition. If psychoanalysis is indeed as Rycroft characterises it, 'a biological theory of meaning', it is at once clear how important, indeed how central, it might be to that 'very significant amendment of orthodox Marxist thinking about art' which is beginning to emerge from Timpanaro's and Williams' timely indication of the degree to which the biological has been ignored in much left aesthetics. I have thus chosen this subject in the hope that it will take us at least one step further towards that elusive enigma, the material basis of aesthetics, though I am far from thinking that psychoanalysis can, of itself, provide us with a complete answer.

We will soon be tugging at the beard of the prophet himself but first I must deliver my second much briefer prelude, that concerning my own relationship to psychoanalysis. What I am going to say will be critical of Freud and so I want to state quite bluntly at the outset that he has had more influence on my thought, and not just on my *thought*, than any other writer I have read. For many people Freud is a 'classic', an intellectual dinosaur whom one encounters, if at all, by digging backwards from Sartre, Marcuse, or whatever. But I spent my childhood in a world which seemed somehow hermetically sealed off from post First World War culture and ideas. My father's own intellectual titan was Karl Barth who, though he died as late as 1968, possessed the last considerable, medieval mind to arise within the Protestant tradition. His theological system was often called 'Neo-Orthodoxy', a reaction, provoked by the First World War, against the humanising 'immanence' of 19th century German Liberal Protestantism. Barth engaged in a Kierkegaardian disparagement of human reason and postulated the Unknowable, Unspeakable Otherness, the *mysterium tremendum* of an utterly transcendent God, hidden as much as he was revealed in his one moment of revelation through 'The Christ'. He then devoted some six million words in twelve volumes of *Church Dogmatics* to describing the indescribable. I should be truthful: as a child I only managed to get through a short version, *Dogmatics in Outline*. But my family was much more 'evangelical' than Barth himself. I lived within a *milieu* in which even evolution was not yet a closed issue. At the Sunday School I went to, we were repeatedly shown film-strips about the Piltdown Man, the implication being that all the evidence about evolution had been similarly rigged.

Given this background, my encounter with Freud had at least something in common with that of many of those who came across his ideas for the first time before the First World War. Freud, for me, was a *modern*: he was one of the means through which I was able to come to terms with and in the end to dispose of my 19th century luggage. I read Freud uncritically, with an almost feverish understanding, but without much knowledge of or feeling for post-Freudian ideas.

Early in 1974, Dr. Charles Rycroft wrote to me concerning my first book, *The Psychology of Gambling*,[21] that the problem with my writing at that time was that I, an obsessional, was using the theories of another obsessional about obsessionality to elucidate an obsessional phenomenon. Similarly, Hans Keller, in reviewing a book of mine, *The Champions*, which was written some time ago but only published in England in 1978, praised my knowledge of classical psychoanalysis but went on to say: 'The author knows (and indeed understands) his Freud backwards, priest-like: not only did Freud never utter a wrong syllable, but to quote any theoretical idea at any stage of his complex development is simply to state fact.' There was much truth in this criticism. Keller ventured to elaborate it by saying that he suspected that I had not myself undergone 'the psychoanalytic experience'. He finished his review with what he called the 'climax' of his assault: 'Mr. Fuller either hasn't had it, or his analytic transference situation was never resolved . . .'[22] In making this perceptive observation Keller was, like Freud, too dualistic. There was, of course, a third alternative: that the book was written in the midst of an 'analytic transference' which was *subsequently* resolved. And this was in fact the case. Paradoxically, it was my experience of psychoanalysis itself that helped me to go beyond my 'paleo-Freudian' credulity. Although Freud remains for me a thinker of almost unparalleled stature, I am now acutely aware of limitations and distortions within his thought and of the way in which these relate not just to his particular historical and cultural experience, his moment of history, but also to the effects of his own psychopathology. Freud was the founder of psychoanalysis but he was never himself analysed, at least not by anyone except himself.

These preludes have been Wordsworthian in length if in nothing else, but I hope that their relevance will become increasingly apparent.

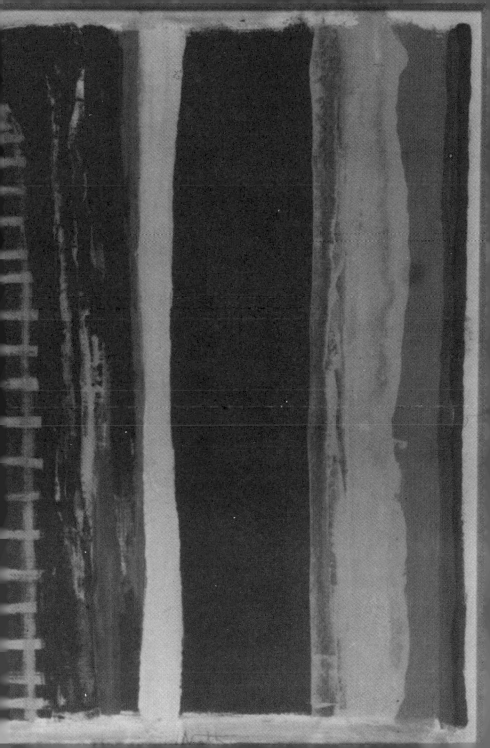

I

MOSES, MECHANISM AND MICHELANGELO

I WANT you to imagine, for a moment, that you are in the Church of San Pietro in Vincoli in Rome and that you are looking as so many have done before you into the face of the Moses of Michelangelo. That expression has been written about so much, subjected to layer upon layer of interpretation. And yet, as you stand there in the cool and gloom of the church, all those words seem irrelevant. You even forget the details and dates which you dutifully read up that morning in the guide-book which you are still holding in your hand. That stony face possesses a tremendous, urgent power. As you look upon it that power reaches you, touches you, moves you *directly*.

Perhaps, after all, you will remember one fact: that the quality *terribilità* was often attributed to both Michelangelo himself, and to Pope Julius II, of whose tomb the Moses forms a part. *Terribilità*: it cannot easily be translated. It is more than the awesome or the sublime. It has much to do with frightening power. It is a word which seems to express exactly the quality which that mighty, marble face, in all its violent serenity, evokes in you. *Terribilità*: as you look, you find yourself thinking of the demonic creativity of the sculptor who carved the statue; of the megalomania of 'The Holy Father' who lies dead behind it; and of the transfiguration of the ancient Hebrew prophet himself through his encounter with 'God' on Mount Sinai. But, in the end, even if you are as thorough-going an atheist as I, it is the idea of 'God the Father' that this face inevitably evokes. More even than the famous Life Giver of the Sistine Chapel ceiling, the expression of Moses seems to be that of the omnipotent, omniscient Primum Mobile himself, the 'Mysterium Tremendum'. His anger is none other than ὀργή, *orgé*, 'The Wrath of God'.

And, as you stand, quietly shuddering in this formidable presence, let me whisper into your ear something about this mysterious *ira deorum*. It is an idea, an image, a representation of a feeling which one finds in many religions. It lies deep at the heart of Judaeo-Christianity. Rudolf Otto discussed it in some detail in the course of his inquiry into 'the non-rational factor in the idea of the divine and its relation to the rational'.

'But as regards the "wrath of Yahweh", the strange features about it have for long been a matter for constant remark. In the first place, it is patent from many passages of the Old Testament

Michelangelo, *Moses* (detail).

that this "wrath" has no concern whatever with moral qualities. There is something very baffling in the way which it "is kindled" and manifested. It is, as has been well said, "like a hidden force of nature", like stored-up electricity, discharging itself upon anyone who comes too near. It is "incalculable" and "arbitrary". Anyone who is accustomed to think of deity only by its rational attributes must see in this "wrath" mere caprice and wilful passion. But such a view would have been emphatically rejected by the religious men of the Old Covenant, for to them the Wrath of God, so far from being a diminution of His Godhead, appears as a natural expression of it, an element of "holiness" itself, and a quite indispensable one.'[23]

Is this not the impression which you receive from the face of the Moses of Michelangelo? That of an anger which is 'a natural expression' or an 'element' of 'holiness' itself? Now I am far from seeking to imply—as Otto does—that a sense of *ira deorum* is an 'irreducible' element of religious experience, an evidence of the autonomy of the latter, and of the reality of its object—'god'. I am, however, suggesting that this statue is somehow supremely expressive of what is a common and yet not readily explicable human sentiment which is often represented through religious forms.

By linking the expression of Michelangelo's Moses with a religious idea, I do not want to suggest that there is anything ephemeral, disembodied, or vacuously 'spiritual' about this statue. This Moses is a man, entirely and utterly a man. There is about him an intense physicality, a sense of irresistible *bodily* strength, which pervades every part of the statue: the enormous head, the great, jutting sweep of the left arm, those huge veined hands, the mighty legs and feet. Even the tumbling whorls of the beard, so often a stylised appurtenance in sculpture, remorselessly emphasise facticity, corporeal being. Michelangelo has deliberately left Moses with the traditional horns which he sports in medieval imagery. He must have known that these were derived from a mistranslation of the Hebrew word for 'rays of light'. But he retains them to emphasise the sensuality, earthiness, perhaps even the sexual potency of his figure.

Admittedly, the high finish of the sculpture may seem far too smooth for you. Perhaps you long for the relative roughness and resistance you get in the battered head of the figure of *Day*, or the tattered breasts of *Night*, on the tomb of Giuliano de'

Medici; or for the overt unfinishedness of the slaves and captives struggling out of their blocks of raw stone. But even though the polish may irritate you as it sends the eye slipping and slithering, it does not deny interiority, solidity or physicality. You are forever pulling yourself up to test the implied strengths and tensions which seem to become manifest through the tautness or slackness of the marble skin, or the way in which hair or drapery cascades.

Indeed, as you continue looking, you begin to realise that, in its own way, the sculpture is as incomplete and as ambiguous as many of Michelangelo's later works. Part of this sense of in-

Michelangelo, *Moses.*

completeness certainly derives from its context. As your eye begins to wander from the compelling figure of Moses to its surrounds, you come to feel that it cannot *belong* where it is. It is not just that Moses is flanked by two of the weakest and most inept figures Michelangelo ever made: those of Rachel and Leah; nor that he is beneath an upper tier cluttered by the flaccid and indifferent work of Michelangelo's assistants. More important even than that is the feeling that he is not at ease in his central position. Why has he swivelled round to his left? This certainly leaves us with a sense of theatre, of an impending moment, or incident which is at odds with both the apparent repose of the figure itself, and the stillness of the grave. If you continue looking, other details may come to worry you too. Did Michelangelo really intend the head to be *so* long and heavy, or the torso *so* violently compressed? You may be filled with a more intuitive response, a sense that for all its awesome power and vigorous physicality something is not *right* with the figure. As you imagine the gestures a good sculpture teacher might make in front of it, you will remember from your reading of the guidebook something of the trials and tribulations that surrounded the making of the Moses.

It was not intended for this site. It belongs to a much more ambitious project for the tomb which Michelangelo never completed. As Howard Hibbard has written:

> 'Michelangelo conceived the figure . . . for a position many feet above our heads that would have changed its entire proportion—the long face would have been foreshortened, the torso telescoped, the feet and left hand partially hidden. In order to produce this optically corrected view Michelangelo, as he himself said on another occasion, held "the compass in his eyes and not in his hands." Preliminary blocking-out may even have been done with the statue lying on its back, which would have given the possibility of seeing the forms from the desired worm's-eye view. . . . Michelangelo understood the problems of perspective diminution, and apparent distortions in the figure of *Moses* chiefly derive from his desire to accomodate the statue to the position of the viewer below. But none of Michelangelo's works is "correct" in proportion; all express his idea of perfection, or struggle, or longing through an anatomy that is based on study but created by art.'[24]

But before I say any more about this statue, let us look at what Freud said about it.

In his paper, 'The Moses of Michelangelo', Freud cites a variety of interpretations of the sculpture prior to his own, and points out that broadly they fall into two groups: those which maintain that Michelangelo intended to create 'a timeless study of character and mood', and those which argue that, on the contrary, Moses was portrayed at 'a particular moment of his life'. Most of the commentators Freud cites favoured the latter sort of reading. Many thought they could identify the particular moment in question as that immediately after Moses had descended from Mount Sinai. As Freud puts it:

> 'Moses has received the Tables from God, and it is the moment when he perceives that the people have meanwhile made themselves a Golden Calf and are dancing around it and rejoicing. This is the scene upon which his eyes are turned, this is the spectacle which calls out the feelings depicted in his countenance—feelings which in the next instant will launch his great frame into violent action,'[25]

an action through which he will 'dash the Tables to the earth, and let loose his rage on a faithless people'. Wolfflin was one of many who held this view. He spoke of 'inhibited movement' and saw the statue as depicting 'the last moment of self-control before (Moses) lets himself go and leaps to his feet'.

But Freud was not convinced. He noted how such accounts often contradicted each other and ignored what he took to be significant details. He points out that the figure was also intended to form one of six on the base of the never-to-be completed version of the tomb of Pope Julius. 'A figure in the act of instant departure,' he argues, 'would be utterly at variance with the state of mind which the tomb is meant to induce in us.' Freud thus fell back on the view that the Moses was a 'study of character'. Nonetheless, he felt that there was 'something lacking' in this interpretation too. Freud felt the need to 'discover a closer parallel between the state of mind of the hero as expressed in his attitude' and the contrast, first noted by others but accepted by Freud, between Moses' 'outward' calm and 'inward' emotion.

Freud then goes on to say that for many years he had known of the work of Giovanni Morelli, an Italian physician who developed a method of authenticating paintings 'by insisting that attention should be diverted from the general impression and main features of a picture' and by stressing rather the significance of minor details like finger-nails, ear lobes and haloes (Morelli, incidentally, is often claimed as the founder of 'scientific' methods of connoisseurship.) Freud likens Morelli's method to psychoanalysis itself which, he says, is also 'accustomed to divine secret and concealed things from despised or unnoticed features, from the rubbish-heap, as it were, of our observations.'[26] He then focuses upon what he perceives as two troubling details concerning Michelangelo's Moses—the attitude of the right hand and the position of the two Tables of the Law.

Freud says that he has 'no illusions' as to the clarity of his description of what is happening to the right-hand, which is just as well, because it is as opaque as the most meticulous descriptive passages in late Modernist, formalist accounts of sculptural detail. Essentially Freud argues that the way the fingers and the strands of the beard are related can only be understood as the residue of a prior movement, or, as he puts it: 'Perhaps (Moses') hand had seized his beard with far more

Drawings after
Michelangelo's *Moses.*

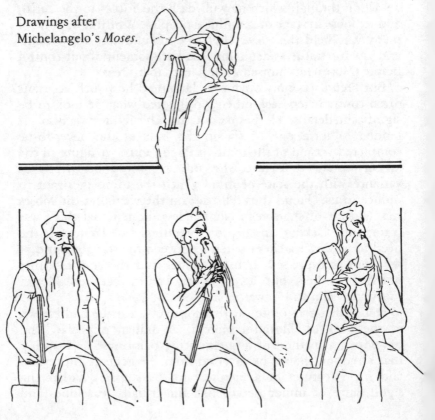

energy, had reached across to its left edge, and, in returning to
that position in which the statue shows it, had been followed by
a part of his beard which now testifies to the movement which
has just taken place.'[27]

Freud then goes on to argue that 'a protuberance like a horn'
on the lower edge of the Tables indicates that they are upside
down, although he maintains, with Thode, that as they are
depicted they are in no danger of slipping. Freud thinks that
the peculiar position of the Tables also indicates a prior
movement. Linking his analysis of the fingers and beard with
that of the Tables, he proposes a *sequence*, which he got an
artist to draw up for him. The first diagram shows Moses sitting
sedately, a calm patriarch with the Tables of the Law held firmly
under his right arm, supported on their bottom edge by his
right hand. The second depicts him after he has seen the
idolatrous Israelites on his left. He is looking towards them in a
state of inchoate rage. The Tables have swivelled upside down,
are in grave danger of crashing to the ground as the hand which
supported them is now grasping the beard in anger. But the
third diagram represents the statue as it is: Moses has drawn his
right hand back across his beard to regain control of the Tables.
He has mastered and overcome his fury, of which only the traces
are left. Thus, as Freud puts it:

> 'What we see before us is not the inception of a violent action
> but the remains of a movement that has already taken place. In
> his first transport of fury, Moses desired to act, to spring up and
> take vengeance and forget the Tables; but he has overcome the
> temptation, and he will now remain seated and still, in his frozen
> wrath and in his pain mingled with contempt. Nor will he throw
> away the Tables so that they will break on the stones, for it is on
> their especial account that he has controlled his anger; it was to
> preserve them that he kept his passion in check . . . He
> remembered his mission and for its sake renounced an indulgence
> of his feelings.'[28]

Freud is evidently delighted with this finding and he sweeps
objections to it—such as the fact that in the Bible story Moses
did let the Tables drop—aside. Michelangelo's Moses, he says,
is 'superior to the historical or traditional Moses'. The sculptor
has 'modified the theme of the broken Tables':

> '. . . he does not let Moses break them in his wrath, but makes
> him be influenced by the danger that they will be broken and
> makes him calm that wrath, or at any rate prevent it from

becoming an act. In this way he has added something new and
more than human to the figure of Moses; so that the giant frame
with its tremendous physical power becomes only a concrete
expression of the highest mental achievement that is possible in a
man, that of struggling against an inward passion for the sake of a
cause to which he has devoted himself.'[29]

The first thing I should make clear is that, in scrutinising this
essay, I have little interest in identifying and elaborating a
specifically Freudian theory of the plastic arts. I want to look at
it from the point of view of my conviction that before we can, as
it were, get good value from psychoanalysis, not just in relation
to art but also to much else besides, then we have to engage in a
thorough-going critique of Freud.

We have good authority for not being too reverential about
Freud's view of art. He himself began the Michelangelo essay by
saying:

'. . . I am no connoisseur in art, but simply a layman. I have
often observed that the subject-matter of works of art has a
stronger attraction for me than their formal and technical
qualities, though to the artist their value lies first and foremost in
these latter. I am unable rightly to appreciate many of the
methods used and the effects obtained in art.'[30]

Even Ernest Jones, who was not over-hasty in identifying any
flaw within his master, begins his chapter on art in his
biography of Freud by saying that both Ernst Kris and Freud's
artist son, Ernst, had counselled him not to write that section
and had given as their reason that 'since Freud had little
aesthetic appreciation there could be nothing worthwhile to say
on the subject.'[31] Needless to say, Jones took no heed of this
advice. He tells us that Freud's enjoyment and appreciation of
the arts—'whether strictly aesthetic or not'—were in this
descending order: 'poetry first, then sculpture and architecture,
then painting, and music hardly at all.'[32]

Freud owned a few pictures: for example, he possessed
engravings by Wilhelm von Kaulbach (1805–74), an artist so
celebrated in his day that he was rated above Leonardo, but
who, as an arid salon painter, is now held in somewhat lower
esteem than Bouguereau or Messonier. He was also a passionate
amateur archaeologist and built up an extensive collection of
statuettes, figurines, and other small antiquities. But here again
it was the subject matter of a piece, above everything else,
which interested him.[33]

Anthony Storr rightly points to an 'uneasy ambivalence' in Freud's attitude towards artists: what he says about them varies 'from denigration to adulation with few connecting links between these opposing points of view.'[34] In one famous passage, Freud described the artist as 'in rudiments an introvert, not far removed from neurosis. He is oppressed by excessively powerful instinctual needs. He desires to win honour, power, wealth, fame and the love of women; but he lacks the means for achieving these satisfactions.'[35] Elsewhere, however, Freud heaped praise on creative writers, in particular, 'for they are apt to know a whole host of things between heaven and earth of which our philosophy has not yet let us dream. In their knowledge of the mind they are far in advance of us everyday people, for they draw upon sources which we have not yet opened up for science.'[36]

Contrary to the popular conception of the 'Freudian' theory of art, Freud himself often asserted that aesthetic experience and such pleasures as those which are to be derived from contemplation of plastic form were *not* susceptible to psychoanalytic inquiry. He once wrote that psychoanalysis 'can do nothing towards elucidating the nature of the artistic gift, nor can it explain the means by which the artist works—artistic technique.'[37] Because he, personally, was unmoved by such things, he projected them beyond the parameters of psychoanalytic research. In general, he seems to have seen form as the sugary coating, a seductive or coquettish inducement, a mere fore-pleasure to the enticements of content. In a letter to Jones of 1914, written after spending an evening in an artist's company, Freud wrote: 'Meaning is but little to these men; all they care for is line, shape, agreement of contours. They are given up to the *Lustprinzip*.'[38]

Despite such unpromising positions, Freud did make a significant contribution to *literary* aesthetics through his book, *Jokes and Their Relation to the Unconscious*. The importance of this has been thoroughly elucidated elsewhere.[39] Suffice it to say, there is not even a hint or an echo of this work in Freud's text on the Moses. Indeed, those who make or enjoy sculpture today are likely to be impatient with Freud's method in this text—but *not* because there is anything specifically psychoanalytic about it. We are simply not very sympathetic to the idea that one should stand in front of a work and seek to unlock its 'secret' before one can even begin to appreciate it.

Nonetheless, Freud's 'Moses of Michelangelo' is a revealing document, revealing if not about the Moses, or Michelangelo, or 'Art', then most certainly so about the man who wrote it. I want to start by contrasting Freud's Moses with his even better known study of Leonardo, which he wrote some three years earlier. Apart from scattered references and certain letters, these are the only texts of Freud's in which he turned his attention to the visual arts. They could hardly be more different: the way in which they differ leads us to an important insight concerning Freud himself.

You will remember that the Leonardo study begins with a detailed examination of the artist's adult, emotional life. Freud is evidently fascinated by the conflict between Leonardo's artistic and scientific interests, which he studies in the light of the painter's psychosexual history. For example, Freud relates Leonardo's notorious tardiness in completing his projects to inhibition. He points out that although Leonardo surrounded himself with elegant young men, he appears to have remained sexually chaste. Freud's argument is that Leonardo's curiosity had been aroused in infancy in the service of his sexual instincts, and that he had subsequently succeeded in sublimating the greater part of his libido into an urge for research, but that his sublimations had become affected by the inhibitions exerted against their underlying sexual impulses.

Freud then tries to clarify these character traits of Leonardo's in the light of a reconstruction of his infancy which Freud based, as it turned out peculiarly unhappily, upon an 'infantile reminiscence' which he presumed Leonardo to have recorded. Freud believed this read, 'when I was still in the cradle a vulture came down to me, he opened my mouth with his tail and struck me a few times with his tail against my lips.'[40] Freud says the vulture scene was not a memory but rather a fantasy which Leonardo had formed at a later date and transposed to his childhood. The fantasy concealed a reminiscence of suckling, or being suckled, which had been transformed by the adult into a disguised, passive, homosexual fantasy.

Freud supports this interpretation with a lengthy speculative excursion into Egyptology which yokes such things as the vulture-headed goddess, called Mut, and *Mutter*, the German word for mother. This is a graceful and dazzling piece of writing, but, even without the blunder which we will come to in a moment, it involves exactly the sort of imaginative intuitions which caused many to say that psychoanalysis was something other than a natural science. Nonetheless, by the end of his book, Freud had managed to convince himself that 'the key to all (Leonardo's) attainments and failures was hidden in the childhood phantasy of the vulture.'[41] An over-enthusiastic disciple of Freud's even detected the 'undeniable' outline of the vulture in Leonardo's painting of *Saint Anne*.

Freud himself connected the vulture fantasy with key biographical details concerning Leonardo—especially his illegitimacy and the absence of a father in his infancy. Freud refers to certain obscure legends concerning the insemination of female vultures, in the absence of males, by the winds. He uses such points to bolster his argument that throughout his life Leonardo remained tied to his mother, as he had done in infancy, by an erotically coloured feeling, and that this tie determined his homosexual tendencies and his sexual reticence alike. Insofar as he discusses Leonardo's paintings at all Freud introduces them as just another item in Leonardo's symptomology. For example, he relates the blissful smile, so characteristic of Leonardo's figures—and especially, of course, of the Mona Lisa—to the painter's feelings about the look of his mother's face.

As is today well known, all this was vitiated by the fact that the infantile reminiscence on which Freud had placed so much emphasis was a mistranslation. Leonardo had not written about a vulture, but about a kite. Worse still, there is evidence to suggest that from 1923 onwards, Freud knew this and made no attempt to admit he was wrong and revise his text. When the vulture is extracted the entire Egyptian excursion and much of the intermeshing fabric of speculative interpretation which he offers melts away leaving, appropriately, but the bare bones of the argument. All this has given rise to a voluminous literature. Without engaging in the cretinous hagiography of those who even went so far as to write books to 'prove' Freud was right,[42] I nonetheless feel that the point could and has been polemically over-played. Freud might just as well have chased a winged hare, but despite this I suspect that his overall characterisation of Leonardo—especially of his homosexuality and relationship to his mother—is not a wild fabrication.

Psychoanalytically, the Leonardo text is of theoretical significance not just for the account which it gives of the origins of one variety of homosexuality, but also for the introduction of a concept that was to become central in subsequent psychoanalytic theory: narcissism. Nonetheless, it is pretty well useless from the point of view of aesthetics. As Edmund Wilson has pointed out, Freud does not try to account for Leonardo's creative abilities, his 'genius'; nor does he have anything to say about what constitutes aesthetic value.[43] Leonardo's paintings are treated very much as if they were 'worth' the same as the disguised sexual fantasy. The Leonardo study is, as Wollheim has put it, 'primarily a study in psycho-analytic biography: and the connexion with art is *almost* exhausted by the fact that the subject of the biography happens to be one of the greatest, as well as one of the strangest, artists in history.'[44]

The *Moses* is, of course, quite a different sort of study. This is apparent even from the *form* of the two papers; Freud's Leonardo is, if nothing else, a consummate piece of writing, whereas there is something stuffy, pedantic and academic about the *Moses*—especially in its interminable citing of prior authorities. But one of the most conspicuous features of the latter is the way in which Freud seems consciously to evade offering *any* psychoanalytic arguments concerning Michelangelo or his work.

This is all the more surprising because there is an abundance of material relating to Michelangelo's life, and a clear correspondence between his psychobiography and the manifest themes of his painting and sculpture. I am sure I have no need to remind you that Michelangelo came from a family that had once been noble but which had come down in the world. As an infant, he was put out to nurse with the wife of a Florentine stone-cutter. His mother gave birth to three more boys but died when he was six. His father, who lived off a dwindling inheritance, was a boorish and aggressive idler. He furiously opposed his eldest son's wish to become an artist—but Michelangelo was soon supporting his father and brothers through his earnings from sculpture. In 1512, Michelangelo wrote his father a letter which gives the flavour of their relationship:

> 'I live meanly . . . with the greatest toil and a thousand worries. It has now been about fifteen years since I have had a happy hour; I have done everything to help you, and you have never recognized it or believed it. God pardon us all.'[45]

Michelangelo's professional relationships were clearly inflected by his family history. His attitude towards his patrons—especially the magnificent Pope Julius II—was characterised by marked ambivalence. In 1505, Julius commissioned Michelangelo to make an almost incredible tomb for him: it was to be on three levels, with 40 figures, and to be finished in five years. Pope and sculptor then entered into a tempestuous relationship: Michelangelo oscillated between masochistic self-abasement—he once appeared before the Pope 'with a rope around his neck' to plead forgiveness—and arrogant defiance; Julius between munificent patronage and sadistic tyranny. Julius compelled Michelangelo, against his will, to paint the Sistine ceiling; despite frequent contractual revisions and fresh designs, Michelangelo proved quite unable to produce the tomb. The saga dragged on long after Julius' death in 1513. Finally, in 1545, Michelangelo was released from his obligations through the hotch-potch we can see in San Pietro in Vincoli today. This was largely the work of assistants; only the Moses and the two weak supporting figures are by Michelangelo.

Michelangelo was, of course, a homosexual. If Leonardo was the painter of the blissful maternal smile, then Michelangelo was the sculptor of the male body in struggle, of paternal power, and the father-son relationship. Many of his best known images—David, God creating Adam on the Sistine ceiling, the representations of the prophets, the slaves, the Moses, and the Son of Man returning in the *Last Judgement*—spring from this nexus. At different moments of his life, the focus of Michelangelo's interest shifted from son to father and back again. The male nude became for him *the* instrument of expression: he was notoriously uneasy with the unclothed female body. Thus the haunting statue of *Night* is transparently that of a youth with female elements less than lovingly added on. The convention by which Renaissance sculptors generally worked their female nudes from male models cannot provide a sufficient explanation of this work, especially when one remembers that towards the end of his life Michelangelo developed an impassioned spiritual obsession for a religious woman, Vittoria Colonna, whom he described in a poem as 'A man, a god rather, inside a woman.'[46] The sub-theme of Michelangelo's iconography—as manifested in the *pietàs* and sculptures of the Virgin and Child—is that of his longing for the lost or absent mother.

Now I have raised these details about Michelangelo *not* in order to make anything of them from a psychoanalytic viewpoint myself—that has already been both well and badly done by others—but rather to point out how strange is Freud's silence on all this. Even if he had ignored those questions of form, aesthetic value, and the artist's relationship to his techniques and materials which caused him, personally, such difficulties, it would not have been hard for Freud to have sketched the kind of psychobiographic portrait of Michelangelo that he had done of Leonardo. The Moses could have provided compelling evidence in any such study: even those who do not give psychoanalysis a second thought admit that the sculpture involved a fusion of elements concerning Michelangelo's conception of himself and his feelings about his powerful patron.

In general, Freud tended to ignore the infant-mother relationship; at least, for him it was eclipsed by the father-son constellation. And yet, although, unlike Leonardo's, Michelangelo's life was redolent with those themes which concerned him most—paternal omnipotence, filial ambivalence, the Oedipal struggle against the father, its repression and consequences—Freud remains silent about these matters. Why?

You will recall that in his characterisation of Leonardo, Freud showed himself to be fascinated by the contradiction between the painter's 'artistic' and 'scientific' interests. Freud attributed ultimate victory to the latter. It has often been recognised that Freud's Leonardo paper contains many autobiographical inflections and distortions. As Jones puts it: 'One has a strong impression that Freud's interest in (Leonardo) was partly personal, since he dwelt on many aspects, for instance the passion for natural knowledge, that were equally true for himself.' Without elaborating this, I want to suggest—and it is a gross simplification that we will have to qualify later—that the *method* in Freud's Leonardo paper corresponds to Freud's 'creative', 'imaginative' or 'artistic' self-conception, whereas that pursued in the 'Moses' can be linked to his 'objective' or 'scientific' aspects. There is even some justification for this view in what Freud himself said about these two works. For example, Gombrich makes this comment on the Leonardo study:

> 'It comes as a relief to the sceptical historian to read in Freud's letter to the painter Hermann Struck (November 7th, 1914) that he regarded it as "half a novelistic fiction"—"I would not want you to judge the certainty of our results by this sample."' [47]

Whereas when Freud wrote of the work he had done on the

'Moses', he stressed how it was based on measurement, observation, and empirical study:

> 'I studied it, measured it, and drew it till I arrived at that insight which nevertheless I only dared to express anonymously in that paper. Only much later did I legitimise this non-analytic child.'[48]

This distinction between the two texts can be supplemented by another suggested, but not elaborated, by Wollheim who writes:

> '. . . if the Leonardo essay concerns itself with expression in the modern sense—that is, with what the artist expresses in his works or with Leonardo's expressiveness—then the Michelangelo essay is concerned with expression in the classical sense—that is, with what is expressed by the subject of the work, or the expressiveness of Moses.'[49]

Within the art community today the word 'expression' is used so loosely that we tend to forget what a precise discipline it once tried to be. Alberti, writing in the early 15th century, was the first theorist to specify expression as one of the necessary branches of knowledge for a painter. He argued that since good painting affects the spectator because he responds to the emotions he sees depicted, an artist should thoroughly study how to render emotions by means of gesture or facial expression, i.e. physiognomy. Leonardo agreed: he, too, stressed the importance of showing the emotions and ideas in a person's mind by means of close study of the musculature of the face. Expression, for both Leonardo and Michelangelo, had its roots in the rigorous study of human anatomy. They were among those Renaissance artists who learned most by dissecting corpses with a scalpel. Expression retained this sense until late in the 19th century. One of the later treatises on it, and one of the most 'scientific' was Darwin's *The Expression of the Emotions in Man and Animals* of 1873. Darwin, however, no longer sought to address himself to artists: he even used photographs rather than paintings as illustrations to his arguments. By this time, developments in classical expression were largely made within the scientific tradition.

One can, however, detect the beginnings of the modern theory of expression among fine artists as early as the 1880s. The term 'expressionism' seems to have entered Germany from France in 1910, where it first received extensive usage in connection with the *Die Brücke* painters, active between

1905–13; later it was used to signify virtually the whole modern movement in the arts in Germany and Austro-Hungary between 1910 and 1924. Expression in this sense referred to the artist's capacity to render his own subjective feelings apparent through his colours and forms: it still had a bodily basis, but this became the unseen body of the artist himself rather than his objectively perceived subjects. Thus, in Abstract Expressionism, the basis of expression is manifested through such phenomena as scale, rhythm, and simulation of somatic processes. Scientific anatomy has virtually no relevance to it.

Freud's 'Leonardo' may have been published at the height of *Die Brücke* German Expressionism, and it may have concerned itself 'with expression in the modern sense'; nonetheless we can be in no doubt that Freud would not have welcomed this connection if it had been put to him. In June 1920, Oscar Pfister (who 'saw' the vulture in *Saint Anne*) sent Freud his book, *The Psychological and Biological Background of Expressionist Paintings*. Although Pfister was sympathetic to the Expressionist movement—and indeed was analysing an Expressionist artist—he saw the Expressionist painter as 'an autistic, introvert type, imprisoned in his own repressions'.[50] Freud wrote back to Pfister that he liked the book very much, but added:

> '. . . I must tell you that in private life I have no patience at all with lunatics. I only see the harm they can do and as far as these "artists" are concerned, I am in fact one of those philistines and stick-in-the-muds whom you pillory in your introduction. But after all, you yourself then say clearly and exhaustively why these people have no claim to the title of artist.' (21st June, 1920)[51]

Freud's Michelangelo text came *after* his Leonardo book; we might say therefore that the Michelangelo is, in some sense, a conscious or unconscious repudiation of interest in the new concept of expression in favour of the old.

When Wollheim originally drew this distinction, he warned that it was over-simple, and indicated that it was significant that there had been a '*continuous* theory of expression in European aesthetic'.[52] Thus the old physiognomic approach to 'expression' is present in a residual form in Freud's Leonardo text, i.e. in his discussion of the 'blissful smiles' on the faces of Leonardo's figures. (Similarly, as we shall see in our last seminar, it may be that even the Abstract Expressionism of recent American art never quite severed itself from physiognomic expressiveness.) In the Michelangelo, too, the new concept of 'expression' may make a fleeting entry when, as Wollheim himself has noted, at the beginning and at the end of his essay, Freud 'endeavours to link, though without saying how, the physiognomy of Moses with an intention of Michelangelo.'[53]

I want, now, to return to my own distinction—that between Freud's Leonardo text as 'half a novelistic fiction', representative of an 'artistic' impulse in Freud (or, if this does not overcomplicate matters, expressive of himself as author) and the Michelangelo as a 'scientific' document, purporting to offer 'objective' knowledge concerning a specific object in the world. I have already said that this is a gross simplification. Gombrich, for example, has argued that in Freud's 'Moses', we are 'fully back in the tradition of 19th-century art-appreciation.' Freud, he maintained, had an approach 'to art that characterised the most cultivated "Victorians" of Central Europe.'[54] In the tradition of the 19th century what was called the 'spiritual content' of a work of art came first, and Freud was firmly within this tradition since, 'he always took it for granted that what we must seek in the work of art is the maximum psychological content in the figures themselves.' Gombrich puts forward the view that, in Freud's paper, 'Michelangelo's statue is approached in the same way in which Winckelmann or Lessing approached the *Laocoon Group* or Goethe the Last Supper by Leonardo.'[55] At first sight, this is not reconcilable with my characterisation of the Michelangelo text as 'scientific'.

Wollheim, however, has suggested that, though Gombrich's account is essentially correct, it should not be taken 'too definitively'. He points out that Freud compares his method of art analysis with that of Giovanni Morelli, and that it was Morelli 'more than anyone else who brought the notion of "spiritual content" in art into disrepute.'[56] Admittedly, Wollheim goes on, Morelli's objections were not against spiritual content as such, but against appeals to it in identification and attribution. Nevertheless, Wollheim comments, 'once Morelli's method had been applied to determine authorship, the old idea of spiritual content had received a mauling from which it could not hope to recover.'[57] Wollheim maintains that Freud is at least as interested in the way in which the spiritual content of a work of art is made manifest as in the spiritual content itself. I, however, would put it this way: although Freud is clearly seeking, as Gombrich asserts, 'maximum psychological content' in the figure itself, he is equally intent upon using a maximally 'scientific' method of making that psychological content manifest—hence his adoption of Morellian, or at least Morellianesque, methods.

Others have prised Freud's methods even further away from the early 19th century spiritual modes of analysing a work of art and claimed, I think convincingly, that Freud's interpretation is 'cinematographic': i.e. the very way in which he looks at the Moses and perceives it as forming part of a 'readable' continuum of events suggests that his perception has been

Edweard Muybridge, *Running Man*.

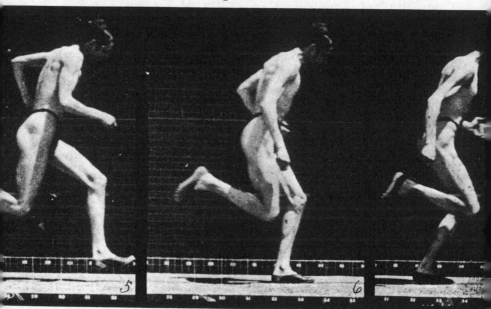

conditioned by the photograph. [58] (As a matter of fact, we know that Freud had a number of photographs of the statue specially made for him so that he could refer to them while he was writing.) Indeed, it is reasonable to raise the question as to whether Freud could have arrived at this reading of the Moses but for the work of Eadweard Muybridge in the 1880s. Muybridge's accurate, sequential photographs of men, women and animals in movement slowly changed the way a number of works of art were seen and interpreted. For example, the Discobolus of Myron was commonly held in the early 19th century to be an exact representation of 'the moment of rest that precedes the throw', but photography of discus throwers in action revealed that they never passed through the position adopted by Myron's model: it is rather a synthesis of several distinct positions, a sculptural representation of a sequence.

As we have seen, Freud not only likened his way of looking at the Moses to Morelli's: he further compared Morelli's method with psychoanalysis itself. Wollheim seems to me much too uncritical in his acceptance of this latter analogy. Although, evidently, there is some truth in it, I feel that the divergences between Morelli's method and psychoanalysis are much more striking than anything they have in common. It is worth stressing that Morelli was a physician, not a psychoanalyst: his connoisseurial method was as closely related to his diagnostic, clinical practice as Freud's approach to Leonardo had been to his. When he adopted Morellian techniques, Freud endeavoured to realise the 'maximum psychological content' of Moses *not* through anything like the 'free association' which got him into such trouble in the Leonardo study, but rather through a very physical examination of the statue's stony body. He examines 'expression', one might say, as Darwin did in *The Expression of the Emotions in Man and Animals*, and not as he, himself, did in the Leonardo.

Wollheim refers to Freud's 'somewhat self-conscious attention to trifles, to measurement, and to anatomical detail' as characteristic of the Morellian method he pursues in 'Moses'; but the 'attention to trifles' which Freud also stressed seems to me not so much a feature of a general correspondence between Morellian method and psychoanalysis as an aspect of the correlation between the former and empirical scientific method which psychoanalysis also happens to share. Psychoanalytic techniques involve no 'measurement' and precious little attention to 'anatomical detail'. These are ways in which psychoanalysis can be distinguished from Morellian methods and 'scientific' medicine alike. A patient in psychoanalysis is not examined according to anything like the method Freud used to produce his 'non-analytic' child, 'Moses'; he rather lies back on a couch and produces his 'infantile reminiscences'.

When Freud first published his Moses essay he did so anonymously. Morelli originally wrote under the false name Ivan Lemolieff. This leads Wollheim to raise what he calls 'the intriguing but quite unanswerable question whether the anonymity of the Michelangelo essay might not have had as one of its determinants an unconscious rivalry with Morelli.'[59] You are probably beginning to feel that my rivalry with Wollheim is so pronounced that it cannot possibly be unconscious. But at the risk of leading others to trace a vulture where there is not even a kite—or, perhaps more pertinently, of building a bridge where there is none—let me say that behind Freud's association of himself with Morelli in this paper, I detect a ghost with a 'terrible gaze':[60] that of Ernst Brücke. Let me explain.

Freud seems first to have come across Morelli's papers when they were translated into German between 1874 and 1876. At this time, Freud, as a 20 year-old biology student, first entered Ernst Brücke's Institute of Physiology in Vienna: he worked there between 1876 and 1882, or 1883. Even when Freud was an old man he said that Brücke had made a deeper impression on him than any of his teachers. 'Brücke,' as Jones puts it, 'was an excellent example of the disciplined scientist that Freud felt he should aim at becoming.' Brücke was a mechanist: indeed, he had been one of the circle of pupils who gathered around Johannes Müller, the father of 'scientific' medicine in Germany.

Müller himself believed that there was something in vital processes which did not admit of a mechanical or material explanation. In effect, he was still a vitalist. But he urged that such explanation be pushed to the limit, 'so long as we keep on the solid ground of observation and experiment.'[61] But, for his pupils, the 'limit' seemed to disappear altogether: they were forever measuring the unmeasurable. The most prominent of these pupils was Hermann von Helmholtz, a man whom Freud was to describe as 'one of my idols'. Helmholtz saw physiology as an extension of physics; indeed, many of his discoveries in physics were derived from his work with the bodies of men and animals. His great physical doctrine of the indestructibility of energy arose out of his study of the heat generated in muscle. Helmholtz believed adamantly, even fanatically, in 'the measurability of all phenomena'. In 1852, he used a pendulum myograph to measure the velocity of the nerve impulse in a frog: it turned out to be 20 metres a second. Only twelve years before his teacher, Müller, had declared that such a measurement would *never* be possible.

Philosophically, Helmholtz and his circle were opponents of *Naturphilosophie* and vitalism which had plagued German science in the first half of the 19th century. 'Our generation,'

Helmholtz wrote, 'has continued to suffer from the thraldom of spiritualist metaphysics. The younger generation will doubtless have to protect itself against the thraldom of materialist metaphysics.'[62] If, as Wollheim put it, Morelli had given 'spiritual content' in art the mauling from which it could never recover, Helmholtz and his circle chased vitalism and its derivatives out of science, and especially out of medicine.

Helmholtz was appointed Professor of Physics in Berlin, in 1871: his circle used to joke that Brücke, in Vienna, was 'Our Ambassador in the Far East'. Helmholtz's notion of the conservation of energy seemed to have rendered possible a quantitative consideration of *all* the processes of metabolism: this, in effect, was Brücke's life-task. In 1874—at the same moment that Morelli's papers first appeared in German translations—Brücke published his lectures on Physiology. These had an unprecedented impact upon the young Freud.[63] Brücke's method became for him *the* model: as we shall see, he later longed to produce a parallel psychology. Brücke stresses that living organisms are phenomena of the physical world: systems of atoms, moved by forces, according to the principle of the conservation of energy. The sum of forces remains constant in every isolated system.

Brücke was a scientist, not a physician: in Vienna, however, he was very closely associated with a group of practitioners of his own generation known as 'The New Vienna School'. These men were imbued with the ideology of mechanism, indeed, some were certainly under the 'thraldom of materialist metaphysics'. Dietl went so far as to announce that a physician must be judged not by the success of his treatment so much as by the extent of his knowledge. 'As long as medicine is art,' he said, 'it will not be science. As long as there are successful physicians there will be no scientific physicians.'[64] Many of these doctors held to 'therapeutic nihilism'. Skoda liked to say that he looked on his patients as objects of research and investigation. As for treatment, he would say, with a shrug, '*Ach, das ist ja alles eins.*' As one authority put it:

> 'This set a bad example. The humane or psychic side of medical treatment was entirely ignored, and a diagnosis confirmed by a post-mortem came to be a sort of shibboleth in Vienna, and snap diagnoses (*Schnell-Diagnosen*) the fashion, even among practitioners who could not have differentiated the pitch and tonality of a heart-sound from a band of music.'[65]

We know, for example, that the Viennese physician, Rokifansky carried out 30,000 autopsies in his own life-time.

Brücke himself was not indifferent to art. His father had been a successful portrait painter and maker of historical pictures. Indeed, in 1846, Brücke had taken up an appointment as a teacher of anatomy in *Akademie der Künste*, the art academy in Berlin. Like Helmholtz—who, as is well known, invented the opthalmoscope and investigated colour vision, especially the sensation of tone—Brücke was intrigued throughout his life by questions of vision, optics, and pictorial representation. Even before he started teaching anatomy in the Berlin art academy, he had published a significant paper on the luminosity of the eye. Later, however, in a much more comprehensive way than Morelli (who was, by comparison, a mere attributor or diagnostician), Brücke toyed with the idea of establishing the material bases of art.

For example, in 1878, soon after Freud had joined him as a student, Brücke published *Bruchstücke aus der Theorie der bildenden Künste*—which was translated into French and published in the same volume as Helmholtz's lecture on *Optics and Painting*.[66] An issue which troubled not just Brücke, but many of his colleagues and followers, was that of the perception of movement through its static representations. Brücke wrote an essay on this subject in 1881 (which again Freud as one of his most faithful pupils would most certainly have read) in which he incorporated Muybridge's demonstration that artists had always wrongly depicted the position of the legs of running horses.[67] Photography was of considerable interest to Brücke's circle. Spector has pointed out how Sigmund Exner, Brücke's assistant who spent his life trying to apply Helmholtzian principles to the study of the nervous system and the mind, approvingly cited Charcot's use of photographs to diagnose certain types of neurosis in his book, *Physiologisches und Pathologisches in den bildenden Kunsten*, of 1889.[68] This is an example of the continuation of a science of expression based on anatomy to which I referred earlier. But it was Brücke himself who in a book which was published within a few months of his death in 1892, took up the cudgels on behalf of the old science of expression within the fine art tradition itself.

Brücke explains at the beginning of *The Human Figure: its beauties and defects* that his purpose is to 'combat erroneous tendencies in the representation of the human body.' The artist, he maintains, ought 'to know the defects of the human body just as a judge of horseflesh knows the weak points in the build of a horse.' Not that Brücke advocated an absolute mimetic fidelity to nature:

> 'No one ever knew so well as Michelangelo Buonarroti how to produce powerful and strangely harmonious effects by means of figures in themselves open to criticism, simply by his mode of placing and ordering them and of disturbing their lines. For him a figure existed only in his particular representations of it; how it would have looked in any other position was a matter of no concern to him. On this account, and not merely by reason of any necessary failure all round, did the tendency to imitate, or even go beyond, Michelangelo proved so fatal to artists of a lesser calibre.'[69]

Brücke argued that the ancients had had 'daily and hourly contemplation' of the human form, whereas, 'we moderns . . . are driven to rely on our anatomical knowledge to guide us among the manifold variations of structure with which we have to deal.' Brücke hoped that his book would be of some assistance to artists, but, he warned, 'No one knows better than an anatomist like myself that perfect insight can only be gained by studying the dead subject scalpel in hand.'[70] Brücke's book, with all its accumulation of detail about what does and what does not constitute a beautiful neck, fore-arm, or breast, seems to us to belong to another world; and so, in a sense, it does. It is one of the last significant instances in Europe of the attempt to root artistic expression materially in observed anatomy.[71]

Let me make my point clear: 'The Moses of Michelangelo', uniquely among Freud's mature writing, makes no reference to psychoanalysis except to liken it to Morelli's 'scientific connoisseurship'. In fact, Freud's method in this paper is *not* really like psychoanalysis, although it is very close indeed to that way of looking and thinking about art and much else besides advocated by Freud's first teachers. Brücke, of course, would not have approved of psychoanalysis. As Jones puts it, 'he would have been astonished, to put it mildly, had he known that one of his favourite pupils, one apparently a convert to the strict faith, was later, in his famous wish theory of the mind, to bring back into science the ideas of "purpose", "intention", and "aim" which had just been abolished from the universe.'[72] I am suggesting that Freud's identification of himself with Morelli in this context was a disguised identification of himself with Brücke's methods, and that it was further the expression of his wish to render psychoanalysis less like the speculative, 'spiritual', 'half-fictional' excursions characteristic of, say, the Leonardo text, and more like the apparent 'scientific certainties' to be reached through Brücke's mechanistic optic, and Helmholtzian physiology. In other words, the Moses text admits of 'intention', and indeed seeks out 'maximum psychological content' (as psychoanalysis did) but endeavours to do so within the infrastructure of a scientific methodology based on anatomy, measurement, and objective observation. This was not like psychoanalysis, although it was the way Freud wanted it to be.

He made that clear at many points in his life. His work with Brücke was on the histology of nerve cells: he studied such things as the spinal ganglia of the Petromyzon, a species of fish. Freud did well at the Institute, found favour with the reserved and authoritarian Brücke, and appears to have intended to spend his life on neuorological research. Brücke himself, however, warned Freud that his 'restricted material circumstances' would prevent him from pursuing a theoretical career. He therefore reluctantly decided to become a clinical practitioner.

Freud longed to remain faithful to what he had learned at the Institute. Brücke died in 1892, and the great Helmholtz in 1895. The following year Freud sketched out a *Project for a Scientific Psychology*, which was not published during his life time. The *Project* is based entirely on Helmholtz-Brücke principles. When it came to light in 1950, it had a comparable effect in Freud studies to the *1844 Manuscripts* in Marx's case. It irrevocably changed our conception of Freud's work. The *Project* opens with the words:

> 'The intention of this project is to furnish us with a psychology which shall be a natural science: its aim, that is, is to represent psychical processes as quantitatively determined states of specifiable material particles and so to make them plain and void of contradictions.'[73]

What follows has been described as psychology 'under the cloak of brain physiology'.[74] More recently, and more controversially, however, the *Project* has been seen as an unequivocally neurophysiological document.[75] Without going into which of these two positions is correct, we can say that it was only with the greatest reluctance that Freud abandoned the attempt to correlate psychology with the physiological functioning of the brain. As Wollheim has said, the model proposed in the *Project* casts a 'long shadow', and I believe a distorting shadow, over much of what Freud subsequently wrote. There was no clear 'epistemological break' in Freud, any more than there was in Marx; this is what makes comments like Timpanaro's, that psychoanalysis arose 'in polemical opposition to materialist psychology', little better than ill-informed nonsense. (In parenthesis, one might add that it was not just psychoanalytic *theory* that Freud sought to caste in a Brückean framework. His therapeutic practice too—some would say with detrimental

Ernst Von Brücke

results—was reflective of New Vienna School traditions. Freud liked to emphasise that, first and foremost, he was a *scientist*, although he doubted whether his 'lack of a genuine medical temperament' had done much damage to his patients: 'They are best helped if [the analyst] carries out his task coolly and keeping as closely as possible to the rules.'[76] Nonetheless, he constantly worried about whether the therapeutic element in psychoanalysis was not compromising the discipline as a science. In later life, he criticised his own earlier attitudes towards technique, admitting that he had overstressed the 'negative' side.) 'The Moses of Michelangelo' then can be seen as a metaphorical plea on Freud's part—or at least an unconvincing attempt to demonstrate—that psychoanalysis was like the old 'science of expression', rooted in the concrete facts of anatomy, rather than the new.

So I have drawn my vulture out of the *method* Freud uses in 'The Moses of Michelangelo', but I now wish to introduce a new and more specific element: that is a correspondence between the physiognomy of Brücke, his facial expression, and that of the statue of Moses with its terrifying gaze. Freud's interest in the statue was a long one. Although he did not visit Rome until 1901, Freud was almost certainly familiar with the plaster cast in the Vienna Academy of Art long before that. Jones tells us that on his first visit to Rome, Freud went to look at the statue many times. Although he once wrote to his wife that he had come to understand the statue by contemplating Michelangelo's intention, he could not, however, have been referring to the interpretation he finally arrived at since he also reported that, as he looked, he expected Moses to start up at any moment.

Throughout his life, Freud had what amounted to an obsession with Moses. The theme crops up again and again in his writing. In the last years of his life he became immersed in the writing of *Moses and Monotheism*, which he once described in similar terms to those which he had used about the Leonardo study as 'an historical novel'. *Moses and Monotheism* embodies a decidedly odd reconstruction of Jewish history: Freud argues that Moses was an Egyptian, who converted the Jews to monotheism but was later murdered by them. Freud's Moses theme led Jones to ask, 'Did (Moses) represent the formidable Father-Imago or did Freud identify himself with him?' He answers, I think correctly, 'Apparently both, at different periods.'[77]

Brücke was certainly a 'formidable Father-Imago'. As Jones puts it, 'Freud always spoke . . . of his respect and admiration for this unchallenged authority, sentiments which were also tinged with awe.'[78] But Jones also tells us that, on his first visits to the statue in 1901, Freud 'used to flinch at the angry gaze as if he were one of the disobedient mob'. From that one must suppose,' Jones writes, that, at this time at least, 'Moses stood for the angry Father-Imago, with perhaps the glare of Brücke's formidable eyes.'[79] This is a reference to the fact that when Freud was a student of Brücke's, he was once late and was reprimanded by the magisterial professor. Freud reported himself 'overwhelmed by the terrible gaze of his eyes', and later admitted that the image of those steel-blue eyes would re-appear at every moment in his life when he might be tempted to any 'remissness in duty or to any imperfection in executing it scrupulously.'[80] Jones further suggests that Freud's first en-counter with the statue was mediated by the fact that, in 1901, Freud was being angrily rejected by his then father substitute, Wilhelm Fliess. Fliess was an associate of the Helmholtz circle with whom Freud had had an intense and emotional in-tellectual correspondence between 1895 and 1900; Freud had confided the draft of his *Project* to Fliess, and much else besides. But all Freud's attempts at effecting a reconciliation were in vain. Something of all this seems to remain in the 'Moses of Michelangelo' paper, which Freud wrote in 1913, and where he recalls that sometimes he has crept into the half gloom of San Pietro in Vincoli 'as though I myself belonged to the mob upon whom his eye is turned—the mob which can hold fast no conviction, which has neither faith nor patience, and which rejoices when it has regained its illusory idols.'[81]

Nonetheless, Jones is undoubtedly correct when he remarks that it is not possible to avoid the 'pretty obvious conclusion' that, in the 1913 paper, Freud had 'identified himself with Moses and was striving to emulate the victory over passions that Michelangelo had depicted in his stupendous achievement.'[82] Being somewhat less credulously sycophantic than Jones, I would make the slight amendment—the victory over passions which Freud *thought* Michelangelo had depicted. In any event, there can be no shadow of doubt that when Freud wrote such things as that Moses 'remembered his mission and for its sake renounced an indulgence of his feelings', or, especially, described the statue as 'a concrete expression of the highest mental achievement that is possible in a man, that of struggling against an inward passion for the sake of a cause to which he has devoted himself', it was he, Sigmund Freud, whom he had primarily in mind—and the cause whose Tables seemed in danger of slipping was none other than that of psychoanalysis itself.

I now want to look more closely at the context in which Freud wrote this paper. Freud was in Rome during the summer of 1912, and, as he had done more than ten years previously, he began to make repeated visits to San Pietro in Vincoli to look at

his beloved Moses. At this time he began to formulate the
interpretation which he was to elaborate in his paper. When he
got back to Vienna, Freud immersed himself in 'Moses'
research. He had special photographs made focusing on those
details crucial to his argument, but he also began to doubt his
own judgement: he came across certain Donatello statues which
raised the possibility that the pose was 'a purely artistic one
without any special ideational significance.'[83] Freud then seems
to have shelved his Michelangelo material for a full year. In
September 1913, however, he returned to it again, and this
time reported that he was absolutely convinced of his reading.
He wrote the text between Christmas of that year and New
Year's Day. However at first he only allowed it to be published
in the psychoanalytic press anonymously, describing it as a
'joke', and saying, 'Why disgrace Moses by putting my name to
it?' (Later, he was to toy with the idea of publishing *Moses and
Monotheism* anonymously, too.)

Unless Freud had some peculiarly urgent psychological
reasons for doing so, it is almost impossible to explain why he
spent so much time and energy on his 'joke', his 'non-analytic
child' at this time. This was a moment of crisis for psychoanalysis, of acute, organisational splits, fissures and dissen-
sions, and also of severe theoretical turmoil within Freud's
own development. You only have to look at the other texts
Freud was working on at the time he was involved with his
Moses paper to demonstrate this. One was the *History of the
Psycho-Analytic Movement*, which, despite its innocuous
sounding title, is a tendentious and polemical document which
Freud wrote to denounce the errors of Adler, and especially
those of Jung (who was then in the process of splitting from
him) and to lay down the history and the law of 'orthodox'
psychoanalysis. The other text which he produced at this time,
however, was his paper 'On Narcissism', the single most important revision that he had introduced into psychoanalytic
theory since its inception and one which even the over-loyal
Jones admitted was 'disturbing' enough to produce 'bewil-
derment' among the early analysts. 'On Narcissism,' Jones
says, 'gave a disagreeable jolt to the theory of instincts on which
psychoanalysis had hitherto worked.'[84] He writes that when the
early psychoanalysts read it, it was at once plain to them that
something would have to be done about the theory to which
they were accustomed.

Thus in 1913, it was not just that Freud felt that Adlerians and Jungians were going after the golden calf—although Freud did write of Jung's work that 'a new religio-ethical system has been created, which, just like the Adlerian system, was bound to re-interpret, distort or jettison the factual findings of analysis'[85]—but also that Freud felt that his own grip on the tables of the law was loosening. The importance of this theoretical crisis in the interpretation of the Michelangelo text cannot be over-emphasised. As Mannoni comments, before 'On Narcissism', 'one could believe that Freud had only to polish an already established theory, defend it, or even invent myths to illustrate it.'[86] After 'On Narcissism', everything was in flux.

I would now like to look very briefly at these two questions separately, that is, at the theoretical crisis which was gnawing at Freud at this time, and also at the organisational crisis which was associated with, but distinguishable from it, and to indicate the relationship between these crises and the method which Freud employs in the Moses text, and also the findings he arrives at through that method.

In 1897, following his father's death, Freud entered upon his historic 'self-analysis', the testimony to which was *The Interpretation of Dreams*, published in 1900, and effectively the world's first psychoanalytic book. Its chapter on general psychological theory, incidentally, is a modified version of the *Project*. In the years immediately following, Freud successively published his work on parapraxes (slips, errors, etc.), jokes, infantile sexuality, and on the meaning of neurotic symptom formation: indeed all the terms and concepts (with the exception of the 'id' and the 'super-ego') by which Freud is popularly and vulgarly known belong to the period 1900 to 1914.

Ernst Kris has written, 'Freud's ideas were constantly developing, his writings represent a sequence of reformulations, and one might therefore well take the view that the systematic cohesion of psycho-analytic propositions is only, or at least best, accessible through their history.'[87] Certainly, there is a great deal of subtle shifting, new discovery, revision, and rejection even in Freud's early psychoanalytic texts. Nonetheless it remains true that, until 1914, the theoretical psychological model which underpinned them all was very similar. Freud assumes a fundamental distinction—that between two different modes of mental functioning, the primary processes and the secondary processes. The primary processes were those modes of mental activity characteristic of the unconscious: primary process thinking manifests such techniques as symbolisation, displacement and condensation (as seen, for example, in dreams). The primary processes, in Freud's view, were characterised by the activity of the sexual instincts, and made use of a highly mobile, libidinal energy, which was free and unbound. The primary processes were held to be governed by the pleasure principle: i.e. the impulses deriving from them constantly sought to reduce tension within the psychic apparatus through spontaneous and immediate discharge.

Secondary process thinking, however, was characteristic of the ego; it involved logic, rationality, grammar—and especially, of course, verbalisation. Secondary process thinking made use of bound energy, and was characterised by structure, and the activity of the ego-instincts. These, Freud never described in any detail, but they roughly correspond to the biological concept of 'self-preservative' instincts. The secondary processes were governed by the reality principle, which caused the ego to seek to reduce instinctual tension in adaptive rather than potentially dangerous ways, since, evidently, immediate discharge of primary process impulses would be disastrous for the organism. The important point is that Freud believed that the psychic apparatus—the very term is indicative—worked to reduce the level of excitation within itself, to avoid tension. Its goal, if you like, was quiescence, or, to be more exact, the maintenance of a low and constant level of internal tension. I will have a little more to say about this model later: for the moment, I would merely remind you that it is based very closely indeed on the thermodynamics of Helmholtz—who was the first to elaborate the distinction between free and unbound energy—and on such physiological concepts as homeostatis, or rather its conceptual precursor, Fechner's 'Constancy Principle'. 'The problem', to quote from Guntrip, 'however, is not whether psychic life has an organic foundation. It has, and no one seeks to dispute that. The question is whether psychic development and functioning, particularly in the human person, can be understood solely from the organic end, and explained in neurophysiological terms, or whether it needs a new terminology appropriate to itself and belonging to a new science that does not, and cannot, operate on the same lines as the so-called natural sciences.'[88] That was a problem which, during those early years of heroic psychoanalytic discovery, Freud never raised.

The 'bewildering' revision which Freud made in his 'On Narcissism' paper (which, you will remember, had had its theoretical precursor in certain passages of the Leonardo text), and which distressed even the most faithful of his followers, was that he snatched the biological function away from the ego, and turned it, too, into a libidinal derivative, a 'vestige of past identifications'. The old distinction between an instinctive unconscious and a purely defensive ego momentarily vanished in Freud's work, and, as Mannoni puts it, Freud's closest followers 'could not accept the idea that this ego, which in effect succeeded the ancient reason, was also a figure of fantasy, an imaginary object, a mirror of mirages—and the agent of madness at least as much as that of reason. Even today, not everyone has accepted it.'[89]

Freud did not hold to the essentially monist position outlined in 'On Narcissism' for long; by 1920, he had fully elaborated a new, dualistic, instinctual opposition—as we shall see. But the moment of 'On Narcissism', a text on which he was working at the same time as the 'Moses of Michelangelo', was, it might be said, the beginning of the end of the heroic period of confident, classical, orthodox, psychoanalysis. ('Now . . . that the ego itself was to be regarded as libidinal, were not the critics right from the start when they denounced Freud's tendency to "reduce everything to sex"?' Jones asked. And what had happened to Freud's previously integral notion of the psychic conflict between two groups of instincts? 'These and similar questions,' he says, 'were thronging in our minds as the great war broke out, and Freud was not able to give any answer to them until after its termination.'[90]) Jones was well aware that 'there was for Freud a security in knowledge of the anatomy and physiology of the nervous system.' (Characteristically, we find Freud writing in 1894 of a wish to 'return to my old pursuit and do a little anatomy' which he regarded as 'scientific' and providing a necessary check on 'speculation'.) 'It was,' Jones writes, 'a long time before Freud brought himself to dispense with the physiological principles of his youth. In a sense he never did entirely . . . a good deal of his later psychology was modelled on them.'[91] But in 'On Narcissism' the 'speculative', 'psychological' investigations moved him further than ever before away from that Helmholtzian model which he held so dear. No wonder that he felt that the tables of the law were slipping away from him. No wonder, too, that through his text on Moses, he endeavoured to deny that this was the case, by 'proving' that he had a firm grasp upon them and, at least metaphorically, rooting psychoanalysis once more in the 'scientific' methodology of his teachers.

Freud wrote 'On Narcissism' under theoretical pressure: the paper—as the editors of the Standard Edition of Freud's work put it—'trenches upon the controversies with Adler and Jung':

'Indeed, one of Freud's motives in writing this paper was, no doubt, to show that the concept of narcissism offers an alternative to Jung's non-sexual "libido" and to Adler's "masculine protest".'[92]

'On Narcissism' was written more or less simultaneously with _The History of the Psychoanalytic Movement_, a text which Freud inscribed with the motto, _Fluctuat nec mergitur_. (It is tossed but does not sink.) In 1911, Freud had effectively driven Adler out of the psychoanalytic movement: the theoretical difference between them was that, in Freud's view, Adler was reducing the significance of libido, 'too much interested in surface psychology and the concept of the ego,'[93] and placing too great an importance on the determinative factor of aggression. Soon after Adler had gone, however, Freud ran into difficulties with Jung. Anyone who thought these controversies were primarily determined by 'scientific' differences would be deluding themselves. Guntrip uses a common comparison when he writes, 'the early history of psycho-analytic theory . . . reads, at times, more like an account of the struggles in early Christian history of the orthodox to defend the true church against heretics and schismatics than an account of a scientific movement.'[94] In order to complete our analysis of the 'Moses of Michelangelo' paper, it is now necessary to refer to Freud's organisational difficulties at the time he wrote it.

Jung began his association with Freud in 1907; Jung came from the bastions of Swiss psychiatry, and as such, was, as one psychoanalyst put it to Roazen, 'to be the Joshua destined to explore the promised land of psychiatry which Freud, like Moses, was only permitted to view from afar.'[95] In addition, Jung was also Freud's first prominent gentile follower, and one of the first who came to him from overseas. Freud had often voiced his fear that after him, psychoanalysis would degenerate into a sect among Viennese Jewish intellectuals. Jung was, in Freud's eyes, a sort of St. Paul who could give him the universality he craved. Freud doted on Jung, who, nineteen years younger than the founder of psychoanalysis, became like a son to him. Freud deluged Jung with letters and manoeuvred him into high office in the growing psychoanalytic institutions and organisations: in Roazen's apt phrase, he cultivated him as the 'Crown Prince', or heir apparent of the psychoanalytic movement. In his turn, Jung reported a 'religious' devotion to Freud, which worried him profoundly as it made him fear 'apostasy'.

Tensions between the two men became apparent early on. One problem was that Jung was interested in religion, mythology, mysticism, and the occult. As it happened, Freud shared these interests—but he was highly ambivalent about this whole territory. (In Freud's attitude to occultism, Jones detected 'an exquisite oscillation between scepticism and credulity.'[96]) Equally, however, Freud endeavoured to isolate these interests, to keep them away from his psychoanalytical 'findings', until he was sure that he had found a material explanation for them: 'you should not for a moment suppose that what I put before you as the psychoanalytic view is a speculative system. It is on the contrary empirical,' he once wrote. Freud, like many obsessionals, placed a tremendous emphasis on 'science' and 'rationality', and he dreaded any contamination with mysticism. It is no coincidence that Freud seems to have begun his intellectual life as a pantheistic adherent of *Naturphilosophie*: then, even before arriving at Brücke's Institute, he had become 'a radical materialist' so fanatical in his affiliation that he almost became involved in a duel with a philosophical opponent.[97] There is no doubt that he felt extremely threatened by Jung's speculative interests. In their correspondence, Freud can often be seen to be urging Jung away from such preoccupations towards the firmer ground of the neuroses.

There were other difficulties too: Jung loathed the organisational work which Freud foisted on him. Freud was further given to interpreting Jung's dreams and actions as indications that he harboured death wishes against him. This mode of argument, though frequently employed by Freud, was not conducive to good personal relations since, of course, to deny the interpretation was to confirm it even more decisively than if one accepted it. This is not to say that there was not any truth in

Freud's observations: Jung was, by all accounts, an exceedingly ambitious man. Nonetheless, it is worth underlining the fact that Freud's self-analysis, on which so much of his psychoanalytic theory was built, was far from being wholly effective: his obsessional character formation was, to put it mildly, pronounced. Not only did he evade critical areas of experience— such as his own relationship to women, from his mother through to his wife—but he was plagued by neurotic symptoms and thoughts until the end of his days. One of these was a tendency to fainting fits.

In 1909, Jung once started talking to Freud about certain 'peat-bog' corpses. Freud became distressed, accused Jung of wishing him dead, and had a fainting fit. After 1910 relations between the two men deteriorated rapidly. By 1912, the rift between the Swiss and Freud's group was apparent to the whole movement. At a psychoanalytic Congress in Munich, Freud bitterly accused Jung and Riklin of 'writing articles expounding psychoanalysis in Swiss periodicals without mentioning his name.'[98]

Abraham, a loyal and talented supporter of Freud's faction, then delivered an over-appropriate paper about the ancient Egyptian, Amenophis IV. Amenophis had wiped his father's name off the ancient monuments and had also founded a new monotheistic religion: Abraham linked the two as manifestations of Amenophis' father complex. This irritated Jung, who defended Amenophis against the charge of parricidal intentions, and argued that many other Pharoahs had eliminated their father's names from the monuments without founding a new religion. Jung claimed that Amenophis had had genuine religious motives. Freud would appear, affectively at least, to have interpreted Jung's remarks in the light of the prior dispute about plagiary, and Jung's position within the psychoanalytic movement. In any event, Freud slid off his chair in a dead faint, and was carried into an adjacent room where, upon waking, he remarked, 'How sweet it must be to die.' Jung reports that when Freud half came to 'he looked at me as if I were his father.' He said he would 'never forget the look he cast at me.'[99]

We need only remind ourselves of the fact that it was precisely at the time of these extraordinary events that Freud— who believed that Moses was also an Egyptian and a founder of monotheism among the Jews—was having difficulty in formulating his idiosyncratic reading of Michelangelo's Moses;

according to Freud's reading Moses was *not* about to be carried away by emotion upon perceiving that the Israelites, under Aaron, had founded a new religion, but had rather constrained his rage and held tight to the tables of the law which the historic Moses, in fact, had let drop. (The confusion of identification implicit in this material about who, for Freud, was father and who was son, may not be wholly projections of Jung's, but may also be reflective of that ambivalence which, as we have seen, characterised Freud's attitudes towards Father Imagos.) Of his fainting, Freud admitted to Jones that 'some piece of unruly homosexual feeling' was at the root of the matter.

From this point on relations between Freud and Jung became appalling; their letters became increasingly involved with poking at each others symptoms. In 1913, Jung finally had had enough: he went into open rebellion against Freud, and wrote him the sort of letter sons dream of sending their fathers:

> 'I am objective enough to see through your little trick. You go around sniffing out all symptomatic actions in your vicinity thus reducing everyone to the level of sons and daughters who blushingly admit the existence of their faults. Meantime you remain on top as the father, sitting pretty. For sheer obsequiousness . . .'

and look at Jung's wording!

> '. . . nobody dares pluck the prophet by the beard and inquire for once what you would say to a patient with a tendency to analyse the analyst instead of himself. You would certainly ask him, "Who's got the neurosis?"' [100]

Jung said that he was no longer going to be taken in by Freud's 'tricks' and that he would 'start telling you in my letters what I really think of you.' Freud broke off relations at once. He met with Jung only once more, at a psychoanalytic Congress in autumn 1913. Back from this Congress, Freud himself finally managed to pluck the prophet by the beard: the secret of Michelangelo's Moses became clear to him, as he simultaneously drafted his 'History of the Psycho-Analytic Movement' and his 'On Narcissism'. No wonder it seemed to him that Moses had kept his 'passion in check' and 'remembered his mission' for the sake of a 'cause' to which he had devoted himself.

The official accounts of these events, especially that to be found in Jones's hagiographic biography, dwell upon the

theoretical differences between the two men. The problem, at
this level, was really that Jung was a vitalist (i.e. his fundamental philosophical position corresponded to that which
Brücke-Helmholtz had, in Freud's view, banished forever).
Jung held that 'no psychological fact can ever be exhaustively
explained in terms of causality alone; as a living phenomenon,
it is always indissolubly bound up with the continuity of the
vital process, so that it is not only evolved but also continually
evolving and creative.'[101] He questioned Freud's opposition of
libidinal to ego instincts, and saw creativity as the result of the
denial of other human capacities than the sexual; he believed
that the neurotic *chose to make* a particular use of his past,
rather than that his present actions were determined, or wholly
determined, by that past. It is true that soon after leaving
Freud, Jung went down a bizarre and unintelligible path.
However, Roazen, whose brilliant biography, *Freud and his
Followers*, is an essential antidote to Jones, seems to me absolutely correct in writing, 'Few responsible figures in
psychoanalysis would be disturbed today if an analyst were to
present views identical to Jung's in 1913.'[102] I also agree with
his observation that, although Freud's essay 'On Narcissism'
was an attempt to establish an alternative to Jung's asexual
libido, 'Freud included so much in his concept of narcissism
that to a modern reader it may be difficult to understand how
Freud is really differing from the monism of which he accused
Jung.'[103]

The point is that Jung was insisting upon an aspect of
psychoanalysis quite incompatible with that neuro-physio-
logical model on which Freud was constantly struggling to
base his 'science'. But that incompatibility was *not* something extraneous which could be banished by getting rid
of Jung. Nigel Walker has pointed out that Freud's use of the
concept of homeostasis, through his hypothesis that 'the
nervous system is an apparatus having the function of
abolishing stimuli' is the unifying concept in psycho-analysis
which links together the wish-fulfilment explanation of dreams,
the defence mechanisms of the ego and the repetition com-
pulsion.[104] But, whatever its value in biology, homeostasis as a
metaphor (and, Freud's longings notwithstanding, it could
never be more than a metaphor) of psychological processes is at
best of very limited validity. Am I then advocating abandonment of Freud's mechanism in favour of Jung's monistic

vitalism? Of course not. But, as Donald MacKay has put it:

'When a computer is set up to solve an equation, there are at least two distinct ways—two sets of terms—in which we can explain its behaviour. First, to the electronic computer engineer, on the one hand, a complete explanation is possible in the language of electronics, whereby the working of every transistor can be accounted for without ever mentioning the equation being solved. On the other hand, to the computer user, the whole performance is equally clearly determined by the equation he has set up and its boundary conditions. But, of course, any idea of a conflict here would be ridiculous. The two explanations in terms of physical causation and mathematical determination are not rivals, but are logically complementary.'[105]

MacKay goes on to say:

'There are good grounds for arguing that exactly the same holds good for explanations of human behaviour both in physical terms of brain mechanisms and in personal terms of motives, thoughts and choices. To argue "it wasn't you who chose, but your brain" would be as absurd as to claim that a computer's behaviour was determined not by the equation it was solving but by the currents in its circuits. Each explanation in fact reveals a true and important aspect of the situation which is ignored in the other. Both mental and physical categories of explanation are needed in order to do justice to the mysterious unity we call a human person.'[106]

Although, evidently, the psychological stands in a specific relation to the neurophysiological, the search for as direct a correspondence as fascinated Freud, is as foolish as to seek a direct correspondence between the mathematical equation, and the computer circuitry. There are many respects in which the analogy with which Freud worked got him into insoluble difficulties. As Guntrip points out:

'Freud arbitrarily equated unpleasure with increase, and pleasure with diminution, of excitation, without taking into account the *total situation* of the satisfaction of a need in and for object-relationship. . . . If tension *qua* tension were unpleasant in itself and the aim were simply its reduction, then any method of relieving excitation would be as good as any other, i.e. autoeroticism would be as satisfactory as object-love and much more easily come by.'[107]

This is an argument to which we will have reason to refer once more in our later seminars.

Why did Freud cling to this unsatisfactory model? The answer is implicit in what I have already said. In part, his affiliation was culturally determined. Freud was trained within a milieu of a mechanistic 'scientific materialism'. Now, as must be clear from what I have already said, I am myself a thorough-going materialist: I have much more respect for the outlook and achievements of Helmholtz and his school than is fashionable today when *both* modern science *and* 'Western Marxism' are deeply penetrated by idealist tendencies. Nonetheless, Helmholtz himself predicted the thraldom of materialist metaphysics, and there is no doubt that in the hands of some of his followers, his ideas became a faith, an ideology, as John MacMurray calls it 'a theology of science',[108] according to which that which was not measurable, which could not be reduced in the end to the laws of physics, was not true and possessed no reality. (The disregard for the whole person and his feelings was not, of course, only characteristic of Freud: I have already indicated how such attitudes pervaded New Vienna School medicine.) But I do not think that Freud's craving for a neurophysiological substructure to his psychology was only a culture phenomenon: it had much to do with his particular psychological make-up. For example, Dr. Charles Rycroft has suggested to me that Freud's insistence on the Constancy Principle, the homeostatic concept that the psychic is always pressing towards a state of minimal excitation and virtual quiescence, relates to his tendency to neurotic fainting fits. (Similarly, Guntrip argues that, 'it cannot escape notice that the propounder of the theory of a death instinct was all his life preoccupied with thoughts about death'.)[109] And, of course, our text, 'The Moses of Michelangelo', manifests a similar distortion: the 'scientific' method of Morelli, and beneath it, that of Brücke and Helmholtz are deployed, but to what end? Towards a fantastic, and idiosyncratic reading of the Moses, which tells us more about Freud's subjectivity than it does about the statue itself.

There is, of course, a wider context to the 'Moses of Michelangelo' text, which was hinted at in the observation of Jones that the problems raised by 'On Narcissism' were thronging in the minds of psychoanalysts as the great war broke out. It is platitudinous to point out that this war was a water-shed in the history of Europe and that it marked a cultural

Marcel Duchamp, *Nude Descending a Staircase*, 1912.

transformation which extended far beyond the narrow limits of the psychoanalytic community. At this moment of history the very polarity on which Freud had based his life and work between 'science' on the one hand, and 'speculation' on the other, between the 'rational' and the 'irrational', seemed to be dissolving in that bloody conflagration which engulfed Europe between 1914 and 1918. At this time, the dreams of the Enlightenment, of the progressive 'liberal' bourgeoisie—to the pessimistic flank of which Freud belonged—were rudely extinguished. The opposition between the old methods of

Freud's teachers, and the irrational, no longer seemed to hold good.

Take one small example: that of aesthetics. Freud's teachers had painstakingly studied the basis of static representation of movement in the laboratories, using sequential photographs: then, suddenly, all that seemed swept away. That nude descended her staircase in her own way in 1912: art and the empirically perceived, 'objective' world seemed about to part company. Even Cubism involved the quest for an entirely new system of representation. The old science of expression, based on anatomy, physiognomy, and empirical observation of nature, seemed to have reached its moment of dissolution. (Whether or not it *had* become culturally irrelevant is a point to which we will return.)

Similarly, the old physics, which for Freud had been that unreachable ground-bed of certainty, the 'truth' with which he wished someday to reconnect his psychoanalytic inquiry, itself seemed to be melting away. There is, it is true, something a bit glib about the way in which Fairbairn and others have accused Freud of having a 'pre-Einsteinian'[110] scientific formation, which twisted the model he used as metaphor for the mind; I am mindful of the innumerable appeals to the 'New Physics' by idealists of every persuasion. Nonetheless, Fairbairn's point is essentially true. The Newtonian scheme did propose a dualism of matter-time-space against 'force', so that physics aimed at one all-embracing law which should explain all things as reducible to matter in motion under the influence of force, or energy. This was part of Helmholtz's quest, and, inevitably, of Freud's psychological thinking. But, of course, with the 'New Physics' even this seemingly irreducible dualism withered away.

I have no doubt that all this is reflected, albeit in a remote and mediated way, in Freud's pivotal but problematic text, 'On Narcissism'. Here, for the first time, Freud theoretically dissolves the rational ego into the maëlstrom of libidinal irrationality. Here, Freud abandons that dualism which was so characteristic of his thought before and after this moment. 'On Narcissism' is foreshadowed in passages of the Leonardo text; again, we can see how it was that when Freud came to write 'The Moses of Michelangelo' at about the same time as 'On Narcissism' he symptomatically expressed his wishful commitment to the old 'scientific' materialism of the 19th century, to Helmholtzian physiology and Brückean tables of the law.

Whatever else it may or may not be, I am convinced that the paper—the only mature text of Freud's which makes no mention of psychoanalysis except to make an improbable connection between it and Morelli's 'scientific' connoisseurship—was an attempt on Freud's part to deny the role of psychoanalysis in the dissolution of the old 'theology of science', the old mechanistic physics, the old aesthetics, and the old 'Enlightenment'-derived ego itself.

Ernst Gombrich has written that it would be a mistake to underrate the force of tradition in Freud's choice of the Moses of Michelangelo: 'If there is any work of art that the cultured Jews of Central Europe adopted, it is this vision of the Hebrew leader.'[111] Nonetheless, there were several aspects and attributes of the Moses which made it, as it were, a peculiarly suitable receptacle for Freud's projections. I am not just referring to the fact that Michelangelo's statue sprung out of a comparable nexus of Father-Son conflicts, of confused attitudes of identification with and submission to omnipotent paternalism and triumphant filialism. (We can be certain of one thing: 'some piece of unruly homosexual feeling' entered as much into Michelangelo's Moses, as into Freud's fainting fit.) Beyond all that, and more significantly, the Moses was also carved by someone standing on the pivot of a cosmological upheaval. Michelangelo was, to the end of his days, an over-pious Christian, the artist, par excellence, of Christian cosmogony and Christian eschatology. Simultaneously, he was perhaps the most prominent exemplar of Renaissance 'humanism', an artist, if ever there was one, of 'Man', struggling to become the subject of his own history, of 'Man', actual, physical, corporeal, concrete, from the imaginative perception of whose this-wordly body Michelangelo's art sprang.

There remains an important question: 'Is Freud's interpretation of the Moses of Michelangelo correct?' I do not think that it is. Spector is not alone in pointing to a drawing for the Julius II tomb which indicates that, originally at least, Michelangelo intended that Moses should be depicted staring straight ahead, with each hand supporting its respective Table from the top edge.[112] This was a common enough conventional pose for the Hebrew leader. Although not conclusive, the drawing lends weight to the argument that the positioning of the figure was determined by formal considerations. Spector is convincing when he suggests that Michelangelo 'intended none of the kinds of subtleties Freud speculated about' but put Moses in this position because of the overall placement of figures on the platform of the middle tier of the tomb. Moses was to sit at the right-hand corner: it thus seems probable that Michelangelo twisted the conventional type round to its left for visual reasons.

Nonetheless, there remains a sense in which we are likely to find ourselves indifferent to the accuracy or otherwise of Freud's interpretation. We do not feel that, even if it were true, it would take us anywhere near the peculiar strength of this figure. Wherein does that reside? That is a question which we have not even begun to answer here, but it will recur in connexion with another sculpture, the Venus de Milo. For the moment, I would merely leave you with the idea that, in the hands of someone with Michelangelo's exceptional sensitivity to his medium and materials, the old science of expression did *potentially* enable an artist to produce an enduring representation, which transcended his own time. Ideology is infinitely labile: the underlying 'human condition', at the level of anatomy and biology, remains relatively constant. Furthermore, Michelangelo used the expressive potentialities of stone in relation to anatomy in such a way that they spoke vividly of 'relative constants' at the level of the psychology of emotion: they render manifest the complexities of what Jones calls 'The Father Imago'. Moreover, through circumstance rather than design, the Michelangelo statue is disjunctured within its surrounding context; thus it is sufficiently incomplete, or 'unsealed', for each successive generation, including Freud's, to 'complete' the work anew in ways meaningful to themselves. All these issues, together with that of the creativity of the spectator himself, will be raised again when we begin to look at post-Freudian psychoanalytic thought and its contribution to aesthetics.

II

THE VENUS AND 'INTERNAL OBJECTS'

I N this seminar, we are going to look at Kleinian theory and its relevance to aesthetics. I have selected the Venus de Milo as a specific focus for what I have to say. The last two sessions will be concerned with post-Kleinian theory and its relevance to Post-Impressionism and to contemporary, American abstract painting respectively. You may feel that a leap from deliberations around a classical sculpture to discussions about modernism, and especially the work of a painter like Rothko, will involve an excessive rupture. And so, I would like to float a clue as to what I hope will be an underlying continuity in these last three seminars.

Whereas in examining the Venus we will be concerned with the re-creation of a damaged image of the mother through art, when we talk about Rothko's paintings in particular, I shall argue that what we perceive is, in a sense, the 'negative' of this process: the realisation of a representation of the presence of her absence.

With that enigmatic clue, let us turn to the Venus de Milo herself. Once more, I have to declare an autobiographical interest. I have been fascinated with this work ever since I first came across a reproduction of it when I was a child. I do not share the view that the Venus is aesthetically uninteresting, or sculpturally inept; nonetheless, I am readily prepared to acknowledge that my preoccupation with it—which at times has amounted almost to an obsession—is bound up with exceedingly powerful ideas and affects of a personal kind. For example, the Venus emerged as a recurrent motif at a certain critical phase in my own psychoanalysis. Now if I were about to offer you a highly idiosyncratic reconstruction of the Venus, if I were on the point of claiming that, say, even in the original she

Venus de Milo.

had no arms or whatever, I think that on the basis of what I have told you alone, you would have every reason to be suspicious. My reading of the Venus would be susceptible to the same kind of inquiry as that to which I subjected Freud's reading of the Moses of Michelangelo last time. But, as it happens, I have no such interpretation to offer. I am interested in what it is about the Venus de Milo which makes it such an enduring image, capable of bearing so many reconstructions, so many specific maternal projections, in such widely varying historical and cultural moments.

Discussions of the Venus are notoriously complex. In 1882, a Victorian commentator wrote, 'The peculiarity of the attitude of the Venus de Milo, and the loss of her arms, which might explain it, have given rise to countless theories respecting the action in which she is engaged. Everything about her except her lustrous beauty, even the material from which she is carved, is a matter of dispute.'[1] For much of the 19th century, the dating, attribution and reconstruction of the statue were matters of vigorous controversy. True, in 1894 Furtwängler published an exemplary 'scientific' analysis based upon the scrutiny of details; this was of the kind which Freud had tried to effect upon the Moses of Michelangelo, but Furtwängler reached more convincing conclusions.[2] Today we can at least be more confident about when the sculpture was made, and what it looked like when it was first erected. Nonetheless much concerning the Venus, and especially its discovery, is still far from clear.

I first tried to clarify the circumstances of the Venus' retrieval from the earth some five years ago and I must admit that the mass of conflicting evidence defeated me then. I am not sure that I have mastered it even now. There are so many confused and confusing reports, denials, retractions, and insinuations that it may never be possible to say with certainty what happened. I think, however, that it was something like this.

On 8th April, 1820, a Greek peasant called Yorgos was digging in his field in a mountainous part of the island of Melos near the theatre of the ancient town when the earth trembled and the ground in front of him subsided to reveal a subterranean niche. Yorgos peered in: he had discovered the Venus.

To understand what happened next you must remember that in 1820 Greece was still under the dominion of the Ottoman Empire: indeed it was on the very threshold of its liberation struggle. As soon as she emerged from the ground, the Venus was destined to become entwined within the thongs of conflicting imperial ambitions. News of Yorgos' find came first not to the Turks, but to the French who schemed to acquire the statue for the glory of their nation. Among the humiliating terms forced upon France by the allies after the Napoleonic wars had been the return of 5,000 works of art looted by Napoleon for the Louvre. Injury had been added to insult when, in 1816, the British Museum acquired the marbles from the frieze and pediment of the Parthenon, seized—with the Sultan's consent—by Lord Elgin.

Yorgos, no doubt, knew little of such matters. It seems, however, that about the time he made his find, one Voutier, a marine cadet from a French boat, *L'Estafette*, which was then moored in the harbour at Melos, was hunting for antiquities near the ancient town. Voutier heard about Yorgos' discovery and persuaded the peasant to move the two pieces in which the Venus had been found to a near-by shed. He also made a rapid and not very accurate sketch of the two parts of the figure together with its plinth and terminal figures, or Hermes, of a kind often used for decorating niches.

Voutier told M. Brest about the statue. Brest was a French consular agent on Melos who had been specifically instructed by Pierre David, the French Consul General at Smyrna, to hunt out Greek antiquities. Brest was friendly with the captain of *L'Estafette*; he persuaded the latter to take Vautier's drawing directly to the Marquis de Rivière, French Ambassador to the Ottoman Court at Constantinople. Over the next few days, a number of French boats docked at Melos. The reports of their captains, together with a despatch from Brest about the find were delivered to David in Smyrna. On 16th April, six days after the discovery, *Le Chevrette*, another French boat, came into Melos bearing upon it an admiral, Dumont D'Urville, and one Lieutenant Matterer. The admiral and Matterer inspected the statue and the site and then D'Urville, too, hastened on to Constantinople to impress upon the Marquis de Rivière, the ambassador, the importance of what had been found. Meanwhile Pierre David, no doubt in the hope of advancement within the diplomatic service, deferred his interest in the statue to the ambassador and forwarded the reports he had received to him. The ambassador determined that he would deliver the Venus to Louis XVIII, King of France. (Later the Marquis was to make his own motives clear in the immortal line, 'My girl doesn't have any arms, but that doesn't matter; she can still open the doors of the Institute.') Thus, within days of her discovery, the rights over this marble goddess had, at least in the conjectures of French diplomatic officials, shifted from the peasant who found her, via a humble sea-cadet, through a consular agent, sea-captains, an admiral, a consul general, and an ambassador towards the King himself.

Accordingly, the ambassador put his secretary, one M. Marcellus, in command of *L'Estafette* and its crew and sent the boat back to Melos to pick up the prize. L'Estafette arrived at the island this time on 22 May—but a lot had been happening while she had been away. We do not know what arrangements Brest had entered into with Yorgos, but it appears that an Armenian priest, one Oiciamos, had intervened with a better offer—some say of around 2,000 piasters, about the price of a goat. Oiciamos had been accused of wrong-doing by his spiritual superiors and he had—or so he thought—obtained the statue from Yorgos in the hope of improving his position by currying favour with a Turkish military potentate and prince, Nikolaki Morusi, who had let it be known that he would rather see the statue at the bottom of the sea than in the hands of the French.

Now the official version of what happened when *L'Estafette* anchored off Melos is that the Venus was already tied up on board a Turkish boat. Marcellus intervened and offered Yorgos a third more than Oiciamos had given him, where-upon the Turkish seamen handed over the statue without so much as a whimper. But it is evident that these reports are little more than a leaky cover-up. We know, for example, that on 26th May, Brest sent a consular despatch to his ambassador saying, 'I believe it to be useless to make a report to you of all that we did to obtain it. Marcellus, on his return, will tell you the whole thing.' Whatever Marcellus told the Marquis, 'the whole thing' was never made public. There are many indications of suppression of the facts. For example, Dumont D'Urville—the admiral who, accompanied by his lieutenant, examined the Venus a week or so after it was found—wrote up a report for the official publication, *Annales Maritimes*. Interestingly, his manuscript version survived: among several significant differences between this and the published text is the excision of any suggestion that Marcellus and his men were only able to get hold of the Venus by force. [3]

For thirty years after the incident Marcellus himself published numerous often contradictory statements. Even he eventually came close to admitting that a battle had taken place:

> 'Irritated by the obstacles which I saw multiplying, compelled by I cannot say what instinct, or more—I will confess it—by the ardent desire of a young heart avid to struggle against that which seemed impossible, I resolved to carry away the statue at whatever price. Surely she would later justify the excess of my zeal!'[4]

Even so, he insisted that he had used only the threat of force and not force itself.

It is however highly probable that a pitched battle between the French and the Turks took place. The rumours were there from the start. Some time after the death of Dumont D'Urville in a railway accident, Lieutenant Matterer began to reveal all that he knew about the affair; and Brest, too, confessed in the 1860s to knowledge of the fracas. According to these accounts, when *L'Estafette* laid anchor the Venus was standing on the beach, surrounded by Turks under the command of Oiciamos. They were preparing to load the statue onto a Turkish boat. Marcellus had a crew of 50 who disembarked, armed with cudgels and sabres, and set upon the rapacious foe. The Turks endeavoured to flee dragging the Venus with them across the rocky shore by tugging at the ropes in which it was harnessed. After a struggle, the Turks were routed and Marcellus carried off his prize.

Such an incident would certainly have had serious diplomatic repercussions. It seems, however, that although Nikolai Morusi, the Turkish prince, was a hater of the French in general he was a friend of the Marquis de Rivière, the French ambassador. The Turks may have been duly compensated and the whole business hushed up.

My own view is that the battle almost certainly did take place. I am much less certain, however, about how much damage was done to the statue, by whom, before, during or after the fracas. One French writer, Jean Aicard, ammassed a great deal of evidence in the 1870s which appeared to demonstrate that those who recorded their recollections of the Venus before it left Melos—including Brest, Dumont D'Urville, Matterer, and another local peasant, Antonio Bottonis who was interrogated by Jules Ferry, then the French ambassador, in 1873—all believed that what they had seen was a statue of a woman holding an apple in her left hand.[5] Aicard is convinced that the left arm was broken off only in the battle on the beach. Certainly another significant deletion between the manuscript and published versions of Dumont D'Urville's report is the removal of the phrase, '*elle representait une femme nue dont la main gauche relevée tenait une pomme.*'

Whether or not one accepts Aicard's view, there is no doubt that the Venus arrived in Paris bearing the signs of relatively recent injuries. Marcellus was quick to blame these on the way that Oiciamos had dragged the Venus down from the mountains to the shore, and thence onto the Turkish boat: 'It is to the jolts and accidents of these journeys that one must attribute the recent injuries that can be noticed on the bust of the Venus and, above all, the degradation of the pleats of drapery which fall so lightly in waves over the knees.'[6] But Marcellus seems to me the least credible of all those whose testimonies have come down to us. He invariably wrote of the sculpture in an over-emotional way. Apparently, on the ship leaving Melos he fell on his knees in front of it and recited Homer. When he reached France, he referred to it as 'My Venus, my goddess, my beauty and my prize!' He also changed his mind about what had happened over and over again. Oiciamos was aware of the value of what he was handling and is unlikely to have mistreated it in the manner Marcellus suggests, except, of course, in the heat of battle. There can be no doubt that serious violence *was* inflicted upon the statue soon after its discovery. Marcellus certainly knew more about this than he made public.

In order to understand the next phase of this strange saga you have to realise that, like many Greek sculptures, the Venus was in fact carved out of several pieces of marble: the upper and lower parts of the torso, the left arm, left foot, and a piece of the right hip were made separately and these 'part-objects' were then put together. When Marcellus left Melos he certainly carried off with him the naked upper half; the draped lower part; a left upper fore-arm, which he described as 'shapeless and mutilated'; a left hand holding an apple; and other fragments. He probably, for example, also took the inscribed block which was attached to the front of the plinth on which the statue stood, although he denied this and claimed that it was only collected six months later when the Marquis de Rivière, the ambassador, visited the scene of the crime. (The Marquis was certainly sold two arms of very inferior workmanship by one enterprising islander: it subsequently took a while to eliminate even these from inquiries.) Amongst the material which turned up at the Louvre were also a left foot, of quite different proportions from those of the Venus, but found near by, and three terminal figures. But the statue did not reach Paris until February of the year after that in which it was found. The reason for the long delay is not clear, but reports suggest that the precious cargo was held up at Marseilles. Inevitably, as soon as the Venus arrived in the capital, it was met with a great flurry of attention from leading *savants*, writers, and artists.

One of the mysteries surrounding the Venus would almost certainly never have been resolved but for the fact that Jacques Louis David, the great classical painter, was at this time in exile as a result of his association with the deposed Napoleon. David was fascinated by news of the discovery and wrote to one of his pupils, Le Baron Gros, requesting a drawing of the Venus. Gros commissioned an artist, one M. Debay, to carry this out. Debay made his drawing while the statue was still in the laboratory at the Louvre; he drew in place the fragment of left fore-arm which accompanied the statue and also, more significantly, the inscribed block which had once been attached to the plinth. The block bears an inscription to the effect that a sculptor called (Ages)andros made the work. (The first four letters of the name are missing.) There is a copious literature on the inscription as revealed through this sketch: but, as Furtwängler underlines, the character of the epigraphy is such that it could have been made 'anywhere between 200 B.C. and the Christian era', with the nearest parallels coming from 150 to 50 B.C.[7]

This block was a very great embarrassment to the 'experts' who were assessing the sculpture. The King had already been sent word that he was to be presented not just with the finest Greek original female nude to have survived from antiquity, and the only one with an intact head attached, but also that he was to be given a work by the great fourth century sculptor, Praxiteles. There was no credible way of denying that the inscribed fragment belonged to the statue since it clearly fitted the right side of the plinth.

These circumstances precipitated a complex and unseemly power struggle in the highest echelons of French cultural life. Quatre-Mère de Quincey, permanent secretary of the Académie Royale des Beaux Arts, rushed out a paper which argued that the statue was a genuine work by Praxiteles. Characteristically, his argument relies largely on 'spiritual' estimation: 'It is a work

Venus de Milo as drawn by Debay.

which offers us, together with the highest idea of imitation of the feminine nature, the greatest character of forms, the most happy mixture of truth and of greatness of style, of grace and nobility, that it must have come out of the studio, or the school, of Praxiteles.'[8] To refer back to our last seminar, it was exactly this mode of attributing authorship to a work of art which Morelli was to discredit half a century later. But, having made his identification, Quatre-Mère de Quincey then had to dispose of all the many facts, and as it happened people and objects too, which refused to go along with it.

He argued that the statue had originally formed part of a group, with Mars the god of war, but that it had been restored in antique times; thus the block, with the tell-tale date and authorship, could be discounted. The piece of marble used to patch up the plinth had *par hasard* born the inconvenient inscription. He also attributed the fragment of the left upper arm, and the left hand bearing an apple, to some late restoration. He supported this with an outrageous argument concerning the statue's alleged left foot. The Venus had arrived at the Louvre with a left foot crudely pushed into place. Now Quatre-Mère de Quincey declared that this was too badly done to be part of the original statue, as indeed it was. But it offered not the slightest evidence of an antique restoration! The foot had been picked up some way from the main find; it was sandalled, whereas the Venus' attached right foot is nude. It was also of quite different proportions. This left foot clearly had nothing to do with the statue at *any* time.

The argument of Quatre-Mère de Quincey and others, that the Venus had been subjected to an antique restoration sounded more credible than it does to us not just because of his great reputation as an archaeologist, but also because so little was then known about Greek carving techniques. There was a widespread—but quite erroneous—belief that ideal, classical figures must have been carved from a single piece of marble, whereas the Venus came in several disparate parts, from different blocks of marble, of differing quality. Indeed, Quatre-Mère de Quincey found it necessary to speak frankly to his readers of the fact that once he had eliminated what he regarded as antique restorations, he was still left with a Venus in two parts. Nowadays, however, the fact that a statue is made from several pieces is one of the ways in which it can be identified as a Greek original rather than a Roman copy. Quatre-Mère de Quincey and his colleagues also failed to realise that the 'inferior workmanship' of the statue's extremities was characteristic of Greek art, where those parts which will not engage the spectator's full attention are often much less thoroughly worked. But despite what he perceived as difficulties to his thesis, Quatre-Mère de Quincey concludes with a re-affirmation that the statue was by Praxiteles, and a recommendation that it should never be restored, but should be left for ever in the mutilated state in which it was found.

Quatre-Mère de Quincey's reading of the sculpture was,

however, strongly opposed by the redoubtable Clarac, Conservateur du Musée Royal des Antiques. Clarac believed that the statue belonged to the era of Praxiteles, but he thought that the inscription gave the real name of the sculptor and that, for some inexplicable reason, it was carved and fitted into place 250 years after the Venus was made.[9] Clarac did not, however, go along with the idea of a full-scale antique restoration. He believed the Venus to have been a free-standing, single figure—though possibly related to other single figures—indicating the victory of the goddess in the judgement of Paris. He thus held that the 'inferior' left hand, and the piece of the upper left arm, belonged to the original work. Clarac supports this view with technical arguments concerning the weathering and grain of the marble, the data for which he received from the Louvre's restorer, M. Lange.

There are indications in Clarac's text that he may have been privy to Marcellus' confidences concerning the circumstances of the statue's discovery, and of the battle on the beach. Marcellus, himself, incidentally put forward the most extreme of the 'antique restoration' hypotheses, arguing that the left arm and the hand holding an apple must have been added by 7th or 8th century Christians!

Clarac's reading of the sculpture was in any event an acute embarrassment to those who wished to present it to the King as unequivocally a fourth century work by Praxiteles. Despite his high position, Clarac was excluded from the setting up of the figure which was carried out 'clandestinely and hastily'. His text on the work was never delivered to the King. Most strangely, the inscribed block which threw such a grave question mark over the attribution of the Venus to Praxiteles was conveniently 'lost', never to be refound, soon after Debay made his drawings. (Furthermore, a dedicatory inscription which had once been situated immediately above the niche in which the statue was found was also brought from Melos to the Louvre and 'lost'. This could also be definitively dated as belonging to the period after 200 B.C. It was only preserved diagrammatically in Clarac's text. The left foot—such a poor witness to an important argument in Quatre-Mère de Quincey's interpretation—suffered the same fate.) As M. de Longpérier wrote, 'Someone told King Louis XVIII that the statue was the work of the celebrated sculptor of Phryne (Praxiteles), and I believe that this was the reason for the loss of the inscription.'[10]

The statue was duly presented to the King on 1st March, 1821, and it had exactly the kind of cultural success which had been hoped for. The Venus was the envy of the Western world! The King of Bavaria optimistically put in a claim that it belonged to him; he had recently bought an amphitheatre in Melos and maintained that the Venus had been found on his ground. The English immediately—and equally optimistically—launched an expedition to Melos in the hope of finding something resembling the Venus' identical twin. In France sculptors, poets, painters and authors enthused uninhibitedly upon the statue. A long book could be written tracing its influences and effects in art, literature and aesthetics.

The Venus became deeply embedded within European culture, but in such a way that it was able to survive radical shifts of taste and to transcend national chauvinisms. From the beginning, it fascinated not just the eclipsed and exhausted residual pockets of Neo-Classicism, but also successive generations of Romantics. Not only Chateaubriand, Lamartine, Victor Hugo and Saint-Victor were seduced by it, but so were much younger Romantic writers: Gautier and Alfred de Musset were among those who had been children when the statue arrived in Paris who wrote poems about it as adults. In Germany, Heine proclaimed the Venus as 'Our Lady of Beauty', and even the English responded without letting their jealousy get the better of them. In his novel, *The Newcomes*, Thackeray makes Clive Newcome write to Pendennis of his first visit to the Louvre in the 1830s:

> 'I shall come and live here, I think. I feel as if I never want to go away. I had not been ten minutes in the place before I fell in love with the most beautiful creature the world has ever seen. She was standing silent and majestic in the centre of one of the rooms of the statue gallery, and the very first glimpse of her struck one breathless with the sense of her beauty. I could not see the colour of her eyes and hair exactly, but the latter is light, and the eyes I should think are gray. Her complexion is of a beautiful warm marble tinge. She is not a clever woman, evidently; I do not think she laughs or talks much—she seems too lazy to do more than smile. She is only beautiful.'[11]

And so on, and so forth, up to the desire to 'bring a spotless kid, snowy-coated, and a pair of doves, and a jar of honey—yea, honey from Morel's in Piccadilly, thyme-flavoured, narbonian' to sacrifice to 'acknowledge the Sovereign Loveliness, and adjure the Divine Aphrodite'.

The Venus became one of the sights of Paris. Most 'cultured' visitors went to pay hommage to her, and many recorded their responses. Freud, in Paris for the first time in 1885, wrote home to his bride, somewhat coolly:

> 'I also saw the famous Venus de Milo without arms and paid her the usual compliment. I remembered that old Mendelssohn (the father in the Mendelssohn Family) writes about her from Paris as of a new exhibit without much enthusiasm. I think the beauty of the statue was not discovered till later and there is a lot of convention about it. For me these things are of more historical than aesthetic value.'[12]

(In the light of what I will say later about the Venus, it may be worth inserting here the speculation that Freud's indifference to the 'aesthetic' aspects of this statue, as contrasted with his obsession with Michelangelo's Moses, may relate to that central lacuna in his 'self-analysis', reflected in all his subsequent theoretical work, i.e. his over-estimation of the father-son relationship and under-estimation of that between the child and the mother. More generally, his response may indicate his striking inability to look too closely at any of his attitudes, affects or relations towards women.)

Perhaps the most remarkable cultural feat of the Venus in the 19th century, however, was its ability to stand as an epitome for two such distinct movements as French Romanticism, in the early part of the century, and the classicism of what has been called the British 'Victorian High Renaissance' of the 1870s and 1880s. It is not easy to think of another representation which could have survived this transition. For the insipid, idealising fantasists of British classicism, the Venus was not so much an object which excited passions as an unsurpassable ideal. For example, Leonée and Richard Ormond have rightly pointed out that most of the figures in Albert Moore's paintings, whether depicted clothed or nude, seem to reflect the Venus de Milo.[13] The torso of the figure in *A Venus* of 1869 is, as Hedberg has pointed out, modeled after the statue;[14] whereas, as Maas has observed, *Forget-me-nots* is based on a reverse print of it.[15] Further specific and general references to the Venus can be traced in the work of Leighton, Alma-Tadema, etc.

It was not however just a question of the chronological survival of the Venus' influence. She did not fade in France when she became trapped within this peculiarly thin, synthetic

Venus de Milo, Restoration by Ravaisson.

and idiosyncratic genre here. For example Rodin—whose imagination was utterly unlike that of a Moore or a Leighton—was also deeply affected by the sculpture. He wrote of it:

> 'Behold the marvel of marvels! This work is the expression of the greatest antique inspiration; it is voluptuousness regulated by restraint; it is the joy of life cadenced, moderated by reason . . . The artist in those days had eyes to see, while those of today are blind; this is all the difference. The Greek women were beautiful, but their beauty lived above all in the minds of the sculptors who carved them.'

Rodin claimed he was a classicist, a follower of Greek and

Gothic sculptors; but Clark seems right to call him 'the last heir of the great romantics'. The contradictions hypostasised within the Venus de Milo—its 'naturalism' versus its idealisation, its energy versus formal stasis, its fragmentation versus its formal perfection—are those which seem to flow through much of Rodin's work.

Nonetheless, responses to the Venus in the 19th century were confined neither to romantic raptures, nor to classical idealisations, nor yet to improbable conjunctions of the two. The desire for reparation and restoration—which involved quite a different way of looking and re-acting—was continuous from the time of the statue's arrival in Paris until the 1890s. This phenomenon manifested itself not just in the learned journals, though it was peculiarly rife there, but also in popular magazines and even novels. It erupted in France, where it amounted to a minor national obsession, and also in Germany, Britain and Scandinavia.

These restorations were sometimes put forward only in words; more usually, they were accompanied by line drawings. Not infrequently, they were physically effected upon a life-size plaster cast of the statue, which was then photographed and published, and/or put on exhibition. Restorations were, however, rarely based on a rigorous, physical examination of the statue, and of such of the fragments found with it as had survived. Many quite transparently have much more to do with the fantasies of those who put them forward: they are projections. The commonest type of 'evidence' presented is that of 'precedent' or 'prototype': a Greek statue, figurine, coin, or whatever is found vaguely resembling the Venus *and* the particular restoration which the author prefers; this is then cited as the 'source' of the statue, and as 'proof' of the correctness of the author's preference.

Here, I can only hint at some of the more prominent versions, most of which were subject to contentiously defended variations. From the beginning, many interpreted the statue as having formed part of a group. Often, she was assumed to have comprised an element in a 'Judgement of Paris' scene, or, alternatively, to have been linked to an Eros. Saloman, however, eccentrically 'proved' that the statue had formed part of a gymnasium decoration and had stood at one side of Herakles as Pleasure, holding a dove in her extended right hand, and balancing Virtue on the other side.[16] After saying that the problem of the statue's restoration could not be solved, Reinach, somewhat desperately, grouped her as Venus with the Poseidon of Melos.[17] The most popular group theory, however, linked her, as Venus, with Ares, or Mars, the god of War, a peculiarly persistent hypothetical companion for our statue. Extraordinary care was lavished on defining his precise relationship to the Venus. Quatre Mère de Quincey thought she had been depicted endeavouring to appease his anger; Ravaisson, also of the Louvre, argued that Venus and Ares formed an amorous pair, or *couple conjugale*.[18] Many followed him. Valentin, however, would have none of this. He tried to demonstrate that the Venus was a statue of a woman 'defending herself against the outrages of a man.'[19]

Many of those who did not link the Venus directly with Ares in a group nonetheless believed that she had once held a spear, upside down pike, or some other emblem of the god of war. In 1882, Kiel of Hanover published a reconstruction which, in the apt words of one of his critics, 'imagines a lance fixed in the

Venus de Milo,

19th century Austrian Restoration.   Restoration by   Kiel.

hole and held by the goddess with both hands; i.e. Venus as giantess with a spear as thick as a tree.'[20] Overbeck was one of the first to give her a shield, though he thought that she was resting it on a pillar, whereas others situated it under her left foot.[21] Others (Jahn, Preller) maintained she was holding it. Some (Muller, Millingen, Braun and Wittig) that she was gazing at herself in the polished surface of the shield. Rydberg believed that she was exhibiting a shield on which was engraved an inscription celebrating the victory of the Greeks over the Persians. Boehm thought she was actually depicted writing on the inside of the shield; and Walter Copland Perry maintained that she once had a buckler in her left hand on which she was in the act of inscribing the names of fallen heroes.

Some followed Clarac and argued that she was a Venus Victrix exhibiting the apple she had won in the competition with Juno and Minerva (Froener, Aicard). They were somewhat nearer the probable truth, though some of them, like the sculptor Claudius Tarral, an English gentleman resident in

Venus de Milo,

Restoration by Millingen.   Restoration by John Bell.

Paris, embellished their Venus Victrix with unwarranted appurtenances, such as a Cupid darting his arrow, Juno's golden diadem, and Minerva's helmet.[22]

Some believed that she was decking a trophy (Heydermann); whereas Emeric David maintained that the statue was a muse which had once played upon the lyre. A Venus *a toilette* was exhibited in Vienna in 1873; many saw her as about to take a bath. And then, of course, there were the real crazies. One even had her with her arms raised above her head, doing her hair. An Englishman, John Bell, produced an amazing reconstruction of her waving garlands like a Spanish castanet dancer doing a striptease.

Together with these doubts about what the statue depicted there were all sorts of other controversies and speculations concerning it. One, obviously, had to do with its dating. Quatre-Mère de Quincey's attribution was inevitably soon questioned, but a range of alternatives were put forward. Murray, for example, thought it was *earlier* than Praxiteles, indeed that it had influenced him, and encouraged him to go one step further in rendering Venus 'entirely nude without offence'.[23] Valentin situated it 'between Pheidias and Praxiteles'; whereas Saloman saw it as being 'after Lysippe' on account of its undulating forms.[24] Some thought it was an original by Scopas. Tarral believed that the fact it was constructed in pieces made it the work of the second century sculptor of the Laocoon; others like Perry, attributed it to 'that age of genial eclecticism to which we owe such marvels as the Belvedere Torso and the Borghese Warrior.'[25]

Similarly, throughout the century, rumours, counter-rumours, denials and confessions persisted concerning the fight on the beach, whether or not it had taken place at all, and, if it had, what damage, if any, was done to the statue during or after it. One bizarre story surfaced in various versions that the statue had been found *intact* and had subsequently been deliberately mutilated. This rumour endured despite lack of any supporting evidence, perhaps because of the rebuttals of the scholars.

Such controversies persisted unabated until 1893, when Furtwängler published his brilliant paper based on thorough-going empirical principles. He maintained that the fragment of left fore-arm and the left hand holding an apple were indeed parts of the original work, not antique restorations. He demonstrated how many reconstructions simply failed to take into account crucial details, such as the direction of the dowel hole for the arm support. He arrived at a Venus with her left arm resting on a pillar and her right arm reaching across to support the drapery above her knee. He admitted, however, that 'the two arms thus restored lend neither unity nor harmony to the composition; in short, their loss is one less to be deplored than might at first appear.'[26] But he also provided an explanation for this disunity beyond that of aesthetic failure because he argued that the Venus was the 'not altogether happy' combination of two entirely independent, traditional types.

Although in his reconstruction, Venus displays an apple, Furtwängler did not agree with those who maintained she was a Venus Victrix, displaying her prize after the judgement of Paris. One major reason he advanced for favouring this unusual pose was that it corresponded with that of 'the highly revered cultus-statue of Melos, the Tyche of the island,' as manifest in its coins and other iconography. (The apple was a symbol of Melos

Venus de Milo, Restoration by Valentin.

whose very name means apple, because the island is, roughly speaking, shaped like one.) Furtwängler thought that the Venus had stood originally in the niche where it was found as part of the decoration of the nearby Gymnasium. he held that 'the artist wished to characterise the Aphrodite of the Gymnasium as goddess of Good Luck, and therefore gave her the pose of the Tyche of the city.' These then were the two elements which the sculptor failed to harmonise.

Furtwängler suggests that those who had found the ghosts of shields in the Venus were not entirely wrong. He argues that although the motive of the left arm supported on a pillar was taken over from the type of the Tyche of Melos, the main design was related to the traditional type for Venus which has her gazing at herself in a shield. Furtwängler maintains that the original which the sculptor had in mind had been lost, but a well-known Roman copy of this type is the Venus of Capua. (He easily refutes one argument, popular in his day, that this figure was a weak Roman variant of the Venus de Milo itself.) He finds numerous residues of the shield-bearing goddess in the Melian statue: the raised foot, the turn of the nude torso to the left, the gesture of the arms are all 'meaningless' when the shield is removed. The sculptor retained them only because they formed 'a graceful pose':

> 'As the shield is not there to keep up the left side of the cloak, and there is accordingly no reason why one side should be higher than the other, both sides have been allowed to slip down as far as they can without falling off. The torso, especially from a back view, gains in sensuous charm by the change, but the drapery would always produce an impression of insecurity even were the right hand still intact to keep it in place.
>
> With the rejection of the shield as mirror the meaning of the drapery and the naturalness of the pose are lost. In the original type the goddess, who is wont to be draped, has partly disrobed for a definite reason, in order to contemplate her own beauty undisturbed. In the Melian type she displays her charms apparently with no object at all, and one does not see why she does not disrobe altogether.'[27]

Furtwängler suggests that the Venus bearing a shield derived from a much older type, that of the armed Goddess of Love, but that this image became progressively 'unintelligible' and was subject to modification. Aphrodite 'lays aside her heavy armour, but keeps the shield to mirror her loveliness'. In the

Venus de Milo, even that has been abandoned but traces of it remain.

Furtwängler began his study by effectively demonstrating the authenticity of the 'lost' inscription: his analyses of the details of hair and drapery provide convincing ancillary evidence in support of his dating between 150 and 50 B.C. But again, those who saw in the statue intimations of High Classicism were not, if Furtwängler is right, entirely foolish. He sees the Venus as the product of a late second century renascence, a reaction against Hellenistic excesses. He argues that the sculptor looked to a model by Skopas: 'the Skopasian groundwork is manifest not only in external details, such as the arrangement of the fillet of the hair . . . but in the attempt to impart fire and vitality to the expression.' But whoever made the Venus may also 'in his adaptation of the Aphrodite of Skopas' have 'consciously emulated the style of some . . . Pheidian prototype.' Thus Furtwängler concludes:

> 'The artist took his motive from a creation of Skopas which he modified considerably, and contaminated, not altogether happily, with the type of the Tyche of Melos. At the same time he strove to import to it something of Pheidian grandeur. So far then he showed independence in his modification of the style, inasmuch as he drew his inspiration from older Attic art, and sought to emulate it. Call him "eclectic" if you will, he was at least a man who could make a traditional type his own, and reproduce it with all the freshness of a new conception.'[28]

Is Furtwängler's view that the Venus was a late second century product of a classical revival, containing echoes of High classicism, and local, specifically Melian features, as it were refracted through a post-Hellenistic perspective, correct? Only a foolish man would unequivocally shout 'Yes'! Here we are in waters as murky as New Testament studies. When we have to appeal to hypothetical, lost original sources, comparable to 'Q', evidently we are beyond the terrain of certainty. Nonetheless, Furtwängler's paper was as important in Venus de Milo studies as, say, Weiss and Schweitzer's almost simultaneous discovery of primitive Christian eschatology was in Jesus studies. Even if it is still possible to raise telling questions concerning his restoration, as Collignon did soon after it was published,[29] most of the prevalent types of speculation about the Venus were finished for ever by what Furtwängler wrote. His dating is almost certainly correct. Indeed, to this day, only cranks have

Venus de Milo,
Restoration by Furtwängler.

actually put forward alternative restorations. For example, in 1958, Elmer G. Suhr published a book in which he argued that 'it is quite evident that we have here another version of the Heavenly Aphrodite spinning her golden thread of life.'[30] Unfortunately, this little better than laughable reconstruction was bolstered only by arguments concerning the shape of the moon's shadow when projected to the earth, and a conspicuous contempt for empirical evidence in favour of intuitive, cultic speculation.

Now it is true to say that by the time Furtwängler's paper appeared some connoisseurs had already begun to question the supreme status which had been accorded to the Venus. (As early as 1880, Walter Pater had written, 'the Venus of Melos, for instance, is but a supremely well-executed object of *vertu*, in the most limited sense of the term.'[31]) But there can be no doubt that Furtwängler's essay hastened the expiration of a certain type of superlative response. In Britain, Victorian classicism was simultaneously waning. Within 'High Culture' at least the Venus seemed to be passing into a partial eclipse.

Now in one sense this sort of sliding out of fashion of a work is not at all surprising: by and large the paragons and epitomes of 19th century taste are not those of the 20th century. Take the case of the Apollo Belvedere: this was revered from the time of Raphael to that of Winkelmann, who described it as 'this kingdom of beauty incarnate'. Clark says that at the beginning of the 19th century, i.e. around the time the Venus de Milo was discovered, the Apollo was 'without question, one of the two most famous works of art in the world.'[32] But it has now been thoroughly relegated. Characteristically, Clark himself speaks of its 'weak structure and slack surfaces.'[33] The Apollo has withered in the popular imagination, too. But the passing out of favour of the Venus de Milo was *not* of this kind.

Certainly, as the 19th century came to an end, art historians and aesthetes stopped writing about the sculpture the way they had done. Painters and sculptors were no longer so frequently influenced by it. Or, to be more exact, only those whose sensibilities remained ensnared within the past continued to respond in the familiar ways. For example, Alfred Noyes, an English conservative poet and a vigorous opponent of Modernism in literature and art, published this epitaph to romantic raptures about the Venus de Milo as late as 1907:

Backward she leans, as when the rose unblown
  Slides white from its warm sheath some morn in May!
Under the sloping waist, aslant, her zone
  Clings as it slips in tender disarray;
One knee, out-thrust a little, keeps it so
  Lingering ere it fall; her lovely face
    Gazes as o'er her own Eternity!
Those armless radiant shoulders, long ago
¯Perchance held arms out wide with yearning grace
    For Adon by the blue Sicilian sea.

This indicates that Noyes subscribed to an exceptionally unusual reconstruction. His last stanza ends:

Oh, naked loveliness, not yet revealed,
  A moment hence that falling robe will show
    No prophecy like this, this great new dawn,
The bare bright breasts, each like a soft white shield,
  And the firm body like a slope of snow
    Out of the slipping dream-stuff half withdrawn.[34]

But my point is this: just as all this sort of writing about the statue was becoming patently debased and absurd, and painters were looking to quite different subjects, the Venus sprang into vigorous life again effecting a transformation even more remarkable than her movement in and out of the classical-romantic polarities of the 19th century.

Elsewhere I have described in detail the way in which in the late 19th century a 'Mega-Visual' tradition was brought into being with the emergence of monopoly capitalism: the Venus de Milo seems to make the transition into this new tradition easily and naturally. She seems almost infinitely adaptable to the new forms to which it gave rise. Thus, in the 20th century, there is little point in looking for poems and reconstructions of the Venus; but advertisements featuring her abound. She emerges not just as a 'trademark for art', but in such contexts as posters and promotional material for pencils, paints, cars, carpets, fabrics, beauty-salons, restaurants, towels, slimming foods, beauty products—even insurance brokers. As the Fine Art tradition, and its related literary and critical activities, began to appear perilously historically specific, the Venus slid right out of it into the new, emergent Mega-Visual tradition. Her position now appears more secure than ever, regardless of the relative indifference of painters, sculptors and critics. The floor of the Louvre still wears away disproportionately in front of her every year, and who knows how many soap-stone maquettes find their way into living-rooms and greenhouses everywhere.

Before we turn to the relevance of Kleinian theory to the understanding of the Venus, I want to tell you about a change in my own thinking concerning the statue. When I first started studying the Venus de Milo phenomenon, I felt that here was something which could be explained sociologically. For example, in an article published in the autumn of 1975, I wrote that the Venus de Milo was not one physical thing, 'but countless thousands of images and ideas each of which has a history of its own.'[35] I had in mind 19th century reconstructions, advertisements, a jig-saw, a match-box, the soap-stone maquette that stood on my desk, the sorts of things we have been discussing, all of which bore a representation of the Venus, in some form within them. Relying heavily on Benjamin and Berger, I drew a comparison between the Venus de Milo and the Mona Lisa:

'If I wanted to write a history of the Mona Lisa . . . I would have to analyze the different ways in which it was seen at different historical moments. The history of the painting would encompass not just the development of critical and verbal responses to it, but the kind and number of the copies and reproductions made of it. The meaning of the Mona Lisa no longer belongs uniquely to the canvas hanging behind bullet proof glass in the Louvre. The frequency of its reproduction has fragmented its meaning into many meanings, in part generated by the shifting context of post-cards, ash-trays, popular art books, newspapers, tea-shirts, advertisments, and even postage stamps in which it is reproduced. In a sense, the original has been drained of all possible meanings but one, which has to do with what it *is* rather than what it depicts: a "priceless" painting, the icon or epitome of "Art".'[36]

But I argued the history of the Venus was even more complex still. A statue is three dimensional; it occupies *real* space. I maintained that a change in its surrounding space constituted a change in the original work of art itself. Additionally, I stressed that the Venus itself was a *fragment*:

'It has been said of the Mona Lisa that when it is seen, today, it is seen as the original of its numerous reproductions (each of which had a relatively autonomous meaning in the context in which it was reproduced). But even this cannot be said of the Venus of Milo: the object on show at the Louvre is in no sense the

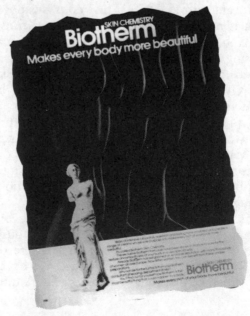

original of the work represented in contemporary reproductions—whether they are two or three dimensional. It is only an ambiguous part of an original, whose appearance has almost entirely been forgotten. Nevertheless—as Kenneth Clark pointed out—"she has held her place in popular imagery as a symbol, or trade mark, of Beauty".'[37]

I asked how this was possible, and noted that Kenneth Clark answered this question just as the idealist critics of the 19th century had done. 'She remains,' he had written, 'one of the most splendid physical ideals of humanity, and the noblest refutation of contemporary critical cant that a work of art must express its own epoch.'[38] I compared Clark's own position to the 'contemporary critical cant' of formalist universalising and went on to say:

> 'There is every reason to suppose that far from regarding the object now displayed in the Louvre as "one of the most splendid physical ideals of humanity", the ancient Greeks themselves would have looked upon it with fear, loathing and incomprehension.'[39]

I described how the Venus now stands, isolated, in a room in the Department of Greek and Roman Antiquities in the Louvre. On the marble floor, there is an inlaid circle, at the centre of which is the pedestal that raises the statue above the crowd of visitors who continuously gather round it, pointing their cameras towards it. The Venus is exposed on all sides. Her back is noticeably coarsely worked and finished, because once she stood close to a wall. Evidently, large pieces of marble are missing: the arms and the left foot have gone; the entire surface is grazed and chipped, so that passages of skin and drapery are severely degraded. The form with which the observer is confronted today is that of a *mutilated woman*.

An idealist critic might say that this did not matter because the average observer engaged in an imaginative completion of the statue. But, I argued, that was not possible: in the 19th century, as we have seen, the reconstruction of the Venus was highly contentious. Moreover, there is no evidence that the average 20th century observer has Furtwängler's, or anyone else's, reconstruction in mind when he or she looks at the Venus. Thus I was able to ask contemptuously where this 'most splendid physical ideal' to which Clark referred, actually was. In the lost original whose appearance was once so hotly disputed and which no one today (including Clark himself) seems to care about at all? Or in the battered, mutilated body upon which we gaze today, yet which would have been so repugnant to the Greeks themselves?

And so I wrote:

> 'Manifestly any given object (e.g. the Mona Lisa) is seen differently, and therefore acquires different meanings, in successive historical moments. (An image is literally re-created each time it is seen.) But, in this case of the Venus, there is not even a fixed object which has remained the same, or similar, through the passage of time. Almost certainly a characteristic of the original statue was its sense of wholeness: the dominant feature of the surviving part is that of fragmentation.'[40]

Thus I could maintain that the idealist assumption of a continuous, unchanging, perceptual response to an enduring, culture free physical ideal had only been maintained through verbal trickery: Kenneth Clark talks about the Venus de Milo as it appears today *as if* it were in the same physical condition in which it appeared to the Greeks. I reminded my readers of how even Furtwängler, when he had established the 'correct' reconstruction, implied that the disappearance of the arms was no great loss, and the fragment was better than the whole.

It seemed to me that one had to speak in terms of two different entities, Venus Mark One, and Venus Mark Two: the condition of ambiguous fragmentation of the latter could, I felt, be related to the culture in which it was resurrected to provide a sufficient explanation of its success. It was, I maintained, the specific physical condition of the transformed Venus that allowed new meanings to become attached to it. I hinted at what some of those relations and meanings were.

French Neo-Classicism had recently declined; the French bourgeoisie had seen the disintegration and fragmentation of what, only a few years before, had been heralded as the style to end all styles, the embodiment of universal, true, eternal ideals. Romanticism had already established itself in its wake, and the cult of the fragment was central to it. The monster and the ruin came into unprecedented prominence. For example, as is well known, in 1816, Byron suggested to Shelley and his wife that they should each write a ghost story; two years later Mary Shelley's *Frankenstein* was published. The story includes the theme of the piecing together from disparate parts of the creature; it involves a similar blending of sentimental humanism and 'scientific' ideas which seems to inform the

Venus restorers. Byron himself, one might recall, faked a limp throughout his life and thus mutilated gave his support to the Greek liberation struggle. He died on his way to join the insurgents just three years after the Venus was found. It is not difficult to see why the fragmented goddess, who had herself been liberated by force from the grasp of the philistine Turks, should have had so much appeal within a culture characterised by such preoccupations.

Similarly, at this time, I thought it worth drawing a parallel between the response to the Venus and the tremendous, contemporaneous interest in men and women 'from the earth'. At the time she arrived in Paris, unsubstantiated 'fossil men' were being discovered in the Paris Basin and elsewhere: there was a new kind of interest in the past as the historicity of nature began to be discovered for the first time. At the *Académie des Sciences*, Georges Leopold Cuvier reigned supreme. Cuvier was the founder of comparative anatomy. It has been written of him that 'his experienced eye could build whole organisms out of parts.'[41] Indeed, Cuvier learned 'the necessary relationship of one part of a body with another so well that from the existence of some bones, he could infer the shape of others, the type of muscles that must be attached, and so on. In the end, he could reconstruct a reasonable approximation of the entire animal from a small number of parts.'[42] Despite this, Cuvier was a pious Christian. He exposed bogus 'fossil men' brought forward by evolutionists with excessive relish. A famous specimen long held to be 'one of the infamous men who brought about the calamity of the Flood', Cuvier identified as the remains of a giant salamander. He also demolished *Homo diluvii testis*, which he incorrectly declared to be the distorted skull of a recent sufferer from hypertosis attached to the vertebrae of an Ichthyosaurus. In a milieu in which intellectuals were interested in comparative anatomy, disputed reconstructions, and contentious historical origins the Venus de Milo could hardly fail to become a cultural focus: indeed some of the responses to the statue we discussed (especially the welter of restorations) do seem to have been not just inflected by, but in some sense displacements from, parallel debates and controversies in the natural sciences.

In that 1975 article, I further emphasised that the Venus' arrival in Paris co-incided with the intensification of the division of labour, the growth of industrial capitalism, and the consequent shattering into specialisms of the cultural fabric. From this historical moment on, the whole man or woman of the 'Greek ideal' belonged to the past; but many longed to equate the shattered and divided with an idealised whole. They, as it were, saw themselves in the broken Venus, but, as the century progressed, so did the tendency to relate to her as if she were an intact, ideal, and unsurpassable whole.

It also seemed possible to explain the Venus' second re-incarnation within the Mega-Visual tradition in a similar way. Although the romantic and classicist revivalist responses to the Venus withered with the waning of those cultural movements through which they had found expression, the Venus remained ambiguous and transformable, as a signifier. The statue still had no arms; its drapery appeared as if it was about to fall away in the second after that depicted. The Venus could do nothing

to defend herself against such revealing exposure. The sense of
time, and the view of women which this involved could be
related to the conventions of the contemporary photographic
pin-up, which frequently depicts a helpless, available woman
the moment before her last item of clothing falls. (Of
course, when the Venus was reproduced as an image within the
Mega-Visual tradition it was most frequently through the
medium of photography.) If that sounds like a banalising
reduction then, I argued, it corresponded to the modes of the
pin-up and advertising image, which were themselves inherently
banalising. They became focused only through emphasis upon
incident, stereo-type, appearance, and the inflation of trivial
promises. Explanations upon these lines, I felt, could much
better explain the survival of the Venus de Milo as 'a trade mark
of Beauty' than any references to enduring ideals permanently
lodged within her.

You will have noticed that my approach to the Venus in 1975
was *relativist*: by this I mean that in attempting to account for
an *apparently* continuous response to the statue I emphasised
the variability of both the signifier and the sign. The physical
condition of the sculpture changed; so did the meaning which
it had for those who looked upon it at different times. I would
not have taken you through what I thought a few years ago in
such detail unless today I still thought that there was much
truth in it. Nonetheless, even at the time, and much more so
now, I felt that something was lacking from my account.

I can best illustrate this by pointing to an improbable
parallel: that of Lenin's view about 'Jesus Christ'. Lenin was
well aware that christological forms were produced by the
processes of history and subject to cultural variation. But he
erroneously concluded from this that the 'Christ-Myth'
theories, put forward by Drews and others, were correct. According to such views, Jesus had never existed at all and it was
only the historically determined fiction of 'The Christ' which
had given rise to the *idea* that there was once a man called Jesus.
But, as Milan Machoveč points out, 'no reputable scholar today
would question . . . that the development took place exactly
the opposite way round: from the historical Jesus to the
theological Christ, not from the mythological Christ to the
allegedly historical (or historic*ised*) Jesus.'[43]
Surprisingly, perhaps, Lenin's position on Jesus was thus

much too idealist. His desire to emphasise the fictional character of 'The Christ' led him to dissolve the concrete, historical man into a series of disembodied abstract relations. As a materialist, Lenin should have realised that if 'The Christ' did not come down from heaven, he came up from a man. It is in this sense that I believe my former view of the Venus of Milo was too idealist.

It is surprising that Lenin made this mistake; after all, he was a vociferous critic of Plekhanov's extreme relativism; and, indeed, it is through scrutinising Plekhanov that I think I can make clear the nature of my own missing element in the analysis of the Venus. Plekhanov polemicised against all 'absolute' values in aesthetics. He held that no criteria should be accepted as scientific except specific or *relative* ones. He saw art works as being 'manifestations and facts generated by human social relations.'[44] Since conditions of social development were relative, so too were 'attitudes in creative work.' The art of different periods could not reasonably be approached with the same yardstick: each epoch has its own standards and criteria peculiar to itself.

Plekhanov's views on aesthetics were, of course, derivatives of his class-relative conception of truth. Plekhanov argues that what looks black to one class seems white to another; one sees truth where the other discerns only falsehood. Thus he concludes that in class society all truth is relative; there can be no absolute truth: 'Art . . . is an expression of truth. Now the truth ought to be recognised by all, but it remains relative as long as there are classes, and our aesthetic notions develop in the struggle of relative (class) ideologies.'[45] Thus Plekanhov held that there could be no materialist criteria for preferring the art of one era over and above that of another. 'Scientific Aesthetics', i.e. the Plekhanov extreme relativist aesthetics, provided no theoretical basis for contending that Greek art must be admired and Gothic art condemned or vice versa, or for accepting some trends while rejecting others.

Despite this, there are many indications that Plekhanov did have decided preferences in the art of the past. For example, as Rosenthal has pointed out, he criticised the 'decadent modernism' of the bourgeois art of his time and held that if anything deserved admiration it was the art of ancient Greece 'when gods were like men, and men gódlike'.[46] He preferred Greek to medieval art, too. Indeed, his relativising of aesthetic experience is subject to all sorts of contradictions, which become apparent in his discussion of the Venus. He writes:

'Turgenev . . . once said that Venus of Milo is more indubitable than the principles of 1789. He was quite right. But what does it show? Certainly not what Turgenev wanted to show.

There are very many people in the world to whom the principles of 1789 are not only "dubitable", but entirely unknown. Ask a Hottentot who has been to a European school what he thinks of these principles, and you will find that he has never heard of them. But not only are the principles of 1789 unknown to the Hottentot; so is the Venus of Milo . . . The Venus of Milo is "indubitably" attractive only to a part of the white race. To this part of the race she really, is more indubitable than the principles of 1789. But why? Solely because these principles express relationships that correspond only to a certain phase in the development of the white race—the time when the bourgeois order was establishing itself in its struggle against the feudal order—whereas the Venus of Milo is an ideal of the female form which corresponds to *many* stages in this development. Many, but not all.'[47]

Plekhanov then goes on to discuss the cultural relativity of 'the changing ideal of the female exterior'. Christian art, he says, had its chaste icons, and Christians dismissed the classical Venuses as 'she-devils'. He writes:

'Then came a time when the antique she-devils again became pleasing to people of the white race. The way to this was prepared by the liberation movement of the West-European burghers—the movement, that is, which was most vividly reflected in the principles of 1789. Turgenev notwithstanding, therefore, we may say that Venus of Milo became the more "indubitable" in the new Europe, the more European population became ripe for the proclamation of the principles of 1789. This is not a paradox; it is sheer historical fact.'[48]

Plekhanov appears to believe that the Venus de Milo grew in 'indubitability' at a time when it was unknown and unseen beneath the Greek soil; he seems unaware that she was only found 31 years after 1789. But let that pass because, although it is not 'sheer historical fact', his argument is not thus invalidated. We can still ask whether Plekhanov was right to suggest that the Venus de Milo was no more absolute than the political principles of 1789. A few pages later, he himself provides us with an answer to this:

'The ideal of beauty prevailing at any time in any
class of society is rooted partly in the biological con
mankind's development—which, incidentally, also
distinctive racial features—and partly in the historical conditions
in which the given society or class arose and exists. It therefore
always has a very rich content that is not absolute, not unconditional, but quite specific.'[49]

Now we have seen how Plekhanov has already had to admit that
the form of the Venus de Milo corresponds to *many* stages of
class development—although he offered no explanation of what
it was about it which enabled it to come to life again in such a
different historical moment from that in which it originated. In
this passage, however, he goes far beyond that: the class-relative
component in a work of art here no longer accounts for
everything. An ideal of physical beauty is 'rooted partly in the
biological conditions of mankind's development'—conditions
which, as Timpanaro pointed out, have remained effectively the
same since the beginnings of civilisations. (Indeed, Plekhanov
himself here suggests that variations in responses to such ideals
are likely to be determined by racial rather than class differences.) Thus even Plekhanov, when faced with the Venus de
Milo, was compelled to re-introduce a component of relative
constancy in aesthetic responses to the statue which he rooted in
its appeal to areas of biological experience which have not
proved readily malleable through historical processes. Indeed,
his formulation that there is always a 'very rich content that is
not absolute, not unconditional, but quite specific' is a long
way from his more usual denial of all non-relative components
in aesthetic experience. Elsewhere, Plekhanov reduces art to 'a
manifestation of ideology' wholly determined by the economic
base; here he appears to be saying no more than that art, at least
art such as this, has an ideological element together with
elements which derive from more constant areas of experience.
Thus, even for the supreme relativist himself, it appears that,
whether he admitted it or not, the Venus de Milo was *much*
more 'indubitable' than the principles of 1789.

Much of the pleasure that we can derive from this statue
today depends upon the expression which the artist has
achieved through his mastery of human anatomy and
musculature on the one hand, and of his techniques and
materials on the other. The potentialities of our bodies are
much the same as those of the ancient Greeks. One reason why

this statue remains transparent to us and can communicate to us actively, and not just as a relic or museum piece, is because we share that common physical condition. It is true that there is much style and ideology in the Venus' anatomy: for example, only an expert is likely to realise today that the equilateral triangle formed by the points of the breasts and the umbilicus is a self-conscious return to the proportions of High Classicism, i.e. it was determined by socio-historic factors. Nonetheless this body is not frozen within such ideology: the Venus transcends it both at the level of particularity and at that of generality. She is not just an ideal, but also a vivid portrait: despite the Attic serenity of the face, the right cheek is rather larger than the left, and the corners of the mouth are not exactly alike. But the musculature of her body is immediately readable according to our knowledge of anatomy. This is not entirely destroyed by fragmentation. We can still see a muscle on the left shoulder which indicates that the left arm must have jutted out at an angle to the body, whereas, on the right side the chest muscle just below the arm pit tells us that the right arm clung closely to the torso. This is not to imply, of course, that the Venus is a mere passive reflection of bodily data like a wax-work, or those uninteresting cast 'sculptures' recently offered by American artists like Duane Hanson. The Venus has been sensitively constituted through the process of carving: each muscular tension and inflexion has been feelingly wrought from resilient stone. Here again we can bring to the statue not just our knowledge of the body itself but also, as it were, our knowledge of its limitations in expressing itself vividly through such a medium as marble, limitations which have in no way been transcended by subsequent technological advance, or socio-economic transformations.

Earlier, you may remember, I quoted somewhat mockingly from Walter Copland Perry, a Victorian idealist who posited the Venus as 'a form which transcends all our experience, which has no prototype or equal in the actual world', but if one looks at his text on the Venus as a whole one realises that he was closer to understanding its survival than the cultural relativists. Thus Perry writes of the 'vivid freshness of the flesh and the velvet softness of the skin, in which it stands unrivalled in ancient and modern art. The extraordinary skill with which minute details, such as folds of skin in the neck, are harmonised with the ideal beauty of the whole is beyond all immitation and all praise. The

life-like effect of this wonderful masterpiece is greatly enhanced
by the rare and perfect preservation of the epidermis and by the
beautiful warm yellowish tinge which the lapse of centuries has
given to the marble.'[50] Perry raises here not just the relative
constants in our response and that of the Greeks (i.e. the
statue's relation to bodily potentialities) but also the effects of
transformations of the signifier itself (i.e. the 'warm yellowish
tinge' infused by 'the lapse of centuries'.) We will return to the
problems raised by the latter in a moment. Here, I want to
emphasise that despite the idealism of his approach and the
extravagance of his judgements, this is a very *physical*
description of the statue, one which focuses upon the expressive
correspondence between the wrought marble and the potentialities of the body, a correspondence which seems to me to
have been largely unaffected by changes in either economic base
or superstructure, or both.

As we saw, Plekhanov slipped back from class-relative to
racially relative criteria: for him, the form of the Venus de Milo
could be fully appreciated only through a correspondence with
the ideals of the white race at a certain phase, or certain phases,
of its development. From a thoroughly materialist perspective,
however, it is easy enough to dispose of this position. Timpanaro argued not just that the socio-historic was penetrated by
the biological, but that the latter was itself emmeshed within
the physical. There are sculptural elements which are not just
class transcendent, but which are also racially transcendent, in
that they pertain to areas of the experience of reality which are
common to all those who have human bodies. (Such elements
are also, in my view, gender transcendent.)

This is not to deny that, just as there are undoubtedly class,
culture, and gender determined elements in the Venus (as in
most other works of art) there are also racially determined
elements. For example, I do not regard it as a co-incidence that
the finest white marble sculptures in the world have been made
by white peoples, whereas the finest ebony carvings have been
made by blacks. Nor can it be denied that this Venus celebrates
and idealises a specific racial type. Nonetheless, the attempt to
reduce its aesthetic value to racial variables seems to me fundamentally wrong-headed.

It is not just that the critical component of the working of the
materials is transparent to all racial types. In his essay, *Laocoon*,
Della Volpe writes: 'Sculpture is the expression of values or

ideas by means of a figurative language of non-metaphorical volumes and surfaces leading into depth. It is a language of free three-dimensional visual forms.'[51] Such a 'language', however, differs from any verbal language in that it is largely culturally and historically transcendent. It is accessible to those who are subject to the common physical conditions of human existence, such as being in space, subjection to gravity, etc.

Much that is significant about the Venus relates to these areas of experience. For example, art-historically, the Venus can be contrasted with the relatively flat, planar, profiles of comparable sculptures, like the Venus of Capua, which preceded it; as Clark has put it, the genius of the sculptor of this Venus resided in the fact that he redesigned the figure *in terms of depth.*[52] Even without any knowledge of what had and had not been achieved in prior sculptures of the female figure, however, the expressive force of that tremendous, swivelling movement of the torso, turning on an axis almost as violent as that which can be seen in Rubens' famous painting of a *Woman in a Fur Coat*, remains apparent. Indeed, one of the many creative contradictions of the statue—like those between the ideal and the specific portrait, the 'timeless' and the momentary, etc.—is that between the aggressive assertion of the upper body and the tranquil stasis seemingly implied by the unseen lower limbs. Such dynamic contradictions—whatever part conventions played in their determination—give expression to the energy and imagination of the man who wrought this work. They do not seem to me to be in any way dependent upon class or racial specificities.

This point can perhaps be underlined by comparing the Venus with a sculpture of a black woman by the white artist, John de Andrea. Della Volpe has emphasised the cardinal difference between the expressed and the unexpressed in sculpture by contrasting the corpses of Pompeii carbonised by larva with genuine sculptures representing the same subject. The de Andrea is a solidification of the unexpressed. Its forms are little better than awkwardly preserved data. But such a judgement has nothing whatever to do with the racial type depicted: de Andrea's representations of white women are equally fatuous. An effective sculpture could have been realised using the body of either racial type as its 'subject matter' base.

By emphasising these 'constant' or 'relatively absolute' elements in the experience of the Venus de Milo, am I then

John de Andrea,
Untitled, 1970.

jettisoning the relative components, which so preoccupied me a
few years ago, altogether? Most certainly not, because, when all
this has been said, we are still left with a key question: 'What
effect has fragmentation, i.e. changes within the physical status
of the signifier itself, had upon the way the work is seen?'

Now I have already pointed out how Furtwängler himself was
by no means happy with what he nonetheless believed to be a
correct reconstruction: the loss of the statue's arms was, you will
remember, 'less to be deplored than might at first appear'. This
was in fact the view of many previous restorers: no one, as far as
I know, vigorously urged that the statue should in fact be
repaired according to their restoration. As far back as the 1870s,
Jean Aicard had written:

> 'In truth, if the Venus de Milo had appeared to us intact,
> immaculate, still holding the glorious apple, she would not have
> dominated the modern spirit as she has done. The symbolism of
> her attributes would not have been felt by the vast majority, and
> she would have been simply, in our eyes, the heroine of the

judgement of Paris, instead of becoming the general type of beauty.

What a singular thing! It is precisely in losing an attribute which made her, in the eyes of the Ancients, the representation of Woman herself, that she was able to become the expression of the Eternal Feminine for us moderns. It is this which has made her popular; it is through this that she has been able to become a favourite subject of decoration; it is for this that one finds her in rooms devoid of all luxury as well as on the precious furniture of the palaces of Europe; it is this which has inspired the artists who have dreamed of the missing arms of the Venus de Milo.'[53]

I have already criticised Kenneth Clark for writing of the Venus de Milo *as if* it was intact; however, elsewhere, when considering the Laocoon—a sculpture whose arm was actually repaired soon after its discovery—he comments:

'Antique art has come down to us in a fragmentary condition, and we have virtuously adapted our taste to this necessity. Almost all our favourite specimens of Greek sculpture, from the 6th century onwards, were originally parts of compositions, and if we were faced with the complete group in which the Charioteer of Delphi was once a subsidary figure, we might well experience a moment of revulsion. We have come to think of the fragment as more vivid, more concentrated and more authentic. That revelation of personal sensibility, the quality of the sketch, to which Croce has given a philosophic justification, is overlayed and smothered by labour. We can test this by imagining, or seeing in a cast, a fragment of the Laocoon, for example the father's torso and thigh. How life-enhancing they are when allowed to make their effect by formal qualities alone, without encumbering detail. There is scarcely another nude in which emotion is communicated with such absolute mastery of means. The accessory snakes and sons seem to lessen the immediacy of this effect.'[54]

Clark advises that we should mistrust an aesthetic which habitually prefers the part to the whole. But how is it that the fragmented Venus can appear, to us, more 'vivid' and 'authentic' than the lost whole?

Part of the answer, at least, seems to me straightforward. It has been suggested in the quotation from Aicard. Fragmentation physically stripped the Venus out of its original signifying system—if Furtwängler was right, a highly complex one involving traditional types for the Venus, the apple as sign, the cult of Tyche peculiar to Melos, Greek athletic practices, and late second century attitudes towards both Hellenistic and high Athenian civilisations. When the arms were lost, the statue was no longer locked so firmly into this intricate set of ideological relations. Its meaning became more ambiguous, and hence more open to annexation by subsequent signifying systems. The disappearance of the arms also served to shift the focus from the statue's cultic, and other historically specific relations, on to those relatively constant elements which we have been discussing. Something similar could also be said of many of the great survivors of painting and sculpture. The Moses of Michelangelo, the Mona Lisa, and the horses of Venice, for example, are all fragments or elements which have been prised out of a complete composition to which they once belonged or, as in the case of the Moses, for which they were originally intended.

But I do not think this can be the whole story. More powerful forces are also involved in determining the present preference for the fragment. In order to expose them, we must turn again to psychoanalysis.

When I was in the middle of my original work on the Venus de Milo in 1975, I went to a lecture by a leading authority on Kleinian psychoanalysis, Hanna Segal, who demonstrated that 'there can be a psychoanalytic view of art which can contribute to our understanding of artistic form and process no less than content.'[55] Her lecture forcefully brought home to me at the theoretical level the inadequacy and lacunae in my 'social history' approach. As I listened, I became aware that the story of the Venus, its resurrection and reconstitution, could almost be taken as a paradigm of the Kleinian view of art.

The next day, I wrote excitedly and no doubt confusedly to Hanna Segal. I poured out details of the comings and goings of boats in Melos harbour a century and a half ago, mysterious fights on the beach over the statue of a beautiful woman, lost fragments, and Victorian restorations. Perhaps not surprisingly, she did not reply. But at least her lecture made me aware of the way in which I had used historical and cultural information about the Venus to evade confronting the urgent emotions which it evoked in me, to avoid, if you will, my aesthetic experience of it—and, more especially, the determinants of that experience. It was to be a long time before I could integrate all the different levels into a coherent view; my 1975 article, for example, made no mention of psychoanalysis from start to finish. But Kleinian theory—despite the grave reservations which I now have concerning many aspects of it—provided me with the 'break-through' I needed.

I am afraid that the account which I can give you of Klein and her theories here can only be of the most rudimentary and schematic kind. It is perhaps appropriate that, to those of you who wish to investigate her work further, I can recommend Segal's two introductory books.[56] But I may perhaps differ from Segal in my belief that Klein's theories can only fully be understood if one takes her own psychological make-up, the organisational history of the psycho-analytic movement, and the overall cultural and historical situations in which she worked into account. John Padel, himself a distinguished British analyst, has had to warn Klein's followers, 'there is no understanding without history.'[57] Evidently, this is something I cannot even sketch, but must only hint at here.

Klein was born in Vienna in 1882; she first involved herself with psychoanalysis in Budapest in 1910. She thus entered the movement towards the end of the heroic years of Freud's first phase, at a time when the great organisational and theoretical controversies were erupting. Klein was analysed first by Ferenzci, and, in the early 1920s, by Karl Abraham in Berlin. Though she was never herself close to Freud, Ferenzci and Abraham were the most intimate of Freud's inner circle of disciples after the rupture with Jung.

In her own psychoanalytic work, Klein specialised in dealing with children. This brought her into conflict with Anna Freud, who was also pioneering the same field, but with very different theoretical and clinical approaches. Klein's relations with members of the Berlin and Vienna Psychoanalytical Societies became less than comfortable. In 1925, however, Ernest Jones invited her to lecture in England, where she settled the following year. Her clash with Anna Freud emerged forcefully at the Innsbrück Congress of 1927—where Klein dogmatically preached infant analysis for all. Nonetheless, she was able to carry on working for a few years relatively uncontentiously within the British Psychoanalytic Society. She gathered around herself a number of co-workers and disciples.

But soon there were problems. For example, one of the most prominent of Klein's early supporters in the British Psychoanalytic Society, Edward Glover—who had himself also been analysed by Abraham—turned against Klein. Klein's daughter, Melitta Schmideberg, who had sided with her mother during the latter's divorce, and had subsequently passed through analysis with Glover into the psychoanalytic movement, followed her analyst and publicly took up sides against Klein. The accusations stressed the incompatibility between her work and Freud's. And then, in the late 1930s, many analysts from Austria and Germany fled from the Nazis to live and work in Britain. They were not sympathetic to the permeation of Kleinian ideas within the British Society. Finally, in 1938, Freud and his daughter, Anna, came here.

At the time of Freud's death it must have seemed that an eventual split within the psychoanalytic movement was, yet again, virtually inevitable. The polemic and vitriol put out by both sides was deafening. However all parties recognised the undesirability of further factional splits: so-called 'Controversial Discussions' were held in 1943, in which theoretical differences were openly explored. Organizationally, these gave rise to a so-called 'Gentleman's Agreement'—hardly an appropriate description since the major antagonists were women; training facilities for analysts were divided into three groups, (Anna) Freudian, Kleinian, and so-called 'neutral' (within which the most fruitful subsequent theoretical developments were to occur.) This agreement held, and indeed survives to this day—although the era of major 'theoretical' disputes with organisational implications may be largely (though not entirely) superseded. Certainly, the most 'orthodox' of psychoanalytic societies contains a wider range of theoretical variations than those which divided Anna Freud and Klein.

What were the theoretical underpinnings of the Kleinian controversy? I have already described how Klein entered the movement at a critical moment in its history, a moment when, you will remember, Freud's original instinctual opposition had fallen into disarray and his structural metaphors for psychological entities required drastic revision. Freud's own last major theoretical work, *The Ego and the Id*, was published in 1923: in it, he proposed a new topography of the psychic apparatus, introducing the terms 'Id' and 'Super-Ego' for the first time. In essence, Anna Freud followed that tendency in Freud's later thought which invested a new importance in the *ego*; her work stressed the onset and growth of self-awareness. She related the classical Freudian phases of libidinal development to the emergence of a sense of identity. Anna Freud's influence was most strongly felt in America, where such workers as Hartmann and Rapaport extended her 'ego psychology' through their preoccupation with problems like adaptation, and the so-called 'conflict free' areas and 'autonomous functions' of the ego. It could be said that this tendency, which largely as a result of the growth and commercialisation of psychoanalysis in America became dominant, was primarily concerned with rediscovering and re-instating the 'rational' ego as opposed to the irrational unconscious, which, at various critical points in Freud's metapsychological development, had appeared on the verge of vanishing altogether.

Klein, however, had very different interests, although she too developed all her major theories from hints, question marks, and insights to be found in the later Freud. Unfortunately, I do not have time to follow Klein's theories as they emerged, and must content myself with a thumb-nail sketch of certain features of her finished 'system'. Like Freud's, Klein's was always an *instinct*-based psychology, but, unlike the 'classical' psychoanalysts, Klein took literally Freud's speculative, late opposition of the Life and Death instincts—first put forward in *Beyond the Pleasure Principle*, in 1920. (Glover later accused Klein of 'deviation' from Freud;[58] Guntrip perceptively remarked, 'Mrs. Klein's "deviation" from Freud consists, in fact, of the radical development of Freud's own greatest deviation from himself.')[59] Klein lays great stress on the innate ambivalence between love and hate which, she maintains, derives from this fundamental opposition. She sees the destructive drives, sadism and aggression of the infant as being a defensive turning away from the self of this inherent, self-destructive Death instinct.

Klein gives a peculiar importance to the earliest months of life. Her system focuses upon the way in which the infant supposedly copes with its over-bearing instinctual drives in relation to the Mother and her breast. The criticism has often been made that, although Klein paid lip-service to the importance of the environment, she could not bring herself to allow for its influence on the child's development. The quality of mothering (a central pre-occupation of later full 'object relations' theories) could have no real influence on the instinctually determined inter-play of love and hate postulated in the Kleinian system. Roazen has credibly related 'the increasing need in (Klein's) writings to justify the mother and accuse the child' to her personal and 'theoretical' differences with her daughter, Melitta.[60] Certainly, one of the more problematic late Kleinian concepts is her attribution to infants of innate *envy* of the Mother's breast and its creativity.

Given her emphasis on aggression, the infant emerges in Klein's writing as truly monstrous. She writes herself:

> 'The idea of an infant from six to twelve months trying to destroy its mother by every method at the disposal of its sadistic trends—with its teeth, nails and excreta and with the whole of its body, transformed in phantasy into all kinds of dangerous weapons—presents a horrifying, not to say unbelievable picture to our minds.'[61]

But all Kleinian writers emphasise how the infant's desires in relation to the Mother's body are bound up with frustration, envy, hatred, and destructiveness. Segal comments:

> 'These desires also involve objects phantasised inside mother's· body, and in relation to them the infant also has greedy libidinal desires and phantasies of scooping them out and devouring them or, because of his hatred and envy, aggressive phantasies of biting, tearing and destroying.'[62]

In Kleinian theory, phantasy (spelled with a 'ph' to differentiate it from those usages which refer only to a *conscious* psychic process) plays a part quite unprecedented in Freud. Susan Isaacs' study of phantasy, one of the theoretical contributions to the 'Controversial Discussions', is still the most authoritative Kleinian exposition of the subject.[63] She describes phantasy as the mental expression, the 'psychic representative', of instinct, and emphasises the 'wealth of unconscious phantasies' dating back to the earliest months of life— especially those involving violent, sadistic attacks on the mother's body. What an outside observer might describe as a mechanism, a subject experiences as a phantasy. According to Kleinians, defences are erected against phantasies which show 'the same protean and kaleidoscopic changes as the contents of a dream'. Therapeutically, a Kleinian analysis focuses upon the interpretation of them.

Klein's view of ego-development differed sharply from Freud's. Klein maintained that a rudimentary ego was innate (whereas in Freud, the ego becomes differentiated from the id only as a result of the operation of the reality principle.) But Klein saw the growth of the ego as being the product of a continual process of projection and introjection. Introjection is the process by which the functions of an object, i.e. a person, in the outer world are annexed by the subject's mental representation of that object, or, as Rycroft puts it, the process 'by which the relationship with an object "out there" is replaced by one with an imagined object "inside".'[64] Projection is the reverse process by which aspects of the self—such as impulses, wishes, or internal objects—are treated as aspects of objects in the external world. The process is nuanced by the fact that representations of objects which are introjected can themselves have been distorted by projections. As Guntrip puts it, in the Kleinian conception,

> 'We live in these two worlds at the same time, one mental and the other material, the one a perpetuation of the past and the other an exploration of the present, and we are involved in both of them in situations and relationships which rouse in us excitements, emotions and impulses of all kinds. It is impossible to keep the two worlds of outer and inner reality, of conscious and unconscious mental life, entirely separate.'[65]

Fairbairn has pointed out that in Klein's work, Freud's original distinction between the conscious and the unconscious becomes less important than the distinction between these two worlds of outer reality and inner reality.[66]

In place of Freud's succession of libidinal phases, Klein postulated two 'positions' which, she argued, the developing infant had to work through during the earliest months of life. The first of these was the so-called 'paranoid-schizoid' position, characterised by a process known as 'splitting'. Essentially, the infant is seen as dividing the representation of the breast into two, the 'good', satisfying, succouring breast, and the 'bad', denying, frustrating breast. Usually (though of course there are individual variations) the infant seeks to introject the 'good' breast which forms an internal source of well-being and the basis of later autonomy, and to project his own aggressive feelings onto the 'bad' breast, which he conceives of as a terrifying persecutor. In the paranoid-schizoid position, the mother is not yet a 'whole object' for the infant. As Hanna Segal puts it:

> '. . . the infant lives in a world of part objects: the mother's breast, hands, eyes, holding arms. These objects are not only anatomically part objects; they are also split in his mind into very good and very bad ones. The very young infant sways between

states of blissful satisfaction where he feels united or fused with his ideal objects and states of hatred and persecution when he feels his objects are totally bad. His love is directed to his ideal objects and his hatred to the bad objects conceived as the sources of all his pain and fear.'[67]

The 'paranoid-schizoid' position is succeeded by the 'depressive position'; now this is really the determinative moment in the Kleinian scheme of things, displacing the classical Oedipal complex as the decisive developmental event. In the depressive position the infant learns to accept ambivalence, and to acknowledge that 'good' and 'bad' are but aspects of the same 'whole object', the mother, out there in the world, whom the infant *both* loves *and* hates. Let me quote Segal again:

'The "depressive position", as described by Melanie Klein, is reached by the infant when he recognizes his mother and other people, and amongst them his father, as real persons. His object relations then undergo a fundamental change. Where earlier he was aware of "part objects" he now perceives complete persons; instead of "split" objects—ideally good or overwhelming persecuting—he sees a whole object both good and bad. The whole object is loved and introjected and forms the core of an integrated ego. But this new constellation ushers in a new anxiety situation; where earlier the infant feared an attack on the ego by persecutory objects, now the predominant fear is that of the loss of the loved object in the external world and in his own inside. The infant at that stage is still under the sway of uncontrollable greedy and sadistic impulses. In phantasy his loved object is continually attacked in greed and hatred, is destroyed, torn into pieces and fragments; and not only is the external object so attacked but also the internal one, and then the whole internal world feels destroyed and shattered as well. Bits of the destroyed object may turn into persecutors, and there is a fear of internal persecution as well as a pining for the lost loved object and guilt for the attack. The memory of the good situation, where the infant's ego contained the whole loved object, and the realization that it has been lost through his own attacks, gives rise to an intense feeling of loss and guilt, and to the wish to restore and re-create the lost love object outside and within the ego.'[68]

This experience of total desolation, then, 'gives rise to reparative impulses—to an overwhelming desire that what has been destroyed must be re-created, reconstructed and regained.' It is important to emphasise that the reparative impulses are directed not only at the mother's body, but secondarily also at other 'internal objects' felt to have been destroyed, which include the parental couple, since during the depressive position the infant is assumed to become aware of parental intercourse. The reparative impulses, 'the wish and the capacity for restoration of the good object, internal and external,' are held to be 'a fundamental drive in all artistic creativity.'[69]

In effect, Segal argues that the artist is working through his infantile depressive position again and is seeking to 'repair' through his artistic activity a harmonious internal world which he feels himself to have had, and to have lost, through his own aggression. But it is not enough for him 'to re-create something in his inner world corresponding to the re-creation of his internal objects.'[70] He also has to externalise the completed object, and to give it a life of its own in the external world.

This side of artistic production was stressed by another early pioneer in Kleinian aesthetics, Adrian Stokes: 'The work of art is esteemed for its otherness, as a self-sufficient object, no less than as an ego-figure.' Stokes was not, of course, a psychoanalyst himself: he was a painter, an aesthete, and a writer about art. Stokes' position was similar to that of Segal's:

'We are intact only in so far as our objects are intact. Art of whatever kind bears witness to intact objects even when the subject-matter is disintegration. Whatever the form of transcript the original conservation or restoration is of the mother's body.'[71]

Thus, for Stokes:

'. . . whatever the projection of narrow compulsions . . . whatever the primitive and enveloping relationships that ensue, the reconstitution or restoration of the outside and independent whole object (expressive equally of co-ordination in the ego) whether founded entirely, or less founded, upon what I have called minimum or generalized or ideal and impersonal conceptions, remains a paramount function in art.'[72]

There are, however, interesting differences between Stokes and Segal. Stokes found elements belonging not just to the depressive position, but also to its precursor, the paranoid-schizoid position in both artistic creativity and aesthetic experience. For him, the artist was not just working through the depressive position, but also necessarily expressing that sense of fusion with the mother (breast), and sadistic attack upon her, characteristic of the earliest stage. As he puts it, 'We can always discover from aesthetic experience that sense of homogeneity or fusion combined, in differing proportions, with the sense of object-otherness.' Thus Stokes argues that negative expressions can figure successfully in art if there is present, as well, 'a reparative nucleus', one sign of which can be a richness or excellence attributed to the medium, or even 'to art in general'. (Roualt and Soutine would appear to be examples of this.) As Stokes writes:

> 'In defining aesthetic form I have indicated that subject-matter is organised under the dominion of two imagos or prototypical experiences that have been introjected: first, the feeling of oneness with the breast and so with the world; secondly, the keen recognition of a separate object, originally the mother's whole person whose loss was mourned in the infantile depressive position. The second postulate is in accord with Dr. Segal's analysis of the aesthetic approach to the solution of despressive phantasies. But is my first postulate (merging with the breast) at variance?'[73]

Here, I merely wish to raise Stoke's question, not to answer it: what he says himself in reply has the aroma of diplomacy. The question of primitive fusion, oceanic feeling, and mergence with the breast as a component in aesthetic experience and artistic creativity will come into clearer focus in our next two seminars: it is something which becomes fully explicable only beyond the Kleinian system. The problem for Segal in admitting such elements was that they smacked of the so-called manic defences, in which the feelings and mechanisms of the earlier position are re-invoked in order to *deny* depressive experience and its concommitant sense of loss, rather than to work it through. There was such a thing as manic reparation, but when manifested in art, in Segal's view, this would lead to sentimentality, over-sweetness, a sense of unreality, and facile idealisation. She gave such elements none but a distorting role in her account of aesthetic experience. Stokes, on the other hand, came increasingly to associate two modes of art—the modelling and carving traditions respectively—with the two positions, paranoid-schizoid and depressive. Whereas his earlier work focuses upon the carving mode, his later subtlety rehabilitates the modelling.

Rickmann—himself an influential follower of Klein—emphasised that 'underlying impulses of destructiveness' provide a 'substratum to Art' and to aesthetic experience, alongside the reparative processes. This is a theme drawn out by Segal too.

She stresses that the aesthetic experience of the recipient of art is not only, nor even primarily, one of sensuous pleasure. Rather she maintains that aesthetic pleasure is derived from our unconscious identification with the artist's depressive struggle and his emergence from it. As she puts it, 'For true reparation to be done, there must be admission of the original destruction—otherwise, there is no true reparation, but only denial.'[74] Thus she writes:

> 'Take, for example, the aesthetic concepts of the ugly and the beautiful; from the psychoanalytic point of view . . . the ugly corresponds to the destroyed, to what is fragmented, lacking in rhythm and wholeness and harmony. I would say the ugly signifies the destruction of the internal world and its results; the beautiful is usually seen as the rhythmical, the harmonious, the whole—corresponding to the experience of a loved, whole, good object and self. Both the ugly and the beautiful are an essential part of aesthetic experience. A work of art devoid of the elements we might call ugly would not be beautiful, but merely pretty.'[75]

She insists that the working through of the conflict must penetrate the work, even if the final outcome is cheerful or serene. Indeed, she suggests that in the most aesthetically satisfying works, the formal resolution is never quite complete:

> 'We must complete the work internally: our own imaginations must bridge the last gap. (Anton Ehrenzweig draws attention to the fact that a drawing is always made with interrupted lines.) . . . It is inferior art which gives us, as it were, all the answers—when we see, or hear, or read it, we may enjoy the experience, but have no wish to repeat it.'[76]

Dali once used the Venus de Milo as the basis for a work of his own, *Venus de Milo aux Tiroirs*: this was a half-scale maquette of the statue with drawers set into the forehead, belly and knees. The handles of the drawers were white, rabbit-tail tufts. Dali explained:

> 'All the drawers had to be put into an ample body not yet having been exposed to the Christian invention of remorse of conscience. This sculpture could cure us of psychoanalysis.'[77]

In fact, psychoanalysis enables us to move towards a closer understanding of the sculpture, and I want to conclude by trying to draw our various threads together.

The sculptor of the Venus rendered an expressive representation of the body of a beautiful, mature, maternal woman—about 30 years old—through the way in which he worked his marble. Evidently, what he did was influenced not only by a specific ideology of the body, but also, in a more general sense, by that of the society within which he worked. But his end product was dislocated from the ideology of his times, on the one hand by his conscious evocation of classical style, and on the other by what is sometimes called his 'naturalism', i.e. his ability to re-create imaginatively through his handling of stone expressive potentialities of the skin, flesh and musculature of the body. Since these are part of the continuity of human physical and somatic being, they provide

Salvador Dali, *Venus de Milo aux Tiroirs*, 1936.

the basis through which his representation was able to remain continuously transparent after its re-discovery in the 19th century. The sculpture's immediate relation to the body is not significantly changed by socio-economic transformations, and this relation forms the *sine qua non* of the statue's survival as something other than a historical document. The statue's *relative* detachment from a specific ideological moment (and hence its accessibility to successive ideological moments) was reflected both in the wide range of credible earlier datings which it attracted, and in its subsequent cultural trajectory.

Clive Barker,
Chained Venus, 1971.

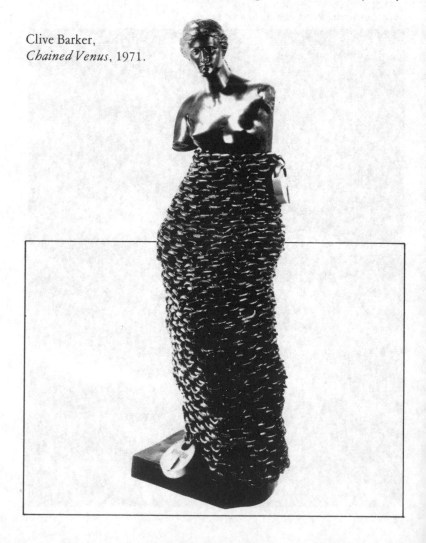

Although I am loathe to admit it, there is therefore some justification to Clark's remark that the Venus is 'the noblest refutation of contemporary critical cant that a work of art must express its own epoch.'

Earlier I described how the disappearance of the arms further released the torso from that specific signifying system within which it was originally produced; but now we are also in a position to explain the apparent aesthetic superiority of the present mutilated version over its original, as described by Aicard, Furtwängler, and, in a more general way, by Clark himself. It seems to me that the totality of injuries which the statue suffered amounted to a relatively drastic change within the signifier itself: the statue now becomes not only the representation of a woman, or an 'idealised' woman, i.e. a goddess of carnal love, but also a vivid externalisation of one of the commonest 'internal objects'. The Venus is now as close to the 'inner' world of phantasy as to the 'outer' world of real, sensuously perceived objects: indeed, as Dali seems to have correctly surmised, she is as 'surreal' as she is 'real'. (It is no coincidence that the Venus makes frequent appearances within the iconography of Surrealism, and that of its successors.)

For the millions who have enjoyed the statue since 1821, she is a representation of the internal 'Mother' who has survived the ravages of a phantasised attack. Despite her fragmentation, the reparative element remains dominant: it is expressed through the fact that the Venus *has* endured throughout the centuries; in the still-evident idealisation in the midst of naturalism; and, above all, in the sense that Stokes pointed out, through the richness and excellence which the classical sculptor so manifestly attributed to his medium.

The injuries which the statue has sustained have simultaneously rendered it, in Segal's terms, a work which we must complete internally, or at least one which refuses to give us all the answers: this, too, seems to increase our aesthetic enjoyment of it. I have already referred to the emphasis which certain Kleinian writers have given to 'underlying impulses of destructiveness' in aesthetic experience. Interestingly, Rickman observes:

> 'Some people feel uncomfortable in the presence of ancient statues which are incomplete; they say that these would be beautiful if they were not mutilated, but as now seen they are horrible and sometimes in their injured state they are even called

ugly . . . it appears that the subject identifies himself with these objects; i.e. he has thought of himself as a mutilated person, or he has identified the statue with someone whom he has in his thoughts mutilated. It would be more correct to say that the sight of the statue rouses unconscious phantasies of re-mutilation, because the phantasy is not roused for the first time by the statue. Its injury awakens the impulse to carry the destruction a stage further. These phantasies can be traced back to the patient's early years and have undergone many modifications, submergences and resuscitations.'[78]

Rickman emphasises that the phantasy of aggressive action remains unconscious, while the affect of fear or horror becomes attached to the external object so that the person does not realise his secret wish: 'the phantasy is kept from consciousness at the expense of the richness of the subject's emotional relation to an external object.'[79] Those who are so affected, Rickman suggests, are suffering from a more widespread neurotic disturbance, in which their mutilation phantasies, and the defences which they successfully or unsuccessfully raise against them, play a conspicuous part; but, for the majority, the component of mutilation enhances aesthetic experience—at least as the Kleinians describe it—through the admission of an original destruction, and of depressive struggle, rather than the 'manic denial' which can be associated with preferences for the over-complete and the uninterruptedly 'ideal'.

Here the Venus can usefully be contrasted with *The Greek Slave*, a sculpture by Hiram Powers, which for a time, enjoyed an even greater popularity in Europe and especially in America, but which is now usually regarded as a discredited piece of kitsch. In one sense, the *Slave* represents a similar subject matter, that of the captive woman: if the Venus de Milo cannot defend herself because she lacks arms, the slave is even more helpless. Her hands are manacled; she is about to be sold. Powers was an American neo-classical sculptor who lived and worked in Italy. He had a taste for Carrara marble. he produced the first of six full-length statues of the *Slave* in 1843; this was conspicuously featured at the Great Exhibition in 1851 and subsequently was shown in Paris. Meanwhile, another version toured America where it was 'widely exhibited . . . in special tents, exhibition galleries, merchants' exchanges, rotundas, etc.—throughout the late 1840s and '50s, and was lavishly praised at every stop.'[80] The *Slave*, too, penetrated deeply into

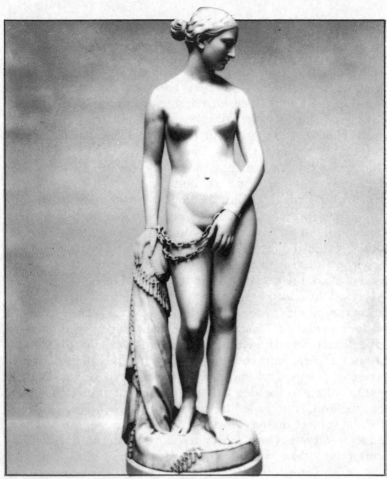

Hiram Powers, *The Greek Slave*, 1869.

19th century culture: innumerable reproductions were made of it, articles and poems written about it, and paintings and sculptures influenced by it. Henry James was one of many who have 'wondered at' *The Greek Slave* phenomenon. In 1903, he wrote:

> 'There were the names that one was brought up to, one of which for reasons I now wonder at, but do not quite seize, was that of Powers, and this in spite of *The Greek Slave*, so un-dressed, yet so refined, even so pensive, in sugar-white alabaster, exposed under little domed glass covers in such American homes as could bring themselves to think such things right.'[81]

But we are now in a position to suggest why the *Slave* has passed into cultural oblivion whereas the Venus has not. Firstly, it must be stressed that Powers—who began as a maker of wax-work tableaux in Cincinnati—could not draw from his materials those representations of 'timeless' biological expression that we found in the Venus de Milo; the smooth surface of the *Slave*'s ideological skin is never ruptured by imaginative, anatomical truth. Now it is easy to point to the elements that made this sculpture a popular success: Victorian Neo-Classicism of this kind was a culturally acceptable vehicle for otherwise socially inhibited representations of nude figures; the Greek independence struggle in Europe, and the American slavery and anti-slavery movements gave it a topical context. But there is nothing about it which can transcend that context. It is so locked within the disingenuousness of the ideological moment which produced it that even lopping off its arms (or any other part) could not release or redeem it.

As it is, the *Slave* is formally all too complete: it offers the eye neither ambiguities, nor resistances. The slickness and virtuosity of Powers' execution amount to a manic denial of depressive struggle, rather than genuine reparation. Formally, the slave is without any elements we might call ugly and this, though it sweetens, lessens and cheapens the work. All this is in such sharp contrast to the degrading nature of the subject depicted that the work is pervaded by a sense of inauthenticity. Indeed, it is the subject matter which reveals that this is a work which indulges *fantasy* (within the restrains of decorous idealisation) rather than working through *phantasy* and achieving reparation. Conscious fantasy is, of course, but the uttermost tip of the iceberg of phantasy, in the Kleinian usage, which reaches deep into the unconscious. It might thus be said that the Venus, in its mutilated state, evokes in its receptive viewers the affects attaching to their most primitive phantasies about savaging the mother's body, *and* the consequent reparative processes; whereas the Slave merely titillates by evoking (within a format of cultural rationalisations) those perverse sexual images which are themselves characteristic defences *against* working through that which gives rise to them. In form, content, and the depth of 'aesthetic experience' which it offers the *Slave* is thus cutaneous: it is held captive within that cultural moment which produced and celebrated it, whereas the Venus is not.

And now, I hope, you will be able to see why I dwelt so long and in such detail on two components in the early history of the resurrected Venus: the fight on the beach, and the reparation or reconstruction of the figure. The fight (or the rumoured fight for if it was only imagined, or greatly exaggerated, then my point would be strengthened rather than weakened) came to symbolise the phantasy of attack on the mother's body, or rather on the internal representation of that body. The Venus was dragged from the earth, a 'timeless' goddess, like some imago salvaged from the unconscious: she was, it seems, subjected to gross ill-treatment, and mishandling, perhaps to actual mutilation. But she survived. And behind all those attempts to lie about what had happened, to cover it up, perhaps even to elaborate it, behind all those rumours about which bits had been broken off by whom, lay those powerful unconscious phantasies concerning the mother's body so vividly described by the Kleinian analysts. Now I am *not* saying that these events were determined (although they *were* necessarily inflected) by the primitive affects which they aroused in those who took part in them. But the rumours of this attack, and indeed of the further sabotage to which the statue was subjected on its arrival at the Louvre, seem to lurk behind the reception of the Venus, to deepen the emotional responses of those involved with it.

Similarly, the phase of attack was superseded by that of reparative drive: it is in this way that we can explain the obsession with piecing together the parts of the Venus into a whole, with repairing and restoring that which has been (almost) destroyed, the reluctance on the part of the savants to believe that the Venus could *originally* have been made up out of parts, and even the 'wild' rumours that she had in fact been found intact. It is in terms of the reparative drives, I think, that we can understand the reconstructive responses to the Venus I discussed earlier. Certainly, the majority of these were something more than objective, art-historical work. As Furtwängler demonstrated, a high proportion of the reconstructions are simply non-starters. They reflected the phantasies of those who proposed them as much as the material possibilities of the statue. Of course, only a few were totally irrational, but the ambiguities within the original forms of the Venus, exaggerated by mutilation, provided a nucleus for a wide range of reparative elaborations.

Hanna Segal observed that under the influence of the
reparative drives, 'Love is brought more sharply into conflict
with hate, and is active both in controlling destructiveness and
in repairing and restoring damage done.'[82] In many of the early
reconstructions, hate (Mars) is presented as being in some way
subdued or tamed by love. Indeed, the tendency to group the
figure with others, despite all the evidence that it was free-
standing and isolated within a niche, suggests that some
restorers were, as one might expect, exerting reparative drives in
relation to internal objects other than the mother's body, itself.
One might, for example, go so far as to suggest that Ravaisson's
'couple conjugale' constitutes an externalisation of the repaired
'parental couple'. Many of the more idiosyncratic versions
seem to retain highly personalised components, which remain transparent despite the numismatic and iconographic
rationalisations with which the restorer surrounded them. (For
example, I am prepared to hazard an entirely unsubstantiated
guess that the differences between such extreme and idiotic
reconstructions as those of Kiel and Bell could be correlated, if
we had sufficient information, with the specificities of their
respective mothers.) Some restorations suggest characteristic
disturbance of the reparative impulses; indeed the bizarre
'pike' and 'stake' versions appear to be representations of the
'phallic woman'.

It should now be growing quite clear that if at one point
we seem to be moving sharply away from the idea of historically
relative responses, we are now very firmly involved with them
again. Perhaps I can put it this way. Both the human body (in
the world) and the Mother's body (of the internal world) are,
relatively speaking, constants of human experience. The Venus
de Milo mark one was (in relatively absolute terms) consummately expressive of the former; in its mutilated state, it has become consummately expressive of the conquest over depressive
struggles surrounding the latter. But the question remains as to
why we should prefer the fragment of this sort to the sensuous
idealisations of the Greeks, or indeed to that total denial of
sensuality in art which led the early Christians, as Plekhanov
pointed out, to regard statues like the Venus de Milo as 'she-
devils'. This is a point which the Marxist art historian, Arnold
Hauser, seems to have had in mind when, after praising
Rickman's observations on responses to mutilated statues, he
went on to say:

'The historical point of view is neglected here, however, as in psychoanalytic writings in general, for otherwise the author could hardly have failed to notice that the enjoyment of or the aversion to fragmentary works of art is, above all, a historical phenomenon, varying with cultural background. The delight in ruins, torsos, sketches, so characteristic of the second half of the 18th century and the subsequent period, is a symptom of the romantic mood, which has now taken hold of the Western world. It is only within this frame of mind that the whole psychic mechanism of frustration, retaliation, compensation, a sense of guilt, and anxiety for restitution, as psychoanalysis describes it, becomes operative and creative in art; it is only from that time on that a torso is felt to be more suggestive and expressive than an unmutilated work of art.

It is since romanticism that art has become a quest for a home that the artist believes he possessed in his childhood, and which assumes in his eyes the character of a Paradise lost through his own fault.'[83]

I do not think there can be any disputing Hauser on this point. Certainly, when Segal says 'the wish and the capacity for restoration of the good object, internal and external' is 'the basis for creative activities which are rooted in the infant's wish to restore and recreate his lost happiness, his lost internal objects and the harmony of his internal world',[84] her insight seems much more true of the Romantic and post-Romantic artist than of, say, the Greek sculptor, or the 18th century Neo-Classicist. This is not to say that in Greek or Neo-Classical art the idea of reparation has no relevance. Indeed, as Fairbairn wrote at a time when he was himself deeply under the influence of Klein, Greek art provides 'the most obvious example' of 'the dominance of the principle of restitution' in art: 'it is hard to imagine any more convincing attempt to establish the integrity of the object than that represented by the symmetry of Greek architecture and by the perfection of form and purity of line, which are such obvious features of Greek sculpture.'[85] The problem is, however, that the Greeks and Neo-Classicists made a different kind of demand of their sculptures than the Romantics and post-Romantics. The Kleinian view posits aesthetic experience as being, in their terminology, intimately related to the working through of depressive struggles. Hence the broken Venus is, with its admission of 'attack', a 'deeper' and more satisfying work than an intact, complete original

which denies it. (As Fairbairn put it in 'The Ultimate Basis of
Aesthetic Experience', 'to appear beautiful, the work of art must
be able above all to produce in the beholder an impression of
the "integrity of the object": but, in order to do so, it must at
the same time provide a release for the emotions which imply
the destruction of the object. Otherwise the conditions of
restitution remain unsatisfied; and aesthetic experience is
accordingly precluded.')[86]

Similarly, contemporary 'taste' commonly prefers the aesthetic experience of Michelangelo's unfinished figures to
that of those which he completed. (One level of expression—
the anatomical—is not necessarily called into question through
recognition of this relativity: indeed, one might say that it was
only because the Greek sculptors so vividly expressed concrete
relations between the marble and the body that Christians
hated their work so much, or that, once fragmented, the Venus
was capable of becoming an epitome of art in the Romantic
era.) However, despite this we know that the Greeks abhorred
any intimation of mutilation in their sculptures. (They would
not have been able to attend to the Venus in its present state at
all, let alone to have derived a deep aesthetic experience from
it.)

Perhaps we can say that an effective work of art is expressive
of potentialities of human experience which remain relatively
constant, and yet not every work of art draws upon the same
components and emotions or combines them in the same
proportions. Within what we now describe as the category of
the 'aesthetic', a range, but by no means an infinite range, of
'basic emotions' and areas of experience are structured within
culturally and ideologically inflected forms, which they may, or
may not, succeed in 'transcending'. The success of the
rediscovered Venus was due in part to the fact that it was found
at a historical moment when concern with one area of experience was beginning to be displaced by a concern with
another: but the form of the Venus, given the effects of history
upon it, was such that it could straddle these polarities, and be
seen as expressive of the gamut from the fully restituted (or
ideal) object (if you were a Leighton or a Moore) to an object
which could also 'provide a release for the emotions which
imply the destruction of the object'. The Kleinian account of
aesthetics, however, can provide us with part of the explanation
as to why the fragment is now often experienced as more

satisfying than the whole: but it cannot, of its own, explain fully why at this particular moment of history, the dominant mode of aesthetic experience should be of this kind.

Moreover, in their emphasis on, perhaps even exaggeration of, the axis of attack-restitution and its indubitable significance to aesthetics, the Kleinians also leave out of account other contributory factors. At one extreme, as Hauser perceived, they are silent upon the relationship of the realised forms to history: on the other, as Stokes saw, they have little to say about the operation of more benign elements from early life—such as the feeling of fusion with rather than attack upon the mother—in much aesthetic experience. The Venus de Milo is a work in relation to which Kleinian considerations seem of particular significance: there are many where they appear to be much less important. But these are issues which we will investigate more thoroughly in our next two seminars.

THE RISE OF MODERNISM
AND THE
INFANT-MOTHER RELATIONSHIP

I BEGAN this series of seminars by pointing to a weakness in the traditional Marxist approach to art, a weakness manifest in the writings of Marx himself, which is immediately raised when we ask the question: How do works of art outlive their origins? I suggested that Sebastiano Timpanaro had pointed to the direction in which we might look for an answer by emphasising the relative biological constancy of 'the human condition', a constancy which underlies socio-economic historical variation. I further argued that psychoanalysis, at least psychoanalysis understood as a theory of biological meaning, could thereby be expected to provide a significant component in any materialist aesthetics.

In these last two seminars we will look at what would be another Achilles' heel of Marxist approaches to works of art, were it possible to have more than one. We will approach the problem of *abstraction*, or, more generally, why it is that certain types of art which seem to bear no discernible relationship to the perception of the objective world not only appear to us to be 'good' but are also capable of giving us intense pleasure.

However I am afraid that once again it is going to be necessary to burrow towards tentative answers in a rather labyrinthine way. To hark back to our last session, it may well appear to you at times that I have arrived here with a bag of disjointed fragments. But I would ask you to bear with me. Although it may sometimes seem that we are toying with an extraneous left foot that got attached to the torso of the argument in error, I think, in fact, it does add up.

I would like to begin by referring to a book called, *On Not Being Able to Paint*, written by Marion Milner, and published in 1950. This book is well-known among educationalists and psychologists, though not, I think, among artists, nor indeed anywhere within the art world. In one sense I suppose that is not surprising: what title could be more seemingly irrelevant to someone who does paint than, *On Not Being Able to Paint*? In fact, however, Milner's book is among the most interesting of all texts by practising psychoanalysts on art.

In her introduction, Milner explains how she had spent five years in schools making a scientific study of the way in which children were affected by orthodox educational methods; she found herself subject to growing misgivings about this work and felt that these misgivings were connected with the 'problem of psychic creativity'. Gradually she came to the view that 'somehow the problem might be approached through studying one specific area in which I myself had failed to learn something that I wanted to learn.'[1] That something, for Milner, was painting:

> 'Always, ever since early childhood, I had been interested in learning how to paint. But in spite of having acquired some technical facility in representing the appearance of objects my efforts had always tended to peter out in a maze of uncertainties about what a painter is really trying to do.'[2]

The choice of painting as the means towards finding out something about 'the general educational problem' was facilitated when Milner discovered that 'it was possible at times to produce drawings or sketches in an entirely different way from that I had been taught, a way of letting hand and eye do exactly what pleased them without any conscious working to a preconceived intention.' The book chronicles her attempt to learn to paint largely through the making of drawings in this way. Now I cannot summarise the richness of Milner's text here, but I do want to focus upon two moments within it. One is what she has to say about her problems with perspective; the other concerns the nature of outline.

Milner explains that at first instead of 'trying to puzzle out the meaning' of her free drawings, she carried on 'trying to study the painter's task from books'. Up until this point she had assumed that all the painter's practical problems to do with representing distance, solidity, the grouping of objects, differences of light and shade and so on were matters for common sense, combined with careful study. 'But,' she writes, 'when I tried to begin such careful study there seemed some unknown force interfering.' It soon became clear to her the difficulty was that 'the imaginative mind could have strong views of its own on the meanings of light, distance, darkness and so on.' A particular instance of this was the interference of imagination in perspective drawing. This is how Milner describes it:

'In spite of having been taught, long ago at school, the rules of perspective, I had recently found that whenever a drawing showed more or less correct perspective, as in drawing a room for instance, the result seemed not worth the effort. But one day I had tried drawing an imaginary room . . . and after a struggle, had managed to avoid showing the furniture in correct perspective. The drawing had been more satisfying than any earlier ones, though I had no notion why.'[3]

It then occurred to her that 'it all depended upon what aspects of objects one was most concerned with':

'It was as if one's mind could want to express the feelings that come from the sense of touch and muscular movement rather than from the sense of sight. In fact it was almost as if one might not want to be concerned, in drawing, with those facts of detachment and separation that are introduced when an observing eye is perched upon a sketching stool, with all the attendant facts of a single-view-point and fixed eye-level and horizontal lines that vanish. It seemed one might want some kind of relation to objects in which one was much more mixed up with them than that.'[4]

Now at first it seemed to Milner that her 'unwillingness to face the visual facts of space and distance must be a cowardly attitude, a retreat from the responsibilities of being a separate person.' But it did not feel to her entirely like a retreat; it felt, she writes, 'more like a search, a going backwards perhaps, but a going back to look for something, something which could have real value for adult life if only it could be recovered.'[5]

Milner had read that 'painting is concerned with the feelings conveyed by space', but she realised that before she herself set out to learn to paint she had taken space for granted and never reflected upon what it might mean in terms of feeling:

'But as soon as I did begin to think about it, it was clear that very intense feelings might be stirred. If one saw it as the primary reality to be manipulated for the satisfaction of all one's basic needs, beginning with the babyhood problem of reaching for one's mother's arms, leading through all the separation from what one loves that the business of living brings, then it was not so surprising that it should be the main preoccupation of the painter . . . So it became clear that if painting is concerned with the feelings conveyed by space then it must also be to do with problems of being a separate body in a world of other bodies which occupy different bits of space: in fact it must be deeply concerned with ideas of distance and separation and having and losing.'[6]

Milner also comments:

'There were many other aspects of the emotions conveyed by space to be considered. For instance, once you begin to think about distance and separation it is also necessary to think about different ways of being together, or in the jargon of the painting books, composition.'[7]

Thus Milner came to see that original work in painting 'would demand facing certain facts about oneself as a separate being, facts, she felt, 'that could often perhaps be successfully by-passed in ordinary living.'

I now want to turn to what Milner says about *outline*. It was, she writes, 'through the study of outline in painting that it became clearer what might be the nature of the spiritual dangers to be faced, if one was to see as the painter sees.' She then points out that, until she set out on this attempt to learn to paint through free drawings, she 'had always assumed in some vague way that outlines were "real"'. In a book about drawing, however, she read that 'from the visual point of view . . . the boundaries (of masses) are not always clearly defined, but are continually merging into the surrounding mass and losing themselves, to be caught up again later on and defined once more.'[8] She then started to look at the objects around her more carefully and found that this was true:

'When really looked at in relation to each other their outlines were not clear and compact, as I had always supposed them to be, they continually became lost in shadow. Two questions emerged here. First, how was it possible to have remained unaware of this fact for so long? Second, why was such a great mental effort necessary in order to see the edges of objects as they actually show themselves rather than as I had always thought of them?'[9]

Milner then says that outlines *put objects in their place*; this seemed the crux of the matter. 'For,' she writes;

'I noticed that the effort needed in order to see the edges of objects as they really look stirred a dim fear, a fear of what might happen if one let go one's mental hold on the outline which kept everything separate and in its place.'[10]

Milner then goes on to describe a key experience:

'After thinking about this I woke one morning and saw two jugs on the table; without any mental struggle I saw the edges in relation to each other, and how gaily they seemed almost to ripple now that they were freed from this grimly practical business of enclosing an object and keeping it in its place. This was surely what painters meant about the *play* of edges; certainly they did play and I tried a five-minute sketch of the jugs . . . Now also it was easier to understand what painters meant by the phrase 'freedom of line' because here surely was a reason for its opposite; that is, the emotional need to imprison objects rigidly within themselves.'[11]

Milner began to perceive that we believe outlines are real (unless we learn to paint) despite the fact that they are, as one 'Learn to

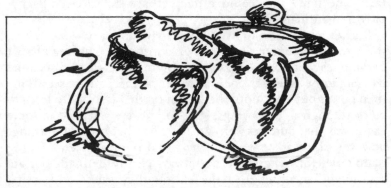

Marion Milner, *Jugs*.

Paint' book puts it, 'the one fundamentally unrealistic, non-imitative thing in this whole job of painting'. But because the outline represents the world of fact, of separate, touchable, solid objects, 'to cling to it was therefore surely to protect oneself against the other world, the world of imagination.'[12]

Milner thus came to see that insistence upon the reality of outline was associated with:

'. . . a fear of losing all sense of separating boundaries; particularly the boundaries between the tangible realities of the external world and the imaginative realities of the inner world of feeling and idea; in fact a fear of being mad.'[13]

She even ventured the aside:

'. . . I wondered, if perhaps this was one reason why new experiments in painting can arouse such fierce opposition and anger. People must surely be afraid, without knowing it, that their hold upon reason and sanity is precarious, else they would not so resent being asked to look at visual experience in a new way, they would not be so afraid of not seeing the world as they have always seen it and in the general, publicly agreed way of seeing it.'[14]

Later, we will return to the question of the relationship between insistence upon perspective and outline and history; however, for the moment let us leave Milner with her intriguing problems over objective space and the rippling boundaries of her jugs, at least for the time being, and pick up another of the pieces that I am trying to fit together in this seminar.

This section, as a matter of fact, concerns me intimately: we have reached what seems to have become a regular feature in these seminars, the autobiographical interlude. Now I want to tell you something about the changes, I would say the growth, in—I'll keep the word for the moment—my 'taste' since childhood.

As far as I can remember, I first became interested in paintings when I was seven or eight years old. My father had a great many illustrated art books, and I would take these down from his shelves and look at them. My family also frequently visited art galleries and stately homes but, significantly perhaps, I think I got more at least at first, from the art books. Initially there was an element of naked sexual investigation about my looking. I saw a lot of different works of art in reproduction, but by and large I was most impressed by those of women without their clothes. At first my art appreciation was accompanied by some guilt feelings; the books belonged to my father and I did not have his permission to gaze upon them. The Oedipal component in this looking is so transparent that it is hardly worth commenting on. Incorporation of visual images is one of the ways in which from infancy to old age we take possession in fantasy of that which we cannot (but wish we could) possess in reality. But despite the primitive character of my interest in art at this time, it would be wrong to suppose that it was entirely without that which someone like Clive Bell might have diagnosed as a rudimentary 'aesthetic sensibility'.

Let me explain more fully: at first, I did not make much distinction between medical books (of which my father also had a great many) and art books. But soon I was aware of a sense of *goodness* when I set eyes upon, say, the Rokeby Venus in reproduction, which I did not feel when I looked at, say, Plate V of 'An Atlas of Gas Poisoning' contained in a *Medical Manual of Chemical Warfare* which illustrated, as it so happens, Blistering of the Buttocks by Mustard Gas. Now this sense of 'goodness' could not be explained by reference to the immediate sensuousness of the subject matter alone, which was often similar in those art books and medical manuals which interested me—though in the latter, of course, it tended to be more explicit. Nor, I think, could it be wholly accounted for by saying that art allowed me to indulge my unacceptable 'instinctual' voyeuristic impulses in an acceptable way. This could be no more than a part of the truth, if that. Borrowing art books was no less an offence than borrowing medical books. Despite the specificities of the latter I soon came to prefer the former.

This rather vague sense of 'goodness' which I derived from certain paintings, even in black-and-white and colour reproductions, had much to do with the development of my 'taste'. If I was a certain kind of writer about art, I would no doubt claim that this sense of 'goodness' and my quest for it represented the awakening of a pure, unsullied, autonomous, 'aesthetic sensibility' to 'Significant Form', or something of the kind, in the midst of all that crudely sexual researching. But personally, I am inclined to doubt this.

To speak formally, for a moment, it seems to me when I look back that my pursuit of 'goodness' was bound up, among other things, with a growing capacity to take greater risks with *outline* in my perception and enjoyment of images. At first, I was not greatly interested in either colour or what is now called the 'materiality' of the paint. Subject matter and drawing were what concerned me most, which was why a black-and-white reproduction was almost as good as the real thing. I began by liking Ingres, where the woman's body was tightly contained within a constraining outline. I progressed towards Botticelli: despite his 'naturalism', his paintings had an abstracted, arabesque quality which was somehow much less insistent on being 'real'. For example, I was fascinated by the fact that in Botticelli's *Birth of Venus* you can still see where the artist changed the position of the outline of the right-arm, a degree of ambivalence which would have been quite inconceivable in a major painting by Ingres. Then I became interested in Modigliani, a painter again who insists on the reality of line— where would Modigliani be without it?—but who often hints at a kind of mergence between the figure bound in by the outline and the background against which she is set. (There are some Modigliani's in which it is hard to tell whether a particular passage of paint is depicting flesh, wall, or both.) Later still, I became interested in Matisse—yes, still outline of course, but in him it becomes provocatively fluid, as tremulous and variable as we see it in the real world, rather than as rigid as the non-painters among us often imagine it to be.

I remember that I was stimulated both to start looking seriously at modern art (which was, of course, ignored when it was not derided within the '19th century' culture in which I spent my childhood) and to paint myself through a triggering contingency: seeing Tony Hancock's film, *The Rebel*. I was fourteen at the time. Some of you may remember what, in truth, was a rather banal plot. Hancock plays a 'modernist' artist of little ability who shares a Parisian garret with a representational artist of great ability. The only thing they have in common is that they are both poor and unknown. One day, Hancock is in the garret and is 'discovered'; however, he is assumed to be the producer of his friend's works. These are duly exhibited and Hancock is celebrated on account of them. But soon the pressure is on him to produce more canvases of similar quality, which, of course, he cannot do. Eventually his friend, who for reasons I cannot recall colludes with the mistaken identity, supplies him with a fresh batch of works. These turn out to be abstract paintings; Hancock is horrified and convinced that 'his' career is finished. But the backers and critics acclaim these abstract works as loudly as they did the representational ones. Hancock, who thought it was all a question of style, shrugs his shoulders and gives up any attempt to make sense of the art world.

All right: the film was silly enough. I'm certainly not recommending it. It may well have been intended as a satire on the values of the art world, but the message I took away from it was that facility in 'objective' representation was not decisive. Up until this time, I had always been relatively indifferent to drawing and painting myself because I was hopelessly inept at what seemed to be the essentials of these practices, and which had indeed been taught as such in my preparatory school, i.e. mastery of such things as perspective and 'realistic' outline. Perhaps at this stage in my life I was simply too dissociated from the external world: anyway, I could not even begin to draw in that sort of way. But, when I saw *The Rebel*, it confirmed a dawning realisation that these were not the only things which counted in image making: this was given tremendous encouragement by a sympathetic art teacher at public school. And so I entered into a prodigious period of pictorial productivity which really persisted, whatever else I was doing, until I was twenty-one. This was checked, at various times, by a desire—never to be fulfilled—to master the 'objective' aspects of drawing. I remember my art teacher once patiently trying to teach me how to draw light and shadow using the surface of an egg as a model—at my own request. It was no use, and I gave up in despair. On another occasion, I abandoned all imaginative explorations, and tried to study artist's anatomy, and 'How to Draw the Nude' books. That did not last either. These two images—both done about the same time, when I was sixteen—indicate the discrepancy between my capacity to depict, as it were, representations of objects in my 'inner' and in the 'outer' world.

As a matter of fact, that discrepancy never was resolved in terms of my practice as a maker of visual images. My 'taste' however did not develop in harness with my creativity. I

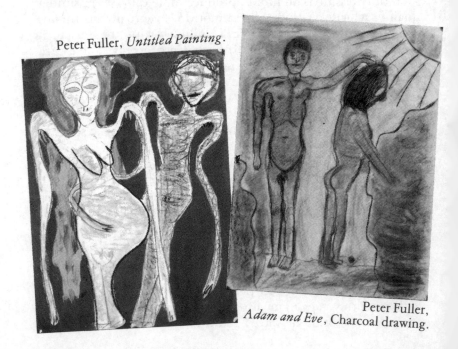

Peter Fuller, *Untitled Painting*.

Peter Fuller, *Adam and Eve*, Charcoal drawing.

continued to admire those who were exemplary of that which I was least able to do myself. (I spent many hours gazing at Leonardo's drawings in a book in the school library.) Of course, I did become increasingly interested in abstract painting; by the time I was fifteen, I had developed a passion for Mondrian. I even remember writing a poem about him in the style of Robert Browning's marvellous 'Fra Lippo Lippi'. Looking back on the development of my relationship to abstract art I am inclined to the view that what was important for me was *the affective meaning of the space*, and that there was a sense in which at times, though not often and not for long, I could do without the presence of the figure itself. At least I am aware that, once established, the trajectory of my pursuit of abstract painting closely paralleled that of my changing interest in the figure. I got to know Mondrian largely through colour reproductions: I did not realise, therefore, just how painterly some of his works are. I read him essentially as a painter of outline, an Ingres, if you like. I responded to something almost clinical, contained and restrained, linear and 'objective' in his 'classical' works. Nonetheless, it was through Mondrian that I went on to look at Kandinsky, and later still, Klee, where I felt lost in a world of almost magical transformations and transfigurations. (On looking back at the copy of Klee's *On Modern Art* which I had in adolescence I was interested to note that I had underlined the words, 'I do not wish to represent the man as he is, but only as he might be'[15]—an idea which was to play a central part in my later aesthetics.)

The painters I was able to appreciate last were those whose space seemed to me to be an attempt to fuse internal and external: this was, of course, something I responded to affectively (often initially by defensive boredom) rather than something I thought through intellectually. Although I looked voraciously at everything I came across, I had difficulty with impressionist painting for a long time, because the concrete world just seemed too subjectivised there, too insubstantial, too close to diffusion and dissolution. (I think the lateness of my interest in colour had much to do with this, too. Again, to speak affectively rather than epistemologically, colour seems to be the most subjective of an object's properties; to depict the world through colour alone felt, to me, like depriving it of actuality and solidity, qualities which, psychologically speaking, were difficult enough for me to recognise anyway.) Much the same went for Cezanne, too. Cubism simply did not interest me, or enter my world, until I was at least seventeen.

But, as my interest in painting deepened, artists who were involved in this fusion came to interest me more and more. For example, among painters of the female figure whom I began to enjoy after initial indifference with what I can only somewhat pompously describe as a sense of 'awakening goodness' were Bonnard and De Kooning. I am not sure when I first began to like Bonnard: I saw the Royal Academy show in 1966. It must have been about that time. But it is only very recently that I have allowed myself to realise just what an important painter he is for me. In his work, the woman is entirely unleashed from her outline. Berger has brilliantly described what he calls 'the risk of loss' in a Bonnard painting, the fact that the figure is 'simultaneously an absence and a presence,' because she is 'potentially everywhere except specifically near.'[16] He describes how in a Bonnard painting one is confronted with 'the image of a woman losing her physical limits, overflowing, overlapping every surface until she is no less and no more than the *genius loci* of the whole room.'[17] You can see this most literally in paintings like *The Open Window* of 1921—and it is by no means the only one like this—where you *sense* the fleshly presence of a woman in the whole picture surface, but you do not at first (and sometimes not even at length) notice that Bonnard has literally included an equivocal representation of a woman, in this instance in the extreme bottom right-hand corner of the picture. Although Berger has described this aspect of Bonnard better than any other writer I have read, he is rather critical of it, indeed of Bonnard's work as a whole.

For myself, let me just say at this stage that this apparent loss of the physical limits of the woman's body, this restless overlapping, was, I think, what prevented me from enjoying Bonnard when I first saw his work. I was frightened by it, and I covered my fear, as is so often the case, with a veneer of indifference. Later, the painter Robert Natkin told me the story of a visit by Balthus to an art gallery where a Bonnard hung between a Picasso and a Soutine. Balthus looked at the Picasso, and then at the Soutine, and finally at the Bonnard—at which he exclaimed, 'Ah! At last, real violence.' I knew what he meant at once. Today I would say that it is this very indeterminacy of outline, the peculiar kind of space one gets in Bonnard which both is, and is not, based on a perspectival

Pierre Bonnard, *The Open Window*, 1921.

pictorial structure, which, in its imagery as well as through the
way that it is painted fuses inner with outer—(it is no accident
that one of Bonnard's favourite themes is an open window
simultaneously revealing interior and exterior, another a body
almost literally dissolving in water)—that accounts for the
intensity of pleasure which I can derive from looking at his
works. Do you know Bonnard's drawings? His lines at first seem
to be a literal con-fusion: he seems to me to draw fluently in a
way which Milner was struggling towards in that moment with
her two jugs.

Now Bonnard offers a highly equivocal sort of space. When
he paints a woman, an interior, or a landscape, he makes it very
unclear indeed who is separate from what, what merges with
whom, who belongs where, out there, or in here. I see works of
this kind as almost, but not quite, the culmination of that
search for 'goodness' which began, I suppose, when I noticed
that slight blurring or warm fuzzing in the outline of the
Rokeby Venus which differentiates it from Ingres, and incidentally from pin-ups. Now I am aware that much of my

interest in certain 'abstract' painters, like De Kooning, Rothko, and Natkin, could be seen as the final step in what has been a relatively continuous, if uneven transformation of an aspect of my taste from the time when I first started poring over Ingres in reproduction. Harold Rosenberg once wrote of De Kooning that in his mature work, 'landscapes and the human figure become in Shakespeare's phrase "dislimned and indistinct as water".'[18] In Natkin one just goes right over the edge. Outline vanishes altogether; one is confronted with a sensuous skin of paint which then bursts open into a limitless vista. One moves into a painted world where nothing is locked by line and everything exists in a boundless and plenitudinous state of transformation and becoming. I look upon it, and find it 'good', though more than a trace of the fear that would have stopped me looking at Natkin at all a few years ago remains. Now I will have a lot more to say about this change in my taste later on. Next time, I will talk in detail about the affective meanings of the space in Natkin and Rothko. But, for the moment, I want to stop here and pick up another of the pieces out of which this seminar is made. This will involve us in a little art history.

Some of you may have an idea of the particular historical perspective with which I have surrounded my art criticism over the last few years.[19] However, for the purposes of our argument it is necessary to outline it briefly here.

I try never to let people forget that the idea of 'Art' (with a capital 'A') is of extremely recent origins. In England, we do not find the words 'Art' and 'artists' used in the sense in which they are used today, i.e. as referring to *imaginative* skills and practitioners, rather than to just *any* skills, until the end of the 18th century. The word 'Art' came into being with the rise of the middle-classes and the emergence of a professional Fine Art tradition. The nature of the Fine Art tradition varied considerably from country to country: for example, in the Italian city states at the time of the Renaissance some artists seemed to spring directly out of the indigenous craft traditions; they were acclaimed as men of 'genius' and, unlike the 'primitives', their own name was attached to their work. In Britain, however, such immediate transcendence out of the craft traditions was not possible. The craft traditions had fallen into decadence *before* the waning of High Feudalism; they were obliterated through the iconoclasm of the British Reformation. Until the 18th century, fine artists were effectively imported. However, everywhere that national Fine Art traditions established themselves they were characterised by a particular *training*. Professional fine artists acquired the skillful use of a specific set of pictorial conventions: conventions of pose, anatomy, chiaroscuro and above all perspective. Now these were not taught as historical variables, but as being the way of depicting 'The Truth'. Hitherto, with Berger, I have argued that these conventions equipped fine artists to depict the world from the point of view of that class which they served, and that only the *exceptions* tried to defy their training by, as it were, forcing the conventions they had learned to serve the point of view of another class. I still consider that there is much truth in this. Nonetheless, I would now maintain that the science of expression, as elaborated theoretically by Alberti and as practised by such artists as Leonardo and Michelangelo, had a concrete, cultural and class transcendent basis in anatomy, which prevented it from being reducible to a mere ideological instance.

It is, however, undeniable that the growth of professional Fine Art traditions was accompanied by the efflorescence of an accompanying ideology of 'Art' which was elaborated by artists, art historians, critics, and later museum officials. This ideology turned 'Art' into a transhistorical universal and projected it, together with its values, back into the earliest known social formations. As the great archaeological discoveries of the 19th century were made, fine artists came more and more to see themselves as the consummation of an unbroken continuum of 'Art' stretching back from the Royal Academy to prehistoric caves.

However, the reality behind this ideological mystification was rather different. Although in every known civilisation men and women had always made visual images of one sort and another, they had done so in a great variety of different ways, and these images had served a multitude of different functions. (Nonetheless, and this is a point insufficiently emphasised in my previous analyses, certain specific practices, most notably painting and sculpture, *can* be shown to have a material continuity since the beginnings of human civilization.) Prior to the rise of the professional Fine Art traditions, there was no equivalent of either 'art' or artists; but Fine Art's mystification of itself allowed it to disguise the fact that its status was changing profoundly with the development of new means of visual image making—like photography and lithography. These really came into their own when monopoly capitalism displaced the old entrepreneurial capitalist system, and the bourgeoisie as a progressive class began to wither. Associated with the emergence of monopoly capitalism was the efflorescence of what I have designated as 'The Mega-Visual Tradition': by that I mean that whole welter of means of producing and reproducing images which includes not just photography, mass colour printing, lithography, and holography, but the moving pictures of cinema and television, too. Indeed, I argue that just as free-standing oil painting was the dominant form of static visual imagery under entrepreneurial capitalism, advertising is the dominant form of static visual image making under monopoly capitalism.

Now this process of displacement of the old Fine Art tradition from the task of conveying the world-view of the bourgeoisie initially had the effect of opening up possibilities for the imaginative artist. He was no longer pinned down within a particular 'visual ideology'. For a very brief period—roughly from the time of Cezanne's maturity in the 1880s until the death of Cubism—what I would characterise as a 'progressive' Modernist movement (or rather plethora of related movements) thus came into being.

Certain of the artists in some of these movements attempted—in some instances consciously, in others not—to act as visual prophets of the new world order which they felt was in the process of coming into being. We must not forget the exhilarating promise which seemed to be implicit in the advance of the bourgeoisie throughout the 19th century, a promise which seemed to be on the very threshold of realisation in the technological progress associated with emergent monopoly capitalism. An attainable vision of the transformation of the world into a place where the problem of need had been solved and natural resources fully socialised seemed to be at hand. I agree with Berger when he depicts Cubism as an attempt (even if it was not recognised as such by those engaged in it) to struggle out of the old perspective-based Fine Art conventions towards a half-expression of a new way of seeing and representing the world appropriate to what seemed to be the new, emergent world order.[20] Actually, this initiative was smashed to pieces by the First World War and the long, and still continuing, series of historic calamities and catastrophes which put an end, forever, to hopes for a peaceful, 'evolutionary' transition to the new Utopia.

By and large, it *is* possible to characterise Modernism after the decline and disillusionment of the great avant-garde movements as a retreat, by artists, from even the attempt to articulate a historic world-view to replace the now displaced 19th century, middle-class optic and perspective. The reasons for this retreat appear to have been two-fold: on the one hand, history seems simply to have dazed and outstripped artists; on the other, the 'Mega–Visual Tradition' continued to pump out an ever escalating quantity of banalising lies as the century progressed, swamping, marginalising, disrupting and eclipsing the products and practices of fine artists.

Thus Berger has described most post-First-World-War Western Art as a sort of epilogue to the European and American 19th century professional Fine Art traditions, an epilogue in which painting is reduced to a dialogue with itself, about itself, because there is no other area of experience upon which it can touch meaningfully, except itself. I have elaborated the notion of the *kenosis* or self-emptying of the Fine Art tradition: kenosis is a term I borrowed from theology. I am using it to refer to the apparent relinquishment of the professional and conventional skills by Fine Artists and to the abandonment of the omnipotent power the painter once seemed to possess to create, like God, a whole world of objects in space through illusions on a canvas. I see this general kenosis as having been ruptured at various points—most notably after the Second World War in Europe, New York, London, Chicago and elsewhere—by tremendous outbursts of expressionism in which artists attempted to find ways of speaking meaningfully of their experience, including historical experience, once more. Nonetheless, the process of kenosis, with these occasional regenerative hiccups, proceeds.

That is the historical perspective which underlies my critical practice. By and large, it still seems to me to be a truthful and a useful analysis. But I now want to modify it slightly. I want to approach the problem in a rather different way.

To this end, I now wish to produce the next fragment of that statue which I am piecing together. It consists of a book by Clive Bell, called simply *Art*, first published in 1914, that pivotal year in the destiny of the old professional Fine Art traditions and, as it turned out, of much else besides. Together with Roger Fry, Bell is often regarded on the Left as the source of all the trouble. Fry and Bell are seen as the theoretical precursors of the self-critical formalism of late Modernism. In them, we find the elaboration of the idea that 'Art' constitutes an autonomous, self-contained, entity which we can only truly experience if and because it evokes in us certain types of *sui generis* emotion, which have nothing to do with other human emotions, or with lived experience beyond the experience of art. Art, they maintain, should thus be appreciated without reference to the representational, psychological, social, political, religious, or other non-aesthetic considerations which it might evoke.

Let me say straight away, to preclude the possibility of misunderstanding, I am absolutely *not* about to re-habilitate Bell: he was opinionated, arrogant, ultimately down-right reactionary—one of the nastiest weeds to have flourished in Bloomsbury, and he got it all (or almost all) wrong to boot.[21] But equally, if I am not going to rehabilitate Bell, I am not going to kick him either: that would be much too easy. The brand of aesthetic formalism to which his kind of critical thinking gave rise has been getting an atrocious press recently. Formalism is no longer a cultural danger or a worthy opponent. On the other hand, I would maintain not just that Bell's book is a key text in the emergent ideology of late Modernism (which it is), but also that embodied within it are kernels of truth which have escaped almost all of those who have put forward critiques of formalism from left positions. With a little help from psychoanalysis, I want to isolate one of those kernels of truth, to extract it, unravel it, and preserve it. It not only constitutes something germane to my argument, but also that which 'Social Criticism', the rising orthodoxy, seems in danger of losing sight of altogether.

Let me explain.

Bell claims to offer 'a complete theory of visual art', and in many ways it is a very simple theory. He argues that 'all works of visual art have some common quality, or when we speak of "works of art" we gibber.'[22] He then asks, 'What is this quality? What quality is shared by all objects that provoke our aesthetic emotions?' And he arrives at what seems to him the only possible answer:

'—significant form. In each, lines and colours combined in a particular way, certain forms and relations of forms, stir our aesthetic emotions. These relations and combinations of lines and colours, these aesthetically moving forms, I call "Significant Form"; and "Significant Form" is the one quality common to all works of visual art.' [23]

You can spot right away the sort of clangers which this rope of reasoning is going to wring from our Bell. What can be the status of 'works of art' which fail to stir his aesthetic emotions? According to the theory, they must lack Significant Form, and therefore, cannot by definition, be thought of as works of art at all. It is, I suppose, to Mr. Bell's credit that he pushed this view through to its logical conclusion: most works of art are not works of art at all. The book is peppered with such observations as:

> 'I cannot believe that more than one in a hundred works produced between 1450 and 1850 can be properly described as a work of art.' [24]

Or again:

> '. . . the Impressionists raised the proportion of works of art in the general pictorial output from about one in five hundred thousand to one in a hundred thousand. . . . Today I daresay it stands as high as one in ten thousand.' [25]

You also quickly come to realise that whatever stir's Clive Bell's aesthetic emotion, it is *not* the products of the professional Fine Art tradition. It is no exaggeration to say that Bell had an almost hysterical disregard for the Renaissance (although he modified this position in his later works) and especially for its discovery of perspective. He calls the Renaissance 'a strange new disease', and 'nothing more than a big kink in a long slope'. He often makes such comments as, 'the decline from the 11th to the 17th century is continuous,' or, 'more first-rate art was produced in Europe between 500 and 900 than was produced in the same countries between 1450 and 1850,' or:

> 'This alone seems to me sure: since the Byzantine primitives set their mosaics at Ravenna no artist in Europe has created forms of greater significance unless it be Cezanne.' [26]

Now the curious thing about the way in which Mr. Bell argues is that it is precisely 'Art' (with a capital 'A') in the historically-specific sense which he effectively denies to be art at all. Art, for Bell—i.e. that which stirs his aesthetic emotions—flourished among the so-called European Primitives of the Dark and

Middle Ages, was all but extinguished by the Renaissance and that which followed it, and came to life again with Cezanne who 'founded a movement', a movement which Bell (writing before the First World War at a time when he would still have described himself as some sort of socialist) described as 'the dawn of a new age'.

What did Bell have against the Renaissance? Well, he felt that during it 'Naturalism' and 'Materialism' had driven out what he called 'pure aesthetic rapture'. He compalined that in the art of the Renaissance, 'intellect is filling the void left by emotion', and that the work of artists was being supplanted 'by Science and culture'. These things, in Bell's view, had nothing at all to do with art: he was even more scathing about 17th century Holland, another place where, he felt art barely existed at all. 'We have lost art,' he wrote of Dutch painting of this period, 'let us study science and imitation.'[27] In short, he complains that 'the outstanding fact is that with the Renaissance Europe definitely turns her back on the spiritual view of life.'[28] Bell could not even accept the Impressionists, because, in his view, they were too scientific.

At this point, I simply want to raise the fact that Bell's view of art is exceptionally close to his conception of religious experience. He says that 'Art and religion belong to the same world. Both are bodies in which men try to capture and keep alive their shyest and most ethereal conceptions. The kingdom of neither is of this world.' He describes art as 'an expression of that emotion which is the vital force in every religion . . . We may say that art and religion are manifestations of man's religious sense if by "man's religious sense" we mean his sense of ultimate reality.'[29] At one point, he even exclaims, 'from the beginning art has existed as a religion concurrent with all other religions.'

Is all this, as Bell himself might have said, mere 'gibbering'? In one sense, yes, I am afraid that it is: but, like religious piffle itself, it does contain that vital kernel which I referred to earlier. It is not enough simply to laugh at Bell and to throw 'aesthetic emotion' out of the window as so many of *both* the 'left' social critics and 'right' formalists have done. We have to do to Bell's aesthetics what Feuerbach did to Christianity: we have to invert them, to locate the experiences which they describe in *this* world, to resolve them into their anthropological and biological determinants. I think this may be possible. For the moment, let us leave Bell with a passage in which he contrasts 'the superb peaks of aesthetic exaltation' with 'the snug foothills of warm humanity'. The latter, he writes, is 'a jolly country':

> 'No one need be ashamed of enjoying himself there. Only no one who has ever been on the heights can help feeling a little crestfallen in the cosy valleys. And let no one imagine, because he has made merry in the warm tilth and quaint nooks of romance, that he can even guess at the austere and thrilling raptures of those who have climbed the cold, white peaks of art.'[30]

We will return to examine those thrilling raptures and those cold white peaks later, but I hope that by now at least some of you will be beginning to see where all our threads are going to be tied. I am suggesting that there is something significant in common between the difficulties Milner had with perspective and outline; the development of my taste from Ingres to Natkin and Rothko; the historical crisis in the Fine Art tradition; and Bell's rejection of the most characteristic products of that tradition in favour of raptures on those cold, white peaks. That something was not just a retreat from experience: it was also a retrieval of it.

You will remember that I made some reference to Adrian Stokes' ideas about 'modelling modes' and 'carving modes'—a distinction which, of course, he regarded as being as relevant within painting as sculpture. Stokes, a Kleinian, tended to associate the carving mode with 'the depressive position', with the separateness, autonomy and *otherness* of the object; whereas he links the modelling mode with the 'paranoid-schizoid' position, with flatness, decoration, and failure to establish a separate identity, or to recognise the distinction and space between the self and the mother.

For a moment, I want to talk in gross generalities. I want to say, preposterously, that, prior to the Renaissance, the ideology of space and its representation in visual images was essentially a projection of the fused and con-fused infantile space of what Stokes calls the 'paranoid-schizoid' position. Before I make what I mean by this a little clearer, I want to offer a warning: it is very difficult indeed for us to think ourselves back into an earlier spatial system, whether we are talking about an his-torical, or a biographical-developmental one. The commonest mistake when attempting to do so is to assume that the spatial system out of which one is, oneself, operating must have dawned upon those who first began to discover it like a self-evident truth, whereas in fact, of course, they felt it as a violent disruption of self-evident truths.

Let me give you a good example of this. Writing in 1876, Leslie Stephens commented on how the emergence of a new cosmology through the rise of modern science changed men and women's perception of themselves and their world:

> 'Through the roof of the little theatre on which the drama of man's history had been enacted, men began to see the eternal stars shining in silent contempt upon their petty imaginings. They began to suspect that the whole scenery was but a fabric woven by their imaginations.' [31]

Now that image seems to me vivid and good: but what is interesting is that elsewhere in the same book, speaking of his own late Victorian age, which was the inheritor of a world in which the old stage cloths had finally been, if not torn down, then ripped to shreds, Leslie Stephens could write:

> 'Our knowledge has, in some departments, passed into the scientific stage. It can be stated as a systematic body of established truths. It is consistent and certain. The primary axioms are fixed beyond the reach of scepticism; each subordinate proposition has its proper place; and the conclusions deduced are in perfect harmony.' [32]

In other words, he saw the Victorian scientific world-view in very much the same way that a medieval school-man regarded his own cosmological world view as a 'systematic body' of eternal truths existing in 'perfect harmony'. Stephens, perceptive as he was, had no intimation of the fact that within thirty years of writing this passage, his cosmology would begin to be devastated as thoroughly as when Newtonian science finally revealed the 'imaginary' character of the medieval world-view. In the first of these seminars, we considered the way in which that water-shed of history, the First World War, was associated with the disintegration of the Victorian way of conceiving of the world, part of which was the rise of a new physics which put everything once more well within the reach of scepticism.

With that warning, let us turn to a text by the mathematician Kline about 'early Christian and medieval artists' who, he says:

> '. . . were content to paint in symbolic terms, that is, their settings and subjects were intended to illustrate religious themes and induce religious feelings rather than to represent real people in the actual and present world. The people and objects were

highly stylized and drawn as though they existed in a flat, two
dimensional vacuum. Figures that should be behind one another
were usually alongside or above, Stiff draperies and angular
attitudes were characteristic. The backgrounds of the paintings
were almost always of a solid colour, usually gold, as if to em-
phasize that the subjects had no connection with the real
world.'[33]

That sort of description of medieval art *seems* true enough to
us: essentially, I think that it is true; but it also leaves out of the
account the degree to which the medieval painting *was* a
depiction of 'the real world' as the medieval painter conceived
it. Certainly, medieval painting is highly conventionalised, but
then, as we have seen, outline and perspective are themselves
conventions. It may be that there was a much greater
correspondence than this quotation implies between the flat,
planar earth of medieval cosmology, with its ascending and
descending angels not subject to the laws of gravity, and its
over-arching dome of a heaven above, and a hell below, and the
flat, two-dimensional, 'unreal' way in which the painter
depicted the world. I suspect that there is a sense in which the
space in medieval paintings is expressive of the way in which
men and women felt themselves to be within their world. We
must therefore be careful when we say that the medieval painter
worked 'in symbolic terms'. Such statements are not entirely
untrue. However they greatly over-emphasise the degree to
which the painter conceived of the 'real' world in one way and
then turned away from it and set about painting another
'unreal' or 'religious' world of symbol.

What I am saying is, of course, that the medieval painter
was—as Milner put it when she had problems with perspective—much more mixed up with his objects than were the
painters of the Renaissance. He made much less distinction
between internal and external space—and religious ideology encouraged, indeed enforced, this confusion. Religious
cosmology was effectively the instituionalised version of a
projection of a subjective space into the real world. Up there,
you have the good heaven with its sustaining and nurturing
deities; down there, the bad hell into which all one's own evil,
destructive and aggressive impulses can be projected. The 'real
world' is no more than an integral part of this system, which is
freely peopled with 'good' and 'bad' father and mother
imagos, and with winged and weightless creatures representing

benign impulses, and hooved and cloven ones standing for bad. This, of course, is what I mean when I say that the conception of space prior to the Renaissance was, if we accept the Kleinian terminology, 'paranoid-schizoid'.

The Renaissance changed that. To persist with our extravagant generalisations, the Renaissance involved that sifting out of mind from matter, of self from other, that recognition of space, distance and separateness which in individual development characterises the achievement of the 'depressive-position'. Evidently, this can today be seen most clearly in those Renaissance paintings in which the conventional means were found for the introduction of the third dimension, that is, the rendering of recessive space, of distance, volume, mass, and visual effects. The initiation of these conventions, particularly through the re-creation of perspective, is, for me at any rate, what makes the painting of Duccio, Giotto, Lorenzetti, and Van Eyck so exciting. By the early 15th century, in the work of Brunelleschi—the elaborator of a complete system of focused perspective and the tutor of Donatello, Masaccio, and Fra Filippo—painting became very like a science; not only was it based upon its own laws and mathematical principles, but it had also become a significant means for the investigation and propagation of knowledge about the external world.

Perspective, too, was *conventional*; I do not wish to be thought to be saying that it allowed 'truthful' representations of the 'real'. Like the medieval spatial representations before it, perspective did not even represent as the eye sees:

'The principle that a painting must be a section of a projection requires . . . that horizontal lines which are parallel to the plane of the canvas, as well as vertical parallel lines, are to be drawn parallel. But the eye viewing such lines finds that they appear to meet just as other sets of parallel lines do. Hence in this respect at least the focused system is not visually correct. A more fundamental criticism is the fact that the eye does not see straight lines at all . . . But the focused system ignores this fact of perception. Neither does the system take into account the fact that we actually see with two eyes each of which receives a slightly different impression. Moreover, these eyes are not rigid but move as the spectator surveys a scene. Finally, the focused system ignores the fact that the retina of the eye on which the light rays impinge is a curved surface, not a photographic plate, and that seeing is as much a reaction of the brain as it is a purely physiological process.'[34]

As I have already suggested, perspective also became inflected by the class interests of those whom the professional artists who elaborated, practised and developed it, served. Nonetheless, when all this has been said, it remains true that perspective was essentially an attempt to explore the character of the world out there, the external world, and the properties and material relations through which exterior space was constituted. Technically, perspective involved a literal carving, pushing or cutting back through the surface of the picture plane. Neither artists, nor other men and women, were any longer so 'mixed up' in the objects which they perceived. *Affective* representations of space became increasingly rare.

As Bell perceived, we can (ignoring for a moment all the possible exceptions, of which there are many) say crudely that this separation out of men and women from the 'paranoid-schizoid' space of the medieval world characterised the task of the painter from the decline of Primitive Christian Art (which, you will recall, Bell loved) to the rise of Cezanne (whom he also loved). (Michelangelo's paintings, for example, seem to me in general less masterful than his sculptures because, in the paintings, he is, as it were, endeavouring to constitute 'real' bodies within what is essentially the older spatial modality and mythology.) During the long period from the rise of the Renaissance, until the emergence of Modernism, painters were, to continue with the Kleinian terminology, working through, or at least within, the 'depressive position'.

At the time of Cezanne, however, we have already seen that the ideological obligation upon artists to elaborate an external world-view was rapidly diminishing. As the painter's cultural position was usurped through the rise of the Mega-Visual tradition, he became in one sense at least, freer. I would also emphasise that, by the end of the 19th century, with the emergence of a new physics—i.e. a new conception of the nature of the physical world—and the transformation of science, the old system of 'objective' perspective representation was itself exposed, except for those who were ideologically over-committed to it, as largely a conventional and historically relative means of representing the world. This was one reason why, as we saw in the first seminar, the generation of Freud's mechanist teachers became interested in the depiction of *movement*. But, evidently, the camera and film played a large part in that too.

At this point, I want to raise a question mark about Cezanne. Much has been written about Cezanne by other Marxist writers, for whom I have the greatest respect. One theory suggests that Courbet produced a 'materialist' view of the world; Cezanne a 'dialectical' view; and the Cubists a 'dialectical materialist view.' It is a 'nice' argument, but I am not sure that it is entirely true.

Certainly, Cezanne's work poses a new kind of relationship between the observer and the observed: it is with Cezanne that we begin to be made aware that what I see depends upon where I am and when. He shows us landscape in a state of change and becoming, from the point of view of an observer who is himself no longer assumed to be frozen and motionless in time and space. But I wonder whether this perceptual reading of Cezanne is not sometimes greatly over-done. Perhaps the real sense in which Cezanne was 'The Father of Modern Painting'—and certainly the sense in which writers like Bell responded and over-responded to him—was that for the first time since prior to the Renaissance, Cezanne mingled a subjective with an objective conception of space, but of course he did so playfully and in an explorative rather than a dogmatically decreed fashion. Bell, it is worth noting here, constantly emphasises in his book, *Art*, that what he takes to be the 'religious' component of Christianity can be separated out from its dogma: 'religion' was, for him, the perception of this mingling of inner and outer. Thus, too, Greenberg writes of Cezanne, 'What he found in the end was, however, not so much a new as a more comprehensive principle; and it lay not in Nature, as he thought, but in the essence of art itself, in art's "abstractness".'[35] I consider that what Greenberg calls here its 'abstractness' is its capacity to be expressive of psychological experience. What we get from Cezanne, I would suggest, is exactly that sensation which Milner was looking for, that 'some kind of relation to objects in which one was much more mixed up with them' than classical, focused systems of perspective allowed.

Interestingly, it was the abstract painter Robert Natkin, of whom I will have more to say next time, who first led me to perceive this aspect of Cezanne when he pointed out how, in many of Cezanne's paintings of Mont Sainte-Victoire, something very peculiar goes on between the foreground and the background of the picture. At moments a branch on a tree in the front seems to be depicted only feet away from others; but soon after, it seems to touch the slopes of a mountain which is 'in reality' twenty miles or so away. This sort of playful toying with his perception of the external world, which involves both the acceptance and also the denial of distance and separation, seems to me to have a lot more to do with the re-introduction of certain kinds of *affects* into painting than with Cezanne's perceptual responses alone.

This is confirmed, I think, when one considers the theme of naked figures in a landscape, with which Cezanne was always fascinated. Towards the end of his life the way in which he handled this subject changed; he became less interested in the eroticism of appearance. Although each of the figures in his groups retained its autonomy, Cezanne sought ways of representing them in which they were simultaneously indissoluble from the ground, water, sky and trees which surrounded them. *Women Bathing* was painted within four years of his death: although the whiteness of the canvas surface plays its part, the painting is anything but loose or unfinished.

Cezanne made it in his studio: if he relied on *petites sensations* they were in the form of memories, rather than of things immediately seen. Anyway, he learned as much from looking at Poussin as at Provence. Like Poussin, Cezanne offers an attempt

Paul Cézanne, *Grandes Baigneuses*, 1899–1906.

at a total view of man-man-in-nature, but it is a very different kind of view from that of the 17th century master. Cezanne refuses focused perspective and breaks up and re-orders his picture space in a radically new way. His memories have been realised, through an elaborate structuring of coloured planes, into a vision of a new kind of relationship between human beings and the natural world which they inhabit. Poussin's totalisation was one of eternal stasis. Cezanne's (although, as I shall argue, it involves a *retrieval* of affects belonging to an early phase of life) is essentially a promise, characterised by *becoming*. It revives the emotions of his individual past, to speak of a possible transformed future.

And now, I hope, you will be beginning to see the point I am getting at. Although the modern movement failed, for reasons we have already explored, to realise a new 'world-view' through painting, in the work of Cezanne himself and of at least some of his successors—e.g. Gauguin, Van Gogh, Matisse, Picasso. Bonnard, Klee, and later De Kooning—it did re-introduce to painting an aspect which had been absent from it, or at least heavily muted, during the era of the dominance of professional Fine Artists. These early modernist painters certainly acknowledged the external otherness, the separateness and 'out-thereness' of the outside world, but having acknowledged it, they sought to transfigure and transform it, to deny, or otherwise to interrupt it, as a means of expressing subjective feelings too. Their new forms emerge as neither an indulgence nor an escape from the world, but rather as an extension into an occluded area of experience.

Now I think that it was only when painters attempted to do this that Bell experienced his 'aesthetic emotion', those strange indefinable yearnings on which he places such great importance. But the point is that this was actually a *new* thing for those who made visual images to explore and to attempt to do. Bell made the mistake of identifying this as the essence of 'art', universalising it, and projecting it back through history, so that any work which did not show this quality could be dismissed as not really worth looking at. (Bell wrote off not just the 'world-view' painters of the Renaissance, of 17th century Holland and of 19th century England, but also, of course, those who were trying to elaborate new world-views through painting in the 20th century—the Futurists and Vorticists, for example.)

This leads us to an important point. Stoke's taste, for most of his life, was for work in the 'carving mode', for art in which the depressive position had been worked through, for the Quatrocento and the High Renaissance. Bell's taste, on the contrary, was for the modified 'modelling mode' (though of course the terms would have been quite foreign to him) for the Christian Primitives and the Post-Impressionists, for an art which as it were, pushed back even further emotionally from the 'depressive position' towards the prior 'paranoid-schizoid' position. (Actually, this polarisation is not fair to either of them. As I said last time, unlike many Kleinian aestheticians, Stokes was prepared to recognise the importance of feelings of mergence and fusion in aesthetic experience. In later life, he became ever more sympathetic to the modelling modes. Whereas Bell, of course, modified his vituperative dismissal of Renaissance 'world-view' painting.)

Bell disguised this. He insisted that he was talking about an autonomous, irreducible aesthetic experience, when in fact he was responding to the capacity of a certain type of visual image to evoke and arouse a certain type of relatively inaccessible—not everyone, he stressed, was capable of aesthetic sensibility—human emotion which he and (I better admit it) I, too, find intensely pleasurable. The nature of that exquisite aesthetic emotion is, I think, rendered all but manifest in that passage about the raptures that can be experienced upon the cold white peaks of art. Bell found in the modern movement, and enjoyed there, a capacity of painting to revive something of the spatial sensations and accompanying 'good' emotions which the infant feels at his mother's breast. By this, however, I mean much, much more than that Bell liked art because he found it to be a symbol of the 'good' breast in the Kleinian sense. Let me explain.

Bell's *Art* is full of indications of resistance: he is peculiarly keen on dismissing any attempt to penetrate or reduce aesthetic emotion. He also engaged, as one might expect, in polemic against psychoanalysis. For example, in a communication called 'Dr. Freud on Art', Bell tells how he once begged a roomful of psychoanalysts,

'. . . to believe that the emotion provoked in me by St. Paul's Cathedral has nothing to do with my notion of having a good time. I have said that it was comparable rather with the emotion provoked in a mathematician by the perfect and perfectly economical solution of a problem, than with that provoked in me

by the prospect of going to Monte Carlo in particularly favourable circumstances. But they knew all about St. Paul's Cathedral and all about quadratic equations and all about me apparently. So I told them that if Cezanne was for ever painting apples, that had nothing to do with an insatiable appetite for those handsome but to me unpalatable, fruit. At the word "apples" however, my psychologists broke into titters.'
Yes, the word was 'titters.'

'Apparently, they knew all about apples, too. And they knew that Cezanne painted them for precisely the same reason that poker-players desire to be dealt a pair of aces.'[36]
It is not clear whether Bell was aware of the transparency of the symbolisation he recorded here. In any event, he goes on to say that the real reason Cezanne used apples was because 'they are comparatively durable' (unlike flowers) and can be depended upon 'to behave themselves' (unlike people). If this story is correctly reported, it is hard to say who was the more stupid: the tittering analysts who uncritically interpreted the *figurative* elements in Cezanne's painting as being straight-forward breast symbols; or Bell himself. What we need to ask of psychoanalysis is not a capacity to unmask subject matter or manifest figurative symbols in painting, but rather whether it can help us to understand those subjective spatial represen-tations which begin to appear with the rise of Modernism, and with Cezanne. I think that psychoanalysis *does* have much to contribute here, or, to be more exact, I think there is much to be learned from a particular tendency within psychoanalysis, the British object relations school, to which Milner, for example, belongs. But before I can clarify this, I have to produce another fragment from my bag of pieces, and that is a short chunk of psychoanalytic history and theory.

Some of you may have noticed the direction in which we are moving through this series of seminars. In one sense, this corresponds simply enough to the chronological development of psychoanalytic theory. We begin with Freud; we moved on to Klein; and now we are about to find ourselves standing in the clear, bright light of British 'object relations' thought. But this trajectory also corresponds to an inverse chronology of human development. My first paper, with Moses as its focus, revolved around aspects of the infant-father relationship and its survivals in adult life. In my second paper, we were involved with the mother, albeit as an 'internal object', and the nature of the reparative processes which could be lavished upon that object when it was felt that it had been damaged or destroyed through the subject's own hate and aggression. In these last two sessions, we are concerned with the earliest infant-mother relationships, but we are focusing on the nature of the infant's experience before he (or she) has become fully aware of himself (or herself) as a being separated from the mother or the world.

I want, now, to return to the British School, and to sketch out aspects of the way in which theory developed there after the arrival of Melanie Klein. You will recall that Freud himself conceived of the infant as auto-erotic and narcissistic. In Freud's view, the baby was motivated by the desire to secure instinctual pleasure by evading tension. Freud postulated three phases of libidinal development—oral, anal, and phallic—prior to the Oedipal conflict and the emergence of so-called 'genital sexuality' involving the desire for objects outside the self. Freud supposed that the infant was only interested in the mother insofar as she served the purposes of the child's auto-erotism, by gratifying instinctual desires such as that for food. As a matter of fact, Freud had only the dimmest conception of the nature of the infant's relations to the mother, which he did not discuss until as late as 1926. Indeed, Freud often writes as if the relationship with the father was more important. (The reasons for Freud's blindness in this respect were at least in part defensive; he never satisfactorily analysed his relationship with his own mother, a fact which led to distorted inflections in his theoretical formulations. There were also cultural factors: given the relative status of fathers in the 19th century, European, middle-class homes, Freud was often unable to see beyond the authority of Moses. As we saw, he was indifferent to the Venus.)

Klein's theories, evidently, were in this respect a real advance on Freud's. Klein gave a centrality to the infant's early relationship with the mother, to the degree that, as Brierley put it, Freud's more orthodox followers found it 'difficult to reconcile Melanie Klein's assumption that the infant very soon begins to love its mother, in the sense of being concerned for her, with Freud's conception that in the earliest months the infant is concerned with its environment only in relation to its own wishes.'[37] Nonetheless, despite Klein's formal assurances to the contrary, it remains true that in her system the course and character of this relationship is determined not so much by the quality of the mothering which the child receives as by the way in which the child plays out its innate, instinctual ambivalence. As we have seen, Klein was concerned with what she took to be the working out of an instinctual opposition between love and hate, which was not greatly affected by the nature of the environment. In general, Klein emphasised, indeed *over-emphasised*, orality, feeding, etc. As Guntrip puts it, 'Mrs Klein states that "object-relations exist from the beginning of life"... but this seems to be something of an irrelevance; it does not matter much whether they do or not if they are merely incidental to the basic problems.'[38]

A decisive step in psychoanalysis, however, was the replacement of dual instinct theory, whether of the Freudian or Kleinian variety, by a full object relations theory, i.e. by a theory in which the subject's need to relate to objects plays a central part. Psychoanalysis arrived at this focus in Britain long before it did so elsewhere. (Only during the 1960s did some American analysts also become involved in this area of work.) The way in which this came about involved a number of disparate, and often seemingly incompatible strands and elements. Here, I can only sketch a few of the more significant.

Some came from the serious critiques of psychoanalysis which were being elaborated *outside* the movement itself. For example, in the 1930s, analysts were often involved in theoretical jousting with members of the Tavistock Clinic. (Glover has written that within the British Psychoanalytic Society, 'suggestions that a closer contact might be made even with more eclectic medico-psychological clinics, such as the Tavistock Clinic, were frowned on.')[39] Nonetheless, at the Tavistock, J. A. Hadfield, who was far from totally rejecting analytic findings, argued against Freud's auto-erotic conception of infancy that the fundamental need of children was for protective love. In the early 1930s, Ian Suttie was one of Hadfield's assistants. Suttie died at the age of 46, in 1935, but the following year his critique of Freud's psychology, *The Origins of Love and Hate*, was published.

Suttie provides a systematic account of man as a social animal, whose object-seeking behaviour is discernible from birth. Suttie abandons Freud's concept of Narcissism arguing that 'the elements or isolated percepts from which the "mother idea" is finally integrated are loved (cathected) from the beginning.'[40] Thus Suttie found it possible to speak of the infant's love for an external object, the mother, from the earliest moments of life. This was not sentimentalisation of the infant-mother relationship; he identified its biological basis clearly:

> 'I thus regard love as social rather than sexual in its biological function, as derived from the self-preservative instincts not the genital appetite, and as seeking *any state* of responsiveness with others as its goal. Sociability I consider as a need for love rather than as aim-inhibited sexuality, while culture-interest is derived from love as a supplementary mode of companionship (to love) and not as a cryptic form of sexual gratification.'[41]

Suttie was not approved of by the psychoanalytic establishment in his life-time. Today, however, many of the criticisms he made of Freud—including his observations of the latter's 'patriachal and antifeminist bias'—are very widely accepted, even within the psychoanalytic movement itself. Indeed, by the 1940s, hostility between the Tavistock and the Institute of Psychoanalysis was diminishing. For example, John Bowlby was analysed by Joan Rivière, one of Klein's foremost followers; Klein herself was one of his supervisors when he was a trainee analyst. In 1946, Bowlby joined the Tavistock, without relinquishing his psychoanalytic associations. Bowlby was further strongly influenced by the work of ethologists, especially Tinbergen and Lorenz. Bowlby acknowledges a debt to Suttie, but in his own work he elaborated a thorough-going critique of Freudian instinct theory: 'in the place of psychical energy and its discharge, the central concepts are those of behavioural systems and their control, of information, negative feedback, and a behavioural form of homeostasis.'[42] Bowlby strongly opposed the idea that the infant's relationship to the mother was based on primary need gratification, such as the wish for food. Bowlby emphasised the need for 'a warm, intimate, and continuous relationship' with the mother 'in which both find satisfaction and enjoyment'. He held that the 'young child's hunger for his mother's love and presence was as great as his hunger for food.'[43] Although retaining psychoanalysis as his frame of reference, Bowlby drew on a mass of empirical data from other disciplines. The fact that he stands at the intersection between psychoanalysis, behavioural studies, ethology, biology, and contemporary communications theory should have rendered his work of enormous significance to all of us on the left, who are looking for a rigorously materialist account of the early infant-mother relationship. Instead, socialists have tended to revile his work without attending to it . . . but that is another story.

Other influences were also inflecting the unique course which psychoanalytic theory was taking in Britain. You may remember that in my last seminar, I referred to Sandor Ferenczi, a close colleague of Freud's until his latter days, and Klein's first analyst. Ferenczi was the leader of the psychoanalytic community in Budapest, until his death in 1933. Guntrip has accurately described the differences between Ferenczi and Freud, differences which were to have tragic consequences for the former:

> 'Ferenczi recognised earlier than any other analyst the importance of the primary mother-child relationship. Freud's theory and practice was notoriously paternalistic, Ferenczi's maternalistic. His concept of "primary object love" prepared the way for the later work of Melanie Klein, Fairbairn, Balint, Winnicott, and all others who to-day recognize that object-relations start at the beginning in the infant's needs for the mother. Ferenczi held that this primary object-love for the mother was passive, and in that form underlay all later development.'[44]

Many of those gathered round Ferenczi developed his approach. Hermann, for example, pointed towards such components in the infant's relation to the mother as clinging and clasping, which could not be accommodated within the traditional Freudian perspective. Alice and Michael Balint began to develop a more radical critique of Freud's theory of narcissism, but Hermann's observations enabled them to progress beyond Ferenczi's essentially *passive* conception of the infant's relation to the mother, to a fuller characterisation of this 'archaic', primary object-relation. In the Balints' view, the infant was 'born relating', even if its mode of loving was egotistic.[45] Early object relations possessed autonomy from erotogenic activities. The Balints came to live and work in Britain, where their ideas had a considerable influence among some Kleinians.

But, within Kleinian circles, parallel critiques and extensions of classical theory had already sprung up independently. Among the most significant was that put forward by W. R. D. Fairbairn, an analyst who, in the middle and late 1930s, was strongly under the influence of Klein. However, between 1940 and 1944, Fairbairn published a series of controversial papers— including, 'A Revised Psychopathology of the Psychoses and

Psychoneuroses' of 1941[46]—in which he essentially revised psychoanalytic theory 'in terms of the priority of human relations over instincts as the causal factor in development, both normal and abnormal'. Fairbairn described libido as not pleasure-seeking, but object-seeking; the drive to good object relationships is, itself, the primary libidinal need. In the words of Guntrip, his most devoted disciple:

'From the moment of birth, Fairbairn regards the mother-infant relationship as potentially fully personal on both sides, in however primitive and undeveloped a way this is as yet felt by the baby. It is the breakdown of genuinely personal relations between the mother and the infant that is the basic cause of trouble.'[47]

Fairbairn, like Klein before him, was something of a systems builder: I do not think that there are many analysts today who make use of all his bizarre terms and constructs. Nonetheless, there can be no doubt that Fairbairn's work—together with the influences coming from Budapest, and the 'Tavistock' critiques of psychoanalysis—paved the way for a great deal of original work in the post-Kleinian tradition on the nature of the infant-mother relationship. D. W. Winnicott, Marjorie Brierley, Marion Milner, Harry Guntrip, John Padel, Masud Khan, and Charles Rycroft were among those who contributed substantially to the development of object-relations theory. Evidently, I am talking about a heterogeneous tradition, one which was characterised by internal contradictions, polemics, and controversies—nonetheless, in my view this tradition represents the most constructive development within psychoanalysis, and that which, incidentally, has the most to tell us about the nature of creativity, visual experience and their enjoyment.

In our next seminar, we will be examining the work of D. W. Winnicott in detail, in relation to certain types of abstract art. Here, I merely wish to point out that it is in the work of Winnicott and his colleagues that we find a focusing upon a transient phase of development which is *between* that of the 'subjectivity' of the earliest moment, in which even the mother's breast is assumed to be an extension of the self, and the more 'objective' perceptions of later childhood. As Winnicott himself put it:

'I am proposing that there is a stage in the development of human beings that comes before objectivity and perceptibility. At the theoretical beginning a baby can be said to live in a

subjective or conceptual world. The change from the primary
state to one in which objective perception is possible is not only a
matter of inherent or inherited growth process; it needs in addition an environmental minimum. It belongs to the whole vast
theme of the individual travelling from dependence towards
independence.'[48]

I will have more to say about this phase next time; meanwhile, I
would just point out that it is characterised by tentatively
ambivalent feelings about mergence and separation, about
being lost in the near, of establishing and denying boundaries
about what is inside and what is outside, and concerning the
whereabouts of limits and a containing skin, so that the infant,
while beginning to recognise the autonomy of objects, nonetheless feels 'mixed up in them' in a way in which the child or
adult does not.

Now all this work has been done *since* that moment when the
psychoanalysts 'tittered' at Bell for saying that 'if Cezanne was
for ever painting apples, that had nothing to do with an insatiable appetite for those handsome but to me unpalatable
fruit.' To say that for Cezanne (or Bell) the apple was a symbol
of the breast tells us rather less than nothing: to say, however,
that the kind of space which Cezanne constructs, with its
ambivalences between figure and environment, foreground and
background, and between concepts and perceptions, is in some
way related to the way in which the infant relates himself to the
breast, the mother and the world is to say a great deal. It is in
the light of this later analytical work that we can best begin to
arrive at a materialist anlaysis of what happens in the outstanding paintings of the modern movement. Through this
work, I can give some theoretical spine to my deeply held
feeling that there are moments in the now threatened modern
movement which are not just examples of kenosis and epilogue,
but genuine extensions of the capacity of *painted* images, and
spatial organisations, to speak of certain aspects of human
experience in ways which simply could not be reproduced in
other media, where space cannot be imaginatively and affectively *constituted* in the same way.

Winnicott himself was very much aware of correspondences
between his findings and the work of many writers and artists;
unfortunately, however, few of those involved in theoretical
aesthetics, or critical work, have attended to his texts. Indeed.

one has to confront the fact that although British 'object relations' theory is well known among clinicians, therapists and educationalists, it has had very little impact upon culture beyond those specific disciplines. Perry Anderson, editor of *New Left Review*, commented on this in his historic 1968 text, 'Components of the National Culture'.[49] Although he acknowledged that the British School of psychoanalysis was 'one of the most flourishing' in the world, he pointed out that its impact on British culture in general has been virtually nil. Psychoanalysis 'has been sealed off as a technical enclave: an esoteric and specialized pursuit unrelated to any of the central concerns of mainstream "humanistic" culture.'[50] Anderson relates this to his 'global' analysis of British culture, to the failure of the British bourgeoisie to elaborate a world-view, to the resultant 'absent centre' of British culture, and its resistance to alien 'impingements'. His analysis is one with which, by and large, I am in substantial agreement. But why has the British achievement in psychoanalysis been so widely ignored on the left which opposes itself to that 'mainstream' whose lacunae Anderson describes? I have not, afterall, noticed much discussion of Klein, Winnicott, Rycroft, etc. in the pages of *New Left Review*.

I cannot attempt a complete answer to this question here, but I would like to throw out two indications. Firstly, I am convinced that what Suttie called 'a taboo on tenderness' operates among many intellectuals, a taboo which is characterised by a radical distrust of those areas of experience which, by their very nature, cannot be fully verbalised. (I have in mind here, for example, the tendency of certain Althusserian writers on art to seek to replace the *experience* of the work with a complete, they would say 'scientific', verbal account of it.) Winnicott wrote that 'the individual gets to external reality through the omnipotent fantasies elaborated in the effort to get away from inner reality.'[51] There are those on the left who never stop elaborating such omnipotent fantasies in the attempt to obliterate the encroachments of a subjectivity which they deny. This is one reason why so many who have any interest in post-Freudian psychoanalysis scuttle across the channel to the structural-linguistic models through which Lacan endeavours to describe the infant-mother relationship. In effect, the very forms in which Lacan casts his work, with all its pseudo-algebraic pretensions, are a *denial* of the affective qualities of precisely that which they purport to describe, whereas Winnicott's 'metaphoric' mode does not allow one any such escape into the irrational 'rationality' of a closed system.

There is another, related reason which is perhaps more excusable: in many of these psychoanalysts there is a trace, and sometimes more than a trace, of philosophical idealism. What they discovered about the early infant-mother relationship sometimes led them, for example, to direct or indirect apologetics for religion. (This was true of Brierley, Guntrip, and Suttie.) But the point is that these writers and researchers were uncovering the material, biological, roots of such phenomena as religious and aesthetic experience: by this, I mean, they were exposing their rootedness in a certain definite, developmental phase. There are times in which, lacking a historical materialist perspective, some of these writers tended to conflate the specific social, cultural religious and artistic forms within which such experiences and emotions were structured and accommodated with those experiences and emotions themselves. (This was never true of Winnicott, or of Rycroft who has, for example, drawn attention to the way in which certain theological concepts were, prior to developments in object relations theory, the most adequate accounts of certain kinds of experience, for which non-theological explanations are now possible.) However, in developing an ideological critique of those social and cultural forms, the Marxist left has, in my view, sadly neglected the major advances made by the British psychoanalytic school into what it is that is structured through such forms. This is one reason why, as yet, there is no adequate Marxist analysis of religion, music, or abstract painting.

In this respect, the Marxist left may be said to resemble Freud himself. We have already had occasion to note how Freud dreaded any potential contamination between psychoanalysis and 'mysticism'. But again, it is important to ask whether in his opposition to certain definite cultural forms, such as religion, and his pathological indifference to others, such as music, and non-representational art, Freud was manifesting not just his commitment to 'science' and rationality, but also his *denial* of significant areas of his own experience.

For example, in his discussion of religion, Freud talked about a mystical state which he described as a feeling of being at one with the universe, which he correlated with feelings of dependency and being overwhelmed. Freud described this feeling as 'oceanic'—a term he got from a friend—but confided that he had never, himself, experienced anything like it. Freud explained this feeling as a regression to the early infantile state when the child's ego is not differentiated from the surrounding external world. Anton Ehrenzweig has observed that Freud is thus claiming that the feeling of union is no mere illusion, but the correct description of a memory of an infantile state otherwise inaccessible.[52] In telling us that he never experienced such emotions Freud is indicating an area of his personality which would appear to be subject to defensive denial: he is pointing to a failure in his historic self-analysis. The oceanic feeling of union does not only manifest itself in mystical or religious forms: it seems to be an important element in certain types of auditory and visual aesthetic experience, too— experiences to which, as we know, Freud was notoriously in- sensitive. On all such experiences and areas of human life, Freud has almost nothing of interest to say: his silence, I am sure, may be correlated with his indifference to and denial of the real nature of the infant-mother relationship, as described in the work done by the British object relations school over the last quarter of a century.

Freud, you will remember, admired the Moses of Michelangelo, but had nothing to say about those 'unfinished' or 'incomplete' works—now almost universally more widely admired—in which the figure seems to be struggling to free itself from (or is it to submerge itself back into) the matter out of which it has been wrought. Evidently, this was partly *culturally* as well as *psychologically* determined: in the 19th century, Michelangelo's late drawings were widely regarded as merely the products of a senile old man who had lost his touch; today, there are many who would acclaim these figures with multiple, ebbing outlines as among the finest which the artist did. My point is that these drawings speak of significant areas of experience which, in the past, tended to be either locked within the mystifications of religion, or denied altogether.

Perhaps I can demonstrate this by referring to a writer whose 'taste' and whose psychoanalytic theories can both meaning- fully be described as being somewhere *between* Freud's and my own, E. H. Gombrich. Gombrich, you will remember, can certainly appreciate the art of Post-Impressionism; he has, however, never enjoyed abstract painting. In his essay, 'Psycho- Analysis and the History of Art',[53] Gombrich draws heavily upon

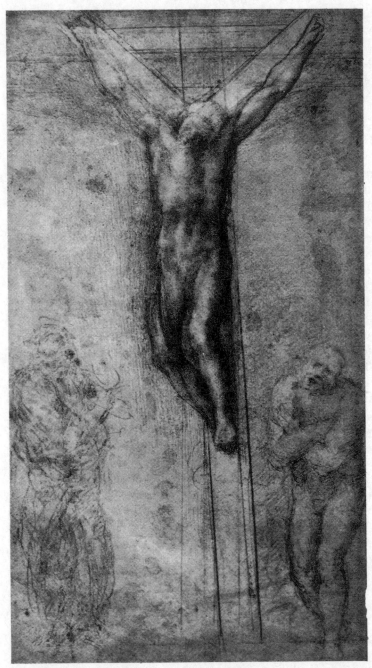

Michelangelo, *Cruxifixion*.

Bonnencontre
(E. Courtois),
The Three Graces,
circa 1900.

the ideas of Edward Glover, and especially on the latter's study, 'The Significance of the Mouth in Psycho-Analysis'.[54] This was written before Glover was deeply influenced by Melanie Klein. (Later, you may remember, he polemicised strongly against her: when her ideas obtained partial acceptance within the British Society, Glover, who had been among its most influential members, resigned and joined the Japanese Society instead.) Gombrich here suggests a wholly oral ontogenesis of aesthetic taste, describing 'oral gratification as a genetic model for aesthetic pleasure'. Gombrich proposes two polarities in taste, the 'soft' and the 'crunchy', which, through Glover's ideas, he correlates with the 'passive' and the 'active', and with 'sucking' and 'biting' oral modes respectively. Gombrich implies that the 'soft' is more primitive and infantile; while the crunchy corresponds with sophisticated, civilised taste.

To make his point, Gombrich takes an atrocious academic painting of the *Three Graces* by Bonnencontre, and, as he puts it, tries to 'improve the sloppy mush by adding a few crunchy breadcrumbs'. He does this by photographing the picture through wobbly glass. 'You will agree,' he writes, 'that it looks a little more respectable'.[55] And, indeed, he is right. It does.

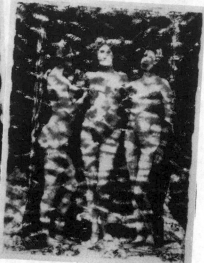

Bonnencontre, *The Three Graces*
seen through rolled glass.

Gombrich explains this by saying, 'We have to become a little
more active in reconstituting the image, and we are less
disgusted.'[56] He repeats the experiment by taking another
photograph through the same glass at a greater distance, so that
the figures are even more shadowy, and their outlines blurred
and dissolved. He comments, 'By now, I think, it deserves the
epithet "interesting". Our own effort to reintegrate what has
been wrenched apart makes us project a certain vigour into the
image which makes it quite crunchy.'
    Gombrich goes on to say:
        '. . . this artificial blurring repeats in a rather surprising way
        the course that painting actually took when the wave of revolt
        from the Bouguereau phase spread through the art world.'[57]
He comments on the blurring achieved by Impressionism which
'demands the well-known trained response—you are expected
to step back and see the dabs and patches fall into place'; and
Cezanne, 'with whom activity is stimulated to even greater
efforts, as we are called upon to repeat the artist's strivings to
reconcile the demands of representation with obedience to an
overriding pattern.'[58] Interestingly, all Gombrich's examples—
the Bonnencontre, Impressionist, and Cezanne's—here are of

the female nude. His conclusion is that whereas 'taste may be accessible to psychological analysis, art is possibly not'.

Now evidently there is much that is true in Gombrich's account, but what is wrong with it is his underlying assumption that the infantile relationship to the mother is instinctual in character, that is, realised exclusively through the mouth and the search for oral satisfactions and reducible to a matter of taste in a limited, oral sense. I doubt whether the reason why the blurred Bonnencontre is more 'interesting' now is simply, or even at all, due to a maturer preference for a later oral phase, for biting over sucking, for crunchy over soft. There are hints that Gombrich, too, realises this because the way he develops the notions of 'active' and 'passive' with reference to the pleasure to be derived from the attempt to 'reintegrate what has been wrenched apart' suggests the kind of Kleinian notion of the restoration of internal objects which we discussed at the end of our last talk. (The differences between the Bonnencontre original, and the 'wobbly glass' versions can be compared with those between the Hiram Powers sculpture and the Venus de Milo.) But we, ourselves, are now ready to go beyond even such Kleinian accounts. I would say that the reason the distorted Bonnencontre is more 'interesting' has to do with its capacity to begin (however thinly and vaguely) to evoke that critical phase, to which Winnicott referred, between experience as wholly subjective, and the achievement of objectivity and per-ceptibility, when the child is relating to another whose otherness is at once recognised and denied; when the existence of the boundaries (outlines) or limiting membranes of the self and of its objects are at once perceived and imaginatively ruptured. An explanation of this order allows us to see the developments in Modernism, to which Gombrich refers, as much more than a change of taste, or the addition of a few breadcrumbs to mush. We can begin to take into account the affective expressiveness of pictorial spatial organisations them-selves. In comparison, Gombrich is merely engaging in a slightly more sophisticated variant of that psychoanalytic 'tittering' in front of Cezanne's apples than that which so understandably irritated Bell.

Indeed, I hope that you will now be able to see that we are ready to leave the Kleinian aesthetics which, up until now, have served us so well. Adrian Stokes, you will remember, found elements belonging not only to the 'depressive position', but also to the prior 'paranoid-schizoid' position in both artistic creativity and aesthetic experience. For Stokes, the sense of 'fusion' was combined, though in differing proportions, with the sense of 'object-otherness'. This led to criticism from more orthodox Kleinians, who felt that, by associating aesthetics and creativity with the 'paranoid-schizoid' position, and its mechanisms, Stokes was characterising them as regressive. But Winnicott rejects the notion of a 'paranoid-schizoid' position, with its overtones of primary insanity, and disjuncture. Indeed, in the work of many of those involved in the British 'object relations' tradition—as Anton Ehrenzweig put it—'the concept of the primary process as the archaic, wholly irrational function of the deep unconscious' underwent a 'drastic revision'.[59] Marion Milner once wrote that this revision 'has been partly stimulated by the problems raised by the nature of art',[60] not least, of course, by much of the art of the modern movement.

We do not have time to go into all the implications of these revisions of psychoanalytic thinking on the nature of the primary process here. Suffice to say that Freud's view of them as something menacing in later life, to be defeated by 'science' and the Reality Principle, or Klein's view of them as an analog of madness have been increasingly eclipsed. To site one specific example, Ehrenzweig drew attention to a distinction between 'the narrow focus' of ordinary attention, and the 'diffused, wide stare' which had its origins in the infantile gaze. This has considerable importance in our understanding of the difference between, say, perspective painting and abstract expressionism. Rycroft has done more work demolishing the view that the primary and secondary processes are mutually antagonistic, and that the primary processes are maladaptive. He has pointed out how the attitude of psychoanalysis towards these processes derives from a paradox:

> 'Since psycho-analysis aims at being a scientific psychology, psycho-analytical observation and theorizing is involved in the paradoxical activity of using secondary process thinking to observe, analyse, and conceptualise precisely that form of mental activity, the primary processes, which scientific thinking has always been at pains to exclude.'[61]

Rycroft, however, emphasises the importance of primary process thinking in many imaginative, creative, and aesthetic endeavours. One might say, therefore, that the re-appropriation of these modes within the modernist tradition was *not* simply a regressive evasion of the world.

In her theoretical paper on art, Milner says:

> '. . . the unconscious mind, by the very fact of its not clinging to the distinction between self and other, seer and seen, can do things that the conscious logical mind cannot do. By being more sensitive to the sameness rather than the differences between things, by being passionately concerned with finding "the familiar in the unfamiliar" (which, by the way, Wordsworth says is the whole of the poet's business), it does just what Maritain says it does; it brings back blood to the spirit, passion to intuition.'[62]

But Milner is not suggesting that the primary processes belong in adult life to a separate category, of no use in understanding the real, as opposed to the imagined or imaginary world. Indeed, she says that 'it was just this wide focus of attention', as described by Ehrenzweig, which made the world 'seem most intensely real and significant' for her. Thus, we might say, those spatial organisations constructed by the early modernists are not merely enrichments of nostalgic fantasy life, but also potentially of our relationship to the world itself. (This seems to me the real secret of Cezanne.)

At one point, while she was trying to overcome her inability to paint, Milner found herself thinking about a statement of Juan Gris, who once defined painting as being 'the expression of certain relationships between the painter and the outside world.'

> 'I felt,' writes Milner, 'a need to change the word "expression" of certain relationships into experiencing certain relationships; this was because of the fact that in those drawings which had been at all satisfying there had been this experiencing of a dialogue relationship between thought and the bit of the external world represented by the marks made on the paper. Thus the phrase "expression of" suggested too much that the feeling to be expressed was there beforehand, rather than an experience developing as one made the drawing. And this re-wording of the definition pointed to a fact that psychoanalysis and the content of the drawings had forced me to face: the fact that the relationship of oneself to the external world is basically and originally a relationship of one person to another, even though it does eventually become differentiated into relations to living beings and relations to things, inanimate nature. In other words, in the beginning one's mother is, literally, the whole world. Of course, the idea of the first relationship to the outside world being felt as

a relationship to persons was one I had frequently met with in discussions of childhood and savage animism. But the possibility that the adult painter could be basically, even though unconsciously, concerned with an animistically conceived world, was something I had hardly dared let myself face.

Looked at in these terms the problem of the relation between the painter and his world then became basically a problem of one's own need and the needs of the "other", a problem of reciprocity between "you" and "me"; with "you" and "me" meaning originally mother and child.'[63]

And now that I have exposed all the fragments of my statue—at least all of those which I have to hand—it only remains for me to attempt to fit them into place. I am suggesting that there is something significant in common between Milner's difficulties with perspective and outline in her attempts to learn to draw; the shift in my taste from Ingres' linearly cloistered figures to the paintings of Bonnard, Rothko and Natkin; the kind of space which begins to manifest itself in paintings with the eruption of the modern movement—say in Cezanne's trees touching and not touching those distant mountains; and poor, dim-witted Mr. Bell's exquisite raptures on his cold white peaks of art.

I am suggesting that what these phenomena have in common is a relatedness to a significant area of experience, that pertaining to a critical phase in the infant-mother relationship; I do not conceive of that relationship as 'a matter of taste', or instinctual orality, so much as a determinative moment in the self's discovery of, and exploration of its relationship to, its world. The nature of the 'primary processes' in this early phase is no longer necessarily opaque to us: 'object-relations' theory, as it developed in the post-Kleinian tradition in Britain, permits us intellectual and affective understanding of this infant-mother relationship. It also causes a revaluing of the 'primary processes', and of the part which they play in the realisation of the full potentialities of the relationship of the self to others and its world. To speak crudely, in the medieval era, the 'primary processes' constituted the *lived relation* of self to the world (e.g. in religious cosmology). But, particularly with the 19th century emphasis upon 'Science', rationality, and inevitable progress, these areas of experience tended to be excluded from the dominant culture, or locked into mystified enclaves—such as religion.

Not even classical psychoanalysis succeeded in penetrating this terrain. In part, this was the result of the deficiencies of Freud's self-analysis, his inability to reach back towards the affects pertaining to this determinative phase in the infant mother relationship, and his consequent misconstruing of the nature of the primary processes. But the world-view of that culture within which Freud was enmeshed reinforced his prejudices and defences, his ambiguous belief in the value of 'science' over and above that of the imaginative faculties. However, 1914–1918 saw the final shattering of that world-view. Those areas of experience which had been denigrated, distorted, eclipsed or excluded flooded back—sometimes in their most archaic and mystifying forms. For example, in the later 19th century Liberal Protestantism in Germany, from Ritschl to Harnack, had effectively purged Christianity of its religious content, through a theology of immanence in which Jesus was nought but a particularly well-behaved bourgeois. The First World War shattered this 'progressive', middle-class faith, and gave birth to a 'mystical' revival, exemplified in Otto's *The Idea of the Holy* of 1917, and a 'Crisis Theology' (soon to be known as 'Neo-Orthodoxy') which re-asserted the transcendence, and unutterable otherness of God. At this time, too, a species of cosmic idealism flooded back into physics as the Newtonian conception of the universe seemed to collapse.

In art, as we have seen, the validity of the focused system of perspective was shattered. But the Modernist enterprise does not seem to me to have been *just* an escape, or a retreat into idealism and 'subjectivity' (although, of course, there were elements within it that could be so characterised). It was almost as if the painter had to go back to experiences at the breast (and before) in order to find again, in a new way, his relationship to others and the world. This, I think, was what happened in the best elements of Modernism—and it was what Bell responded to, though he structured his response in terms of 'aesthetic emotion' and 'significant form'.

Perhaps I can here elaborate an analogy of a kind which I would suspect if it was put forward by anyone except myself! Michael Balint describes a certain type of pathology as a manifestation of what he calls 'basic fault'. In these instances the patient's whole mode of being in the world, of relating to it, and to others is faulty and false; he maintains this can only be overcome if the patient is allowed to regress to a state of dependence on the analyst, in which he can experience a 'new beginning'. (This corresponds to a distinction Winnicott makes between 'true' and 'false' self.) In a certain sense, 1914–1918 exposed the 'basic fault' of European culture: the kenosis of modernism (at least in certain of its aspects) may be compared with the individual patient's *necessary* regression towards a position from which a 'new beginning' (in this instance, presumably, a new realism) was possible. Although he does not draw this comparison, Balint himself implies something similar in his 1952 paper, 'Notes on the Dissolution of Object-Representation in Modern Art'. Balint refers to the disappearance of 'the sovereign, sharply defined and delineated object' from both physics and art; but he ventures the view:

'The present narcissistic disappointment and frightened withdrawal, degrading the dignity of the object into that of a mere stimulus and laying the main emphasis on the sincere and faithful representation of the artist's subjective internal mental processes, will very probably give way gradually to a concern for creating whole and hearty objects. (This is meant in a purely descriptive sense and no value judgement is either implied or intended with it.)[64]

Balint goes on to 'the unavoidable integration of the discoveries of "modern art" with the demand of "mature love" for the object.'[65] But this is already to look forward to the subject of our final seminar, that of the 'promise' inherent within certain of the most emptied-out examples of full abstraction.

IV

ABSTRACTION AND 'THE POTENTIAL SPACE'

I N this, our final seminar, I wish to develop some of the points I made last time. But I want to approach the problems in a different way: by examining my experience of particular works. To begin with a specific painting by Robert Natkin, an American artist. He calls this work *Reveries of a Lapsed Narcissist*, and it belongs to a series, *Colour Bath* canvases. I want to try to describe what happens when you begin to look at it.[1]

At first, your eye responds to the painting's superficial seductiveness and decorative inducements: it is shamelessly beguiling, immediately pleasurable and *engaging*. Nothing in it shouts loudly at you but the apparent taut, stretched surface of paint easily receives your gaze and having done so entertains it, that is continues to hold it through time. Threads of many different colours and iconographic devices like the passages of cross-hatching, the row of dots, and the little blue circle seem to have been woven together to form this surface. Although you can recognise this impression through a reproduction it is, of course, stronger if you are standing in front of the canvas itself. You are aware of the shimmering presence of a myriad of colours including gentle reds and modulating tinges of purple, green, orange and blue; but one is dominant over the others, the intimately sensual pinkness of white flesh.

If you try to find words for what you see the idea of an alluring, suspended cloth—a veil or tapestry, perhaps—will probably occur to you. You might also think of 'suffusion' or 'sheen': but I think you are most likely to pick on the word *skin*. The painting is undeniably saturated with a vibrant sensuality: it is *attractive* almost in the sexual sense. As you look, you are aware of the apparent unity of this seemingly seamless skin of light. You are compelled to confront it as a

whole; your eyes caress and explore it horizontally and vertically almost like hands moving across another's body in the
fore-play to love-making. At first no part of the painting insists
on your attention more than any other, but the paint surface
has a certain translucence, like the skin of a calico veil tailed
goldfish. You may come to feel that it is floating somewhere
immediately in front of—or is it behind—the canvas surface.

About a third of the way down the picture, a little off centre,
there is a roughly rectangular area wedged between two passages
of whitish cross-hatching. As you continue to look at this
constellation it sharpens into a focal point. The rectangle
appears to be 'in perspective': it seems further away from you at
the top than at the bottom. And so it lifts itself upwards and
outwards and the fragile curtain of paint, the sensitive surface or
skin, is apparently ruptured or torn. As you ask yourself where
the rectangular shape is within the picture space you become
aware of what has been imaginatively called 'the hum of light'
which reverberates across the whole surface setting it in motion,
disrupting it, and transforming the way it reveals itself to you,
the viewer. Although you will in fact probably be looking at the
painting in a constant light, it is *as if* it were illuminated
through a succession of continuously changing filters.

All this commotion on the surface draws you *in* through the
skin of paint. In front of the picture itself you may even find
yourself expressing this involuntarily by moving a step or two
closer to it physically. In any event, you discover that the first
phase of your involvement was no more than a prelude or an
overture before the curtain vanished. You come to see that
Natkin began by enticing you with an illusion—the illusion of a
light-filled, elastic membrane of paint like the tinted under-
belly of a gecko glimpsed against a sun-drenched window—
and to accept that what you are in fact confronted with is
nothing more or less than the successive layers of the thinnest of
honey-comb marks laid down gently in whispers of paint upon
the canvas surface. In this work the pigment is as tightly packed,
as literally fleshly, as in any of this series.

But no sooner have you recognised the facticity of the
materials than you become aware of yet another way of reading
the painting. For now it is as if the curtain has risen and yet the
painting continues to suck your eyes into itself, to engulf and
entertain them. The uniform skin of light evaporates in part
because its tenuous existence came about only through the

mixing of colours and the organisation of forms into a shimmering, illusory film on the retina. But as this film distintegrates it gives way to billowing and boundless hazes of colour, to seemingly limitless vistas of illusionary space. The 'foreplay' is over and the eye now seduced is compelled to penetrate deeper and deeper *inside* the painting. You may even experience anxiety as you realise that there is no fixed viewpoint which you can continue to adopt outside the work which will allow you to perpetuate a detached observation of its skin. The iconographic marks, dots, circles and cross-hatchings become more distinct as they seem to detach themselves from the surrounding paint. They too now seem to be floating in space rather than sewn in a fixed position into a surface; because they are drifting as if without gravity you cannot orientate yourself in relation to them. Only by denying the illusion, by moving reassuringly back one step, by seizing again on the fact of the paint on a canvas surface, can you find an anchored raft.

There is only one way to describe this illusionary space and that is to say it is *contained within the painting*. Far from being posited upon an external viewpoint, or even a succession of such external viewpoints, it comes into being between the successive, gauze-like veils of colour as light which Natkin has laid down. There is nothing reticent about this pictorial depth: Natkin pursues a deep, plummeting illusion. This is another reason why, for all the intense pleasure you can derive from looking at this painting, the experience of it can be tinged with an allusive unease, or even fear. It is not easy to verbalise this experience precisely; another metaphor may help. It is almost as if at this level of your interaction with the work the skin had reformed but this time *around you* so that you, originally an exterior observer, feel yourself to be literally and precariously suspended within a wholly illusory space which, like the unconscious itself, contains its own time. Thus when you engage with it receptively this Natkin painting offers the illusion that it is almost a 'subjective object' or a picture of which you are more than a viewer, and almost a literal *subject*.

I have written as if each perceptual stage was experienced separately, successively, logically and verbally whereas in fact the business of seeing is likely to be either more simultaneous or more attenuated than this depending upon the individual observer. There is no 'correct' reading of this painting: everyone who sees it will bring a different history and different expectations to it. Each will take away a distinct experience. Nonetheless. I believe most viewers will probably feel that my analogy with a spectator who begins by watching a performance but who ends up as an actor within it is a fair one. You start by seeing a seductive surface in which 'figure' and 'ground' seem woven inseparably together: but this gives way to an encounter with an infinitely recessive, interior space. This metaphor may suggest cosmic fantasies or Science Fiction excursions; the painting itself, however, has none of that flavour and appears to touch upon more intimate and disturbingly *familiar* areas of experience. But even this is to simplify: my description of filmy skins and vaporous infinities implies that the painting is amorphous, mystifying, vague or accidental. In fact it has a tremulously specific muscular strength. Like many of Natkin's works, it is powerful enough to go on yielding more and more, the more attention that you give to it. Sooner or later, behind the skin, you will also come across the painting's organised, architectural or skeletal *structure*. This recessive space has not been sprayed vicariously like Olitski's mists: it has been constructed consciously and thoughtfully from areas of colour superimposed and set against one another almost like bricks of coloured light.

I want to say something about how I became involved with Natkin's work: in the spring of 1974, I walked into the Holburne of Menstrie Museum in Bath and encountered his paintings for the first time. Characteristically, Natkin's exhibition spilled beyond the walls of the Museum to fill up the City's Festival Gallery as well. I had not heard of Natkin, let alone seen one of his paintings before that moment. I was, however, moved by what I saw. What do I mean by moved? I looked at these canvases which were stretched around me like an ocean of light and I felt that feeling which I spoke about last time, and I felt it to a marked degree: the feeling that these were *good*.

It was not just that the paintings were pretty and 'pleasing to the eye', which as a matter of fact they were. I was also aware that the visual experience which they offered evoked in me significant (and not readily identifiable) emotions. During the process of looking their decorativeness seemed to 'transcend' itself, so that I found my involvement becoming, despite myself, of a much more intense kind than I had at first imagined it to be. For many people who enjoy paintings that experience in and of itself would have been sufficient: the 'goodness' and emotional depth would have been there, for them. They could then choose to indulge the object of their 'taste', or to evade it because it contradicted social, aesthetic, or psychological taboos which they were not prepared to suspend. (I am aware that for certain sectors on the left this is already a controversial formulation because it implies, as indeed I intend to imply, that a viewer's experience of a work is not reducible to his prior ideology but may, indeed, be at odds with that ideology.)

What more was there to be said about this feeling of 'goodness' beyond the assertion of it? It was very difficult to say anything worthwhile about it by reference to existing aesthetic ideologies—least of all those to which I was, myself, most sympathetic. Marcuse once wrote:

> 'Even in its most distinguished representatives, Marxist aesthetics has shared in the devaluation of subjectivity. Hence the preference for realism as the model of progressive art; the denigration of romanticism as simply reactionary; the denunciation of "decadent" art—in general, the embarrassment when confronted with the task of evaluating the aesthetic qualities of a work in terms other than class ideologies.'

'Social criticism' could easily, or relatively easily, account for the specific conventions which Natkin was using, but what could it say about the way in which, for me, he appeared to 'transcend' those conventions? Here that 'embarrassment' to which Marcuse refers becomes acute.

Stylistically, Natkin had much in common with the American 'colour-field' painting tradition. This originated as a minority tendency within the early American Abstract Expressionist movement, where it opposed itself to the discursive brush-strokes of 'gesture' painting. The colour-field artists tended to be reductive in their approach to painting's conventions: i.e., they jettisoned as much as they dared. They concentrated upon single, centralised images expressed in terms of large expanses or 'fields' of colour. The best known—though in many respects the least typical—practitioner in this tradition was undoubtedly Mark Rothko. But, during the 1960s, colour field painting became the most *kenotic* or drained-out element in the repertoire of Modernist painting. The pleasures which it had to offer became predominantly decorative. In 1978, Hilton

Kramer wrote of Natkin that his painting 'remains firmly locked into the safe conventions of the Color-field esthetic, filling the eye with something very nice but not very robust to look at.'[2] I do not agree with this statement, but I can see what Kramer means by it perfectly well. If Natkin is working within an aesthetic, then it is manifestly that of American colour-field painting. In general, this is painting about painting, and the least interesting of all the genres. Of course, Natkin did not abide by all the schematic and reductionist criteria which have come to constitute an orthodoxy for colour-field painters. Far from paring down the conventions of the medium towards the ineluctable flatness of the support, Natkin's work often seems to revel in conservation of painting's traditional conventions such as illusion, allusion, and recessive pictorial depth. Although these technical 'transgressions' manifestly give Natkin's work an affective accessibility lacking in the more clinical products of this tradition, it must nonetheless be admitted that there is no immediate link between them and 'quality'.

But if neither the formalists nor the Social critics could help, there was still something to hold on to and that something was the response which Natkin had evoked in me: my experience of the work as 'good'. In holding on to it, however, I found that I was concentrating upon that about which Marxist criticism (with the exception of Marcuse) had nothing to say. Natkin asked me to write a catalogue introduction for an exhibition which he had in the winter of 1974. In it, looking for a materialist explanation of the effect the paintings had upon me, I found myself writing:

   '. . . the dynamic of our interaction with (Natkin's) canvases took the form of a seduction into an experience where the distinction between the "outside" and the "inside" of the picture became ambiguous. The realisation of this simultaneously involved us in a sense of fear, or horror, and tragedy. It may be possible to interpret these events by saying that Natkin evokes a stage in our development when it was difficult to differentiate between "self" and "not self"; when the skin of our bodies did not provide an absolute, concrete limitation to our sense of our physical being; a stage in which we also lacked the sense of time. The reconstruction of that phase in the present turns out to be fascinating, alluring, and satisfying—though simultaneously frightening and tragic. By now, it should be self-evident that the stage to which I am referring is that before separation from the mother and her breast. Natkin's painting may in part, be seen as an act of reparation for that universally experienced tragedy, an interpretation which is supported by its paradoxically "epic" and "intimate" aspirations. Thus it may be true to say that Natkin's painting recaptures aspects of infantile experience about the nature of time, space, and ourselves which, in adult life, we have been compelled to renounce, defensively, and sometimes to the impoverishment of our perceptions. I am aware that this view may be considered a "wild" or "fantastic" one, and so I put it forward cautiously and somewhat reluctantly. But I do so in preference to stating that in the final analysis we are left with a "sense of mystery" in front of a Natkin canvas. The "sense of mystery" is certainly there, but it, too, must have a material base . . .'[3]

Later—on the strength of what I had already written about Natkin—I was approached to write a monograph on him. At first, I was reluctant to do this. I knew of, and in certain respects was sympathetic to arguments about the role of the monograph in establishing and maintaining the ideology of contemporary art. I was (and still am) repelled by the American art world. But my work on Natkin compelled me to focus on my dissatisfaction with much 'orthodox' left aesthetics—especially of the post-structuralist variety. I had to come to terms with what at first had seemed an 'autonomous' aesthetic experience. Retrospectively, it now seems to me that through this work I drew close to one of the reasons why aesthetic experience within the terrain of the visual just cannot be reduced to ideology *tout court*.

Indeed, it was my work on Natkin that led me to realise how opposed I was to those disciples of Althusser in art history who write such things as:

'. . . there is no such thing as "an artist's style"; pictures produced by one person are not to be centred on him. The fact that they have been produced by the same artist does not link them together, or at least not in any way that is important for the purposes of art history.'[4]

One's approach, this writer feels, ought to be rigorously 'scientific.'

'I deny the existence of an aesthetic effect which can be dissociated from the visual ideology of a work. And I refuse to use even the idea of aesthetic value in art history . . . the pleasure felt by the spectator on viewing a picture, and the correspondence of his aesthetic ideology to the picture's visual ideology are one and the same thing.'[5]

So he concludes that:

'. . . aesthetic effect is none other than the pleasure felt by the observer when he recognises himself in a picture's visual ideology.'[6]

One sometimes wonders why such Althusserians think an encounter with a painting or sculpture is worthwhile at all: their intention seems to be a displacement of the work with a verbal account of it. I think that the only point of writing about art is in order to bring myself, and others, back to the object in ways which enable us to see something we would not have seen before.

Nothing can ever replace truthful and scrupulous attention to the empirical evidence of our eyes and to the affects to which such evidence gives rise in us. The 'visual ideology' (i.e. style) of Natkin's paintings is clear. Kramer identified it accurately. These are American colour-field works. My analysis of this 'visual ideology' is on the record. In my articles on American art, I have identified colour-field painting with a specific conjuncture in American history, and situated it at the inter-section of the escalation of the U.S.A.'s world imperial strength, the need for an evolving 'High Culture', and the destructive and banalising effects of the Mega-Visual tradition of monopoly capitalism.[7] The emblematic function of colour-field painting and the specific class, corporate and national interests which it serves are known to me.

But analyses of this type cannot tell us the whole story. Otherwise it would be quite impossible to differentiate between Rothko, and a run of the mill colour-field painter, or to distinguish between, say, a good Natkin and a bad one. Often the objective difference between a Natkin which works and one which does not can be something as subtle as a nuance of hue or a variation in some particular, perceived effect. Such dis-criminations are not trivial. They are associated with decisive differences in discernible aesthetic effect. But can my per-ception of such differentiations really be solely imputed to my 'aesthetic ideology'?

I am prepared to concede that this *could* be the case. Some formalist painters do not like Natkin because he infringes certain ideological rules about the 'look' of a picture in which they believe. They either just do not feel, or they deny, what I feel in front of a Natkin, at least in part because they are blinkered by their 'aesthetic ideology'. For example, Natkin refuses the conventions of 'reductionism', rejection of 'painterliness', and use of only a 'flat' pictorial space which were, for a time, almost obligatory among practitioners of this genre. I am not arguing that this 'aesthetic' element is necessarily transparent or self-revelatory to all those who approach the painting in good faith, nor am I saying that it will inevitably manifest itself for every individual viewer through whatever ideological structures he or she brings to the work. I am even prepared to concede that there is no guarantee—and certainly no 'scientific' proof—that what one is describing is not largely, or even primarily ideologically determined. Nonetheless, none of these qualifications amount to good reasons for trying to suppress my experience of the work. That is my evidence, the core of my critical project. Certainly, I am well aware that such experience is never 'innocent': that is why I insist upon the need for historical reconstruction. But it is also the reason why I am particularly inclined to attend to experience when it is both powerful and positive, and yet simultaneously embarrassing or challenging because the work's manifest 'visual ideology' contradicts the 'aesthetic ideology' which I hold. Vermeer is as relevant here as Natkin. Sartre pointed out that although Verlaine was a petty bourgeois, not every petty bourgeois was Verlaine. Vermeer, too, was a petty bourgeois. Not only that, but there is not so much as a hint or a trace in any of his paintings that he questioned the ideology of that class sector within which he worked. Nonetheless, it is equally true that not every petty bourgeois and not every petty bourgeois painter either, was Vermeer. Despite his uncritical 'visual ideology' he remains for me one of the most powerful painters of the Western tradition. (Fairbairn had some inkling of why when he observed that 'the principle of restitution' is exemplified in the 'tranquility' of Vermeer's interiors, and the 'meticulousness' of his painting.)

Fortunately, however, not all my arguments in respect of Natkin and the experience he can afford need to be quite so personal. I have seen several individuals *change their minds* about Natkin: by this I mean that at first they 'saw nothing' in his painting, but then the work worked upon them. They came to enjoy it and to be greatly moved by it—a phenomenon which the Althusserian account just cannot explain. Further there is no identifiable class sector to which Natkin's work exclusively appeals. He has been commissioned to produce a mural for the AT&T Corporation's headquarters in New York; and also to produce paintings for the covers of New Left Books paperback editions. His work hangs in the Hirschhorn Museum in Washington alongside Olitski, Bush, Frankenthaler, Louis, etc. as an exemplar of that particular historical 'moment' in the development of American painting. It is also bought by some collectors who otherwise acquire only 'consensus' work, i.e. family portraits, seascapes, animal pictures, 'calendar' land-scapes, etc. Under such circumstances, attempts to explain Natkin's work in terms of a correspondence between the 'visual ideology' of the artist and the 'aesthetic ideology' of the receptive viewer tell us less than nothing.

Of course, not everyone who enjoys a Natkin painting necessarily sees it in the same way. My response is not identical with that of the director of the Hirschhorn. The editorial board of New Left Books does not look at Natkin exactly as the President of AT&T does. But I would argue that these ideologically determined differentiations are *secondary*, i.e. the divergent responses circulate around a core of 'relative con-stancy' common to all those who enjoy Natkin.

In the Venus de Milo, it was much easier to identify that core in terms of the immediate, expressive effectivity of the presence of a powerful representation of a human body. For an idealist critic it would be enough here to fall back on the assertion of an autonomous, irreducible 'aesthetic effect', to explain or describe the mystery. While recognising this experience, we, however, must seek to penetrate it and to reveal its material base. For the moment, let me tentatively formulate the problem this way: while the specific 'structure of feeling', i.e. the assertion of an autonomous domain of the aesthetic, may be ideological, the feelings that are so structured are not. They are aroused because the artist has succeeded in giving effective, pictorial expression, through the material process of his medium, to an experience which is in some way recognised—though not necessarily consciously identified—by his receptive viewers. This experience, I am suggesting, pertains to those elements of the 'human condition' which cannot be reduced to socio-economic variables, however much they may be mediated by them. Thus the phenomenon which in bourgeois aesthetics is described as 'transcendence' may often in fact be a penetration downwards into the obscurely recognised terrain of biological potentiality rather than a reaching 'upwards' into the mythical, Crocean realms of ethereal 'spirit'. As a matter of fact, it is not difficult to establish empirically that there is much in common between the affective responses to Natkin by those who enjoy him from positions within very different 'aesthetic ideologies'. Here I hope that we will be able to penetrate the nature of that 'relatively constant core' more deeply, first by considering this specific structuring of feeling, the 'aesthetic effect' of painting in its historical context, and secondly by correlating it with certain developments in psychoanalysis.

It should be said straight away that 'aesthetic experience' is an elusive category. As Harold Osborne comments, 'What aesthetics is about, what is its subject-matter, and what are its terms of reference have themselves become a subject of aesthetic debate.'[8] He cites, although he does not himself accept, the view that attempts to define aesthetic experience are futile 'because there are neither any psychological features common to all forms of aesthetic experience (following a performance of *Othello*, noticing the leafless branches of a tree patterned against a wintry sky, becoming acquainted with Haghia Sophia, luxuriating in a warm bath), nor is there any way of determining the conditions of all aesthetic experience, nor any criteria common to all specifically aesthetic judgements.' At the end of what I had to say about the Venus de Milo, I, too, suggested that the affects that are structured within what we now call the 'aesthetic' are not the same in all historical periods: the demands the Greeks made of a statue differ from those of early 19th century Romantics. Nonetheless, I think that it is possible to begin to make sense of this category if we seek to comprehend it historically.

Aesthetic experience was not designated as such until the middle of the 18th century; prior to that, the category of aesthetics does not exist in European culture. We find an immediate precursor of the concept in Leibnitz—although he never used the word itself. In 1684, Leibnitz noted that painters and other artists, although capable of sound judgements on works of art, did not know how to render an account of their judgements: if pressed, they tended to reply that what they disapproved of lacked a certain *je ne sais quoi*. Leibnitz maintained that such judgement is based upon knowledge that is clear, but not distinct, i.e. not *rational*. It justifies itself with examples, not demonstrations, and therefore has importance as a standard of taste or of the qualities of the senses only.[9]

Baumgarten was the first to use the word 'Aesthetics' in the mid-18th century. His aim was to throw further light on 'the confused knowledge' provided by the arts as distinct from the sciences, and to elaborate 'a norm of sensitive cognition'. For Baumgarten, as for Leibnitz, that which judges sensible or imaginary presentations is the faculty of taste, or *iudicium sensuum*. Baumgarten was essentially concerned with the nature of apprehension through the senses; his text might be seen as an attempt to illuminate the role of feeling in art. He was reacting against Cartesian rationalism. We find a parallel emphasis in Vico who, primarily with poetics in mind, wrote that 'imagination is so much the more robust in proportion as the reasoning faculty is weak.'[10]

Neither Baumgarten's nor Vico's work was well-known in their day: the category of the aesthetic, for example, does not seem to have been designated as such in Britain before the early 19th century. The important point is that, in the 18th century, evaluative norms in the visual arts were widely assumed to be the canons of beauty which had been elaborated in ancient Greece. Indeed, it was the development of the concept of the 'sublime', in contrast to that of the beautiful, which preceded and accompanied the recognition of a category—the aesthetic—which encompassed both these opposed but related concepts. The sublime was notoriously difficult to define: it had to do with feelings of awe, wildness, greatness, boundlessness, engulfment and inspiring strangeness. Burke made a thorough inquiry into the sublime in the middle of the 18th century. He felt that it was characterised by Vacuity, Darkness, Solitude, Silence and Infinity: he described it as 'tranquility tinged with terror'. Indeed, he even designated terror as its 'ruling principle'. It was also associated with a sense of fusion with the environment: 'the mind is so entirely filled with its object, that it cannot entertain any other, nor by consequence reason on that object which employs it.' Burke saw 'uniformity' as one of its causes: only 'uninterrupted progression' could 'stamp on bounded objects the character of infinity'. Of painting, Burke wrote, 'a judicious obscurity in some things contributes to the effect of the picture' since in art, as in nature, 'dark, confused, uncertain images have a greater power on the fancy to form the grander passions than those which are more clear and determinate.' He was ambivalent, however, about the relationship of the sublime to colour and light for although he held that it was usually realised through 'sad and fuscous colour, as black or brown, or deep purple', he also pointed out that 'extreme light obliterates all objects so as in its effects exactly to resemble darkness'. In his view, the sublime was 'the strongest emotion which the mind is capable of feeling'. It was linked to 'greatness of dimensions', as opposed to the beautiful which Burke saw as consisting in relative smallness, smoothness, absence of angularity and brightness of colour.[11]

Aesthetics make their great leap forward at the level of theory in Kant who attempted systematically to justify the judgements of taste. Kant was anxious not to confine the discipline to art, but saw it as encompassing 'the conditions of sensuous perception'.[12] In his view, taste judged whether a work was beautiful or not; it had the pretension that its judgement was universal without being able to provide any rational demonstration of its rightness. Thus Kant refused the notion of objective rules of taste. Every judgement derived through taste was 'aesthetic' in that its determinative cause was the feeling of the subject rather than a concept of the object. Kant rejected the search for a principle, or universal standard of beauty, as a vain fatigue holding that the very idea that this could be established by means of determined concepts was a contradiction. He stressed a distinction between the subjective and the arbitrary in art and artistic judgement and rejected the necessity of any given rules. He distinguished art and science, art and nature, sense and imagination, and accentuated the spontaneous and original character of the genius provocative of art. However, he tended to fuse the concepts of art and beauty. Drawing on Burke, he contrasted the beautiful with the sublime, which he characterises as a contrasting mode of aesthetic experience attaching to objects devoid of form, objects which involve or evoke an impression of *limitlessness*, like vistas, storms at sea, waterfalls, and mountain ranges.

The point I wish to emphasise is this: the notion of aesthetic experience enters into history in the 18th century, with the rise of a secular, bourgeois culture. It was, in effect, a discipline concerned with sensuous perception and its relatedness to certain significant affective states in the viewer. It may thus be seen as a new, secular, and *potentially* materialist structuring of the 'spiritual', given the withering of the religious and its retraction from wide areas of human experience, including that of iconography. (The sense in which I am using the term 'materialist' here is illuminated when one considers the negative of aesthetic, *anaesthetic*, which as Williams points out was widely used from the mid 19th century to mean 'deprived of sensation or the agent of such deprivation.') For Kant, one should remember, the Christ was little more than a moral exemplar: those sentiments which had been locked within religious structures had to be accommodated within new forms.

From the moment of its formulation, however, the category of the aesthetic was dogged by the enigma of its two contrasting modes—the beautiful and the sublime. The relationship of these to each other and of both to art was by no means clear, or clarifiable. The two modes were distinguishable, but rigorous attempts at definition proved unrealisable. Overlappings were numerous. In particular, the notion that beauty belonged to the province of art (with its relatively small, formed aesthetic objects) and sublimity to nature (with its awe-inspiring dimensions, and seemingly boundless or limitless environments) became increasingly untenable as the 19th century progressed. (It is worth relating the rough-handling Kant gives to the sublime in art, rather than nature, to his own aesthetic preferences. As Körner points out, 'Kant had little feeling for music and his taste in painting would probably have precluded him from calling, say, Matisse a painter at all.')[13]

It would be wrong to think that, even in the 19th century with the rise of bourgeois Fine Art traditions, the aesthetic, in anything approaching the sense in which I have described it, ever achieved a central position within the prevailing ideology of art. (The picture admittedly becomes confused because of the rise during the 19th century of a subsidary meaning of the term: increasingly it comes to be used as synonymous with 'the theory of Fine Arts, the Science of the Beautiful.') For example, in British painting, the artist of the sublime, *par excellence*, the epitome of the painter who sought to create an engulfing limitlessness not just in his subject matters (sea, steam, storms, mountain ranges, etc.) but also through the very ways in which he depicted them, his forms themselves, was Turner. But Turner must be characterised as having stood in opposition to the prevailing 'visual ideology' of his time and to the values and representational conventions of Salons, Academicians, and of the Fine Art tradition itself.

Certainly, one mode of the aesthetic—the pursuit of the beautiful—was more closely emmeshed in the prevailing visual ideology than the other: indeed, one might say that the beautiful often lost its sensuous and affective character and, as in British late 19th century classicism, became effectively ideology, *tout court*. Nonetheless it remains true that the 19th century pursuit of aesthetic experience within painting was often more like a rupture with ideology than a capitulation to it. It seems to me no accident that, in British art, in the 1880s and 1890s, the assertion of the aesthetic dimension was an open protest against the constraining limitations which ideology imposed upon art: the aesthetic movement of the Nineties involved, in however deformed and nugatory a way, a conception of socialism, a belief that the world could be other than the way it was.

Indeed, I would go so far as to argue that the European Romantic and later early Modernist movements of the 19th century involved the awakening of potentialities of sensuous and affective experience, through the appropriation of the 'aesthetic' (especially in its sublime mode) in defiance of the anaesthetizations of the prevailing ideologies of art. One way in which this was formally realised was through an emphasis on *colour* rather than *outline*. Colour proved an excellent way of evoking those sentiments of boundlessness, limitlessness and engulfment which characterised the 'sublime'—or rather that area of experience which the sublime is an attempt to conceptualise. I want to digress for a moment on this aspect of colour.

In an interesting but now forgotten book, Willard Wright argued:

> '. . . Paradoxical as it may seem, all painting up to the time of Turner and Delacroix was an art of black-and-white. Colour played no organic part in the classic pictorial conception. All forms and rhythms were conceived and expressed in *drawing*; and all volumes and tones—namely: the means for obtaining solidity and structure—were produced by the scale of greys.'[14]

However Wright goes on to say that with the modern movement, which he sees as emerging with Romantics like Constable, Turner and Delacroix, all the emphasis is placed upon colour. 'All the activities in "modern painting",' he writes, 'have had one object for their goal—the solution of the problems of colour.' Wright even argues—and here I could not follow him—that modern art thus defined is an entirely new medium which, though legitimate on its own terms, should not be considered as *painting* at all. Thus Wright sees Turner as having sought to heighten the intensity of colour; the Impressionists as having solved the problem of light and vibration; and the Pointillists as having 'carried the science of colour-juxtaposition and the interactivity of complementaries to a coldly intellectual extreme'. Gauguin worked 'exclusively in the decorative values of pure colour'. Matisse devoted himself to 'harmonic relationships of colour'. Wright even saw the Cubists in this way. He described them as seeking to 'eliminate objectivity—the essence of painting—and to achieve form by intersecting tonal planes.'[15]

As for Cezanne, he can speak for himself. He is reported to have said about looking at a picture:

'Shut your eyes, wait, think of nothing. Now open them . . . One sees nothing but a great coloured undulation. What then? An irradiation and glory of colour. That is what a picture should give us, a warm harmony, an abyss in which the eye is lost, a secret germination, a coloured state of grace. All these tones circulate in the blood, don't they? One is revivified, born into the real world, one finds oneself, one becomes the painting. To love a painting, one must first have drunk deeply of it in long draughts. Lose consciousness. Descend with the painter into the dim tangled roots of things, and rise again from them in colours, be steeped in the light of them.'[16]

Do you remember Milner struggling for a way of painting in which she was more 'mixed up' in objects than conventional drawing and perspective allowed? In her search, through painting, for 'a world of change, of continual development and process, one in which there was no sharp line between one state and the next as there is no fixed boundary between twilight and darkness,' she found that she moved from being unable to think about colour to an ever-increasing emphasis upon it. She was aware 'that there was some unknown fear to be encountered in this matter of colour and the plunge into full imaginative experience of it.' But she also recognised the pursuit of colour as having a relationship to 'a warmth and a glow and a delight flooding up from within, dictated by no external copy but existing and developing and changing in its own right.' It had to do with the wish not 'to live amongst the accepted realities of the common sense world,' and the concommitant 'fear of losing one's hold on the solid earth' which that wish evoked.[17] Wright, who was writing in 1923, ventured the prediction that what he designated as 'this new art of colour' (as opposed to painting) 'will in time develop into a source of one of the most intense and pleasurable aesthetic reactions which the world of art has yet known.'[18]

We will return to the aesthetics of colour. But let us continue our consideration of the aesthetic itself. After reviewing usages of the word, Raymond Williams commented that it was 'a key formation in a group of meanings which at once emphasized and isolated subjective sense-activity as the basis of art and beauty as distinct, for example, from *social* or *cultural* interpretations.' Williams thus sees the aesthetic as 'an element in the divided modern consciousness of *art* and *society*'. He describes it as:

> '. . . a reference beyond social use and social valuation which, like one special meaning of *culture*, is intended to express a human dimension which the dominant version of *society* appears to exclude.'[19]

Although Williams considers the aesthetic emphasis 'understandable', he argues, correctly in my view, that there is something irresistibly displaced and marginal about the now common and limiting phrase, 'aesthetic considerations', as contrasted with practical or utilitarian considerations. Nonetheless, his central point remains: the aesthetic is a category which struggles to affirm human potentialities which the dominant version of society (with all its ideological excreta) seems to suppress.

The problem, as I see it, is to identify more precisely what human dimension (or dimensions) is (or are) expressed through the aesthetic category. From Kant onwards, aestheticians have claimed an undemonstratable universality for the judgements of taste—'good taste', at least. The historical specificity of the concept of aesthetics seems, at first sight, to contradict this, to give weight to the notion that aesthetics belong to the province of ideology, *tout court*. I, however, an suggesting that like, say, 'childhood', the aesthetic is a historically specific structuring of certain elements of human experience and potentiality which pertain to that underlying condition of our biological being, and which can be occluded or displaced, but never entirely extinguished, by ideology.

In the 19th century, there were numerous attempts to establish the physiological component in aesthetic experience: in our first seminar, I referred to the work of the Helmholtz School into such things as the representation of movement, optics, the sensation of tone, and the perception of colour. Grant Allen published his *Physiological Aesthetics* in Britain in 1877, in which he defined aesthetic pleasure as 'the subjective concomitant of the normal sum of activity not connected directly with vital functions in the terminal peripheric organs of the cerebrospinal nervous system.'[20] It was once fashionable to hold up work of this kind to ridicule:[21] some of it is archaic, reductionist and mechanist. Nonetheless, I do not think we will ever have an adequate materialist account of aesthetics until we have engaged thoroughly with this type of research. Williams has referred to 'a very deep material bond between language and the body which communication theories that concentrate on the passing of messages and information typically miss.' He points to the importance of what he calls 'life rhythms' in reading and writing, and comments: 'From a materialist point of view, this is at least the direction we should look for the foundation of categories that we could if we wish call aesthetic.' He goes on to say that he reserves the possibility that there may be 'permanent configurations that would account for the responses to which, for example, the concept of beauty point.'[22] What *may* be true in the terrain of language is much more certain to be so in that of the visual (where the relation of the sign to the signified is *never* arbitrary). It is with the visual that the concept of 'aesthetics' has always been seen as having a peculiarly close association.

Nonetheless, physiology on its own will not reveal everything, and some of what it cannot reveal may be explicable in terms of psychoanalysis. Let me refer again to Bell's book, *Art*. Bell believed that 'the starting-point for all systems of aesthetics must be personal experience of a peculiar emotion.'[23] 'The objects which provoke this emotion,' he wrote, 'we call works of art . . . This emotion is called the aesthetic emotion.' Bell thought that, in the visual arts, he could trace the common quality possessed by all works which aroused aesthetic emotion to 'lines and colours combined in a particular way, certain forms and relations of forms.'[24] This was the quality he called 'Significant Form'. When Bell looked back over the painting of the 19th, 18th, 17th, 16th, and 15th centuries he was struck by the *absence* of Significant Form, rather than its presence. I intimated that the 'thrilling raptures' which Bell claimed to have experienced on those 'cold white peaks of art' seemed redolent with emotions deriving from the infant-mother relationship, and I have quoted the Marxist art historian, Arnold Hauser, as saying: 'It is since romanticism that art has become a quest for a home that the artist believes he possessed in childhood and which assumes in his eyes the character of a Paradise lost through his own fault.'[25] What Bell called 'Significant Form' may have been those 'certain forms and relations of forms' which expressed or evoked aspects of that lost Paradise and seemed to posit them as potentialities for the future. How then can we begin to explain the *varieties* of aesthetic experience—for example, the polarity of the beautiful and the sublime? Why should the emotions pertaining to infancy matter to the adult?

Unfortunately, Bell does not have much to say about 'aesthetic emotion' beyond asserting it. Berenson, however, whose aesthetic preferences in art differed greatly from Bell's (Berenson was a Renaissance specialist, opposed to modernism) has described his aesthetic experiences in detail. By contrasting the two, we can learn much about the category as a whole.

Berenson wrote his interesting autobiography, *Sketch for a Self-Portrait*, shortly before his death. The book begins with the words, 'Often I feel like a cow with sagging udders lowing for a calf or milkmaid to relieve her',[26] a metaphor which, while it suggests a peculiarly acute identification with the mother— even to the point of fusion with her—is nonetheless so explicit in its associations that it makes us wonder whether Gombrich was not indeed right when he proposed instinctual orality as a genetic model for aesthetic taste. But all that follows weighs against any such restricted reading. Berenson goes on to speculate about immortality, which he regards as inconceivable, 'unless . . . as mystics tell us, we are to live after this mortal life in God, without memory, without individuality and without an identity of our own.'[27] This thought releases a stream of associations. Berenson recalls that, for the most part, his 'moments of greatest happiness' were those when 'I lost myself all but completely in some instant of perfect harmony. In consciousness this was due not to me but to the not-me, of which I was scarcely more than the subject in the grammatical sense.'[28] Berenson says that this 'ecstasy' overtook him when he was happy, out of doors. He recalls a moment when he was five or six:

> '. . . It was morning in early summer. A silver haze shimmered and trembled over the lime trees. The air was laden with their fragrance. The temperature was like a caress. I remember—I need not recall—that I climbed up a tree stump and felt suddenly immersed in Itness. I did not call it by that name. I had no needs for words. It and I were one.'[29]

Berenson goes on to quote a parallel experience of Thomas Traherne, a poet whom Milner, incidentally, often found useful when explaining her attempt to confront her inability to paint. Traherne once described a moment when he had the feeling that 'the skies were mine and so were the sun and the moon and stars, and all the world was mine and I the only spectator and enjoyer of it!' Berenson identifies his own experience with Traherne's and describes it as 'a revelation, a vision, a psychological equipose'. He says that it provided him with a 'touchstone' which remained 'for seven decades the goal of my yearning, my longing, my desire'. He frequently reproaches himself for not having been true to this feeling, for having betrayed it for intellectual, social, or careerist reasons. He says, however, that at such times 'the feeling of that moment at the dawn of conscious life would present itself and like a guardian angel remind me that IT was my goal and that IT was my only real happiness.'[30] He then describes the derivatives of that experience, including the faculty of melting into a good story 'into its characters, its events, its tempo, to such a degree that', as he puts it, 'my diaphragm loses its flexibility'. He continues by relating this 'IT' to his adolescent sexual desires, saying that when, after puberty, love as yet unmixed with lust began to 'glow' within him, his yearnings and longings were 'for a mystic being in youthful female shape with whom I could aspire to unite myself.'[31] He explains, 'since then every time I was really in love to the degree of obsession, what I wanted was only to become one with the woman of my love—nay to be absorbed by her, to end in her.' He adds immediately:

> 'Through my whole mature life and increasingly with the piling up of the years, I have never enjoyed to the utmost a work of art of any kind, whether verbal, musical or visual, never enjoyed a landscape, without sinking my identity into that work of art without becoming it, although, as in certain pictures and drawings of the 16th and 17th centuries we see tucked into a

corner a tiny figure of the artist at work, so a miniscular observer is always there, watching, noting, appreciating, estimating, judging, always there in moments of utmost sensual and spiritual ecstasy and feeling with the rest, but still there.'[32]

He concludes this remarkable passage by saying that he is, at the time of writing, 'in the decline of my eighth decade' and that he lives 'so much more in the people, the books, the works of art, the landscape than in my own skin, that of self, except as this wee homunculus of a perceiving subject, little is left over.' He says 'A complete life may be one ending in so full an identification with the not-self that there is no self left to die.'[33] In another context Berenson described the aesthetic moment as:

> '. . . that flitting instant, so brief as to be almost timeless, when the spectator is at one with the work of art. He ceases to be his ordinary self, and the picture or building, or statue, landscape or aesthetic actuality, is no longer outside himself. The two become one entity.'[34]

Berenson's account of aesthetic experience interestingly does not correspond at all precisely with his better known theory of art, his view that the *essential* in the art of painting is its capacity to stimulate 'our consciousness of tactile values'. He held that sight alone gave no accurate sense of the third dimension. Drawing on what is now outmoded psychology, he argued that in infancy, 'the sense of touch, helped on by muscular sensations of movement, teaches us to appreciate depth, the third dimension, both in objects and in space.' He says that in the same unconscious years, 'we learn to make of touch, of the third dimension, the test of reality'.

> 'The child is still dimly aware of the intimate connection between touch and the third dimension. He cannot persuade himself of the unreality of Looking-Glass Land until he has touched the back of the mirror. Later, we entirely forget the connection, although it remains true that every time our eyes recognise reality, we are, as a matter of fact, giving tactile values to retinal impressions.'[35]

He goes on to say that painting is an art which aims at giving 'an abiding impression of artistic reality with only two dimensions'. And so, according to Berenson, the painter must do consciously what he believes we all do unconsciously, 'construct his third dimension'.

> 'And he can accomplish his task only as we accomplish ours, by

giving tactile values to retinal impressions. His first business, therefore, is to rouse the tactile sense, for I must have the illusion of being able to touch a figure, I must have the illusion of varying muscular sensations inside my palm and fingers corresponding to the various projections of this figure, before I shall take it for granted as real, and let it affect me lastingly.'[36]

I have not cited Berenson in order to endorse his theory of art: there are plenty of convincing critiques available to those who wish to search them out. However, I do wish to point to the two types of experience which are involved in the 'aesthetic' for him, and which, though related and indeed intermingled, remain distinguishable. One of these types of experience dominates his account of what makes a painting good rather than the other.

Thus many of Berenson's 'aesthetic' experiences, deriving from that moment of union in landscape, are characterised by ecstatic fusion with the environment, loss of limits and boundaries, indeed a seeming dissolution of the ego and the self. But as soon as he comes to talk about his experience with paintings, the metaphor seems to demand of him that he re-inserts 'a miniscular observer' who is differentiated from the environment rather than wholly fused into it. Indeed, in his description of 'tactile values' this emphasis upon the subject as differentiated from 'IT' becomes more and more pronounced. Berenson seems to be correlating the capacity of a painting to give aesthetic pleasure with its ability to evoke the infant's first experiences of the separation of himself from that which surrounds him, with the moment when the self becomes aware of itself as a subject and starts to recognise objects as real, external, and other. It is not a full separation that makes the painting good, but rather its reference to that moment of separating out, of discovery of otherness. Thus, for the moment, we can say that Berenson found his 'sublime' in landscape; in painting, he did not want this. The historical moment he preferred was that of the early Renaissance, of the discovery of perspective, when painters were realising the means of separating themselves out from that which they depicted, and of 'objectifying' their world. Berenson did not like modern painting, though there is some evidence that he admired Matisse.

As for Bell, when he spoke of aesthetic emotion, one suspects that it was something much more like that feeling of mergence and ecstatic union which Berenson encountered in *landscape* rather than in art. Bell actively disliked perspective, the attempt of the painter to make objects look real and other. The point is not, of course, to decide who was 'right'; there are areas and elements of overlap, and mergence in their positions, e.g. on Matisse. What I am saying, however is that aesthetic emotion is involved with this nexus of the submergence of self into the environment, and the differentiation of self out from it. Here the senses of touch and sight, indeed sensuous activity in its entirety, play a part which seems to be prior to (or at least apart from) conceptual activity. The 'sublime' (romantic, colour) emphasises one aspect of this nexus—that of mergence, and union; 'beauty' (classical, outline) and its derivatives stresses the other—that of separation. In reality, there are a miasma of intermediate positions. Bell's aesthetics hypostasised those forms evocative of union in painting; Berenson (who acknowledged union in aesthetic experience) nonetheless insisted upon a much greater component of separating out.

Berenson at least offered a psychological explanation—even if a thin and distorted one—for that type of aesthetic emotion which he demanded of a painting. Bell however insisted on the autonomy and irreducibility of the aesthetic. Before we consider what light psychoanalysis can throw on all this, I would ask you to consider again the battle between the aesthetes and analysts in the early part of this century. I have already intimated that when one reads what many of the analysts were writing about art at that time, one's sympathies are entirely with the aesthetes. In the face of trivialising nonsense about the symbols of manifest content, and of the attempt to explain the aesthetic as a sublimation of libidinal instinctual drives alone, they were perfectly correct to insist upon the autonomy of aesthetic experience. For example, Roger Fry told a gathering of psychoanalysts:

> 'For the moment I must be dogmatic and declare that the esthetic emotion is an emotion about form. In certain people, purely formal relations of certain kinds arouse peculiarly profound emotions, or rather I ought to say the recognition by them of particular kinds of formal relations arouse these emotions.'[37]

Fry was simply insisting that what gives aesthetic pleasure is not the literal, narrative, or 'subject-matter' content of a picture, but its formal structuring in terms, in painting at least, of pictorial space. This was, of course, in sharp distinction to Freud himself who considered the enjoyment of artistic form—which he said he neither appreciated, nor could explain—to be a kind of allurement or, as he calls it, 'forepleasure' to whet the appetite of the viewer for the 'real' meaning, which he derived from the manifest content and its symbolisations.

One should not forget that the painting with which Bell and Fry were predominantly concerned, and to account for which their theories were elaborated, was that of Post-Impressionism, where the indissolubility of form and content is pronounced: an account of Cezanne which ignores the way in which the picture space is constituted and organised is, indeed, worse than useless. But for all their protestations of the autonomy of the aesthetic, the very term 'Significant Form' suggests that these new ways of ordering the picture signified something beyond the terrain of art. In fact, for all his talk about the irreducibility of emotion about form at the beginning of his lecture, this was something which Fry himself was effectively suggesting by the end of it. As he puts it, 'the question occurs what is the source of the affective quality of certain systems of formal design for those who are sensitive to pure form?'[38] He then affirms a familiar idea—that there is a pleasure in the recognition of order and of the inevitability in relations. Then he comments:

'But in art there is, I think, an affective quality which lies outside that. It is not a mere recognition of order and inter-relation; every part, as well as the whole, becomes suffused with an emotional tone. Now, from our definition of this pure beauty, the emotional tone is not due to any recognizable reminiscence or suggestion of the emotional experiences of life; but I sometimes wonder if it nevertheless does not get its force from arousing some very deep, very vague, and immensely generalized reminiscences. It looks as though art had got access to the substratum of all the emotional colours of life, to something which underlies all the particular and specialized emotions of actual life. It seems to derive an emotional energy from the very conditions of our existence by its revelation of an emotional significance in time and space. Or it may be that art really calls up, as it were, the residual traces left on the spirit by the different emotions of life, without however recalling the actual experiences, so that we get an echo of the emotion without the limitation and particular direction which it had in experience.'[39]

As soon as he had finished saying this, Fry dismissed his own words as 'the speculation of an amateur'. Of course, there are not many who today take the concept of a specific aesthetic emotion seriously. Here however, Fry hints at the possibility of the reducibility of that emotion, not in terms of instinctual sublimation, but of its association with 'very deep, very vague, and immensely generalised reminiscences' which underly 'all particular and specialized emotions of actual life'. The very terminology itself is evocative both of the 18th century notion of sublimity, and also of the kind of experience which I described in front of a Natkin. I believe that recent developments within object relations theory allow us to produce a credible account of these kinds of visual, aesthetic experience in something other than their own terms. Psychoanalysis, I am suggesting, now allows us to begin to understand the aesthetic in a materialist fashion and to distinguish it from the correspondence of ideologies to which the structuralist Marxist would reduce it.

I have mentioned how Marion Milner came to react against the conventional character of outline in drawing and to seek a way of representing in which she was much more 'mixed up' in objects than that. This, you will recall, followed an experience in which she watched the play of the surfaces of two jugs. Now what she wrote about this directly stimulated D. W. Winnicott in the elaboration of his major psychoanalytic concept, that of the *potential space*. Winnicott's wife was a potter, so he had many opportunities to observe such phenomena. I want now to say something more about Winnicott's view of early infancy.

It is impossible in words to be completely convincing or wholly systematic about the nature of very early, subjective experiences. Winnicott refers to 'the delicacy of what is preverbal, unverbalized, and unverbalizable except perhaps in poetry.'[40] Feelings and images precede words of any kind: there is a sense in which certain images like Natkin's 'speak' more vividly about what I am going to say now than my writing possibly can. But Winnicott has drawn closer to a convincing account of the earliest phase of the infant's life than any other writer I know. 'There is,' Winnicott once said, 'no such thing as an infant,'[41] by which he meant that whenever one finds an infant, one finds also maternal care without which there would be no infant. In his view the essence of an infant's experience lay in its dependence on maternal (environmental) care. As

Masud Khan has put it, 'For Winnicott the paradox of infant-mother relationship lay in that the environment (mother) *makes* the *becoming* self of the infant feasible.'[42] The mother creates the infant, not just by bodily giving birth to him, but also by supporting him as he finds and realises himself.

In the earliest weeks of life, in the 'ideal' (if not the 'normal') situation, the baby feels at one with the mother, with whom he was indeed somatically at one prior to birth. In this state of primary identification, the baby is unaware of himself as a separate, autonomous human being: he does not realise where he begins and ends, or *that* he begins and ends. Subjectively, he feels completely merged in with the mother-environment. (These concepts invite comparison with the ideas of om-nipotence, infinity, and ubiquity.) Gradually and progressively, given a facilitating environment, the baby becomes dimly aware of the *otherness* of the mother, of the fact that he himself does not flow seamlessly into the world, or into her, but has a separate identity. This process of discovery seems to be a vital period of human growth. During it, the baby necessarily posits the idea of a 'potential space' which Winnicott defines as:

> '. . . the hypothetical area that exists (but cannot exist) between the baby and the object (mother or part of mother) during the phase of the repudiation of the object as not me, that is at the end of being merged in with the object.'[43]

When the infant has begun to apprehend the difference between self and not-self phenomena, development of the ego proceeds by a process which, in one sense, can be seen as a defensive denial of that separation: the infant identifies with, and takes into himself representations of, the mother, and later also of other objects in the environment (father, siblings, etc.) from which he continues to make, strengthen and structure himself.

The idea of this 'potential space' remains, however, of the greatest importance in development, experience, and above all, creative living:

> 'This potential space is at the interplay between there being nothing but me and there being objects and phenomena outside omnipotent control.'[44]

Winnicott suggests that it can usefully be thought of as a 'third area of human living, one neither inside the individual nor outside in the world of shared reality.' The capacity to explore and investigate this 'potential space' in a situation of trust, allows the individual to develop his internal sense of place and integration, his sense of external reality, *and* his ability to act imaginatively and creatively upon the latter. The 'potential space' negates (even as it allows for the 'realistic' growth of) the idea of separation between the baby and the mother: its exploration is thus closely linked with the capacity to *play*. Play is a non-instinctual activity belonging simultaneously to the *inner* and the *outer* worlds: it exists on the borderline between fantasy and action.

Another aspect of this 'intermediate living' in early life are transitional objects, those things, often blankets, cloths, toys, pieces of string, etc. to which children become deeply attached and through which they explore, and sometimes playfully deny, the separateness of and relationships between self, mother, (or part mother, i.e. breast) and the world. The transitional object 'comes from without from our point of view, but not so from the point of view of the baby. Neither does it come from within; it is not a hallucination.' Winnicott once said that his contribution was to ask for this paradox 'to be accepted and tolerated and respected, and for it not to be resolved. By flight to split-off intellectual functioning it is possible to resolve the paradox, but the price of this is the loss of the value of the paradox itself.'[45]

However 'potential space' was not something which the baby could set up and explore on his own. Winnicott constantly emphasised the *social* character of the infant-mother relationship: 'the history of an individual cannot be written in terms of the baby alone.' Cultural and environmental factors, especially the nature and quality of mothering, also had to be taken into account:

> '. . . it is not instinctual satisfaction that makes a baby begin to be, to feel, that life is real, to find life worth living . . . It is the self that must precede the self's use of instinct; the rider must ride the horse, not be run away with. I could use Buffon's saying: *'Le style est l'homme même.'* When one speaks of a man one speaks of him *along with* the summation of his cultural experience. The whole forms a unit.'[46]

Thus Winnicott argues that the experience of this 'potential space' seems related to the presence of a dependable, responsive, caring mother who evokes from the infant's earliest days a continuous sense of *being* (which precedes the use of instinct) and which later becomes the basis of trust. Only then is the infant free playfully and creatively to find himself through a growing awareness and imaginative denial of separation.

Winnicott placed considerable stress upon 'the capacity to be alone', which he regarded as being dependent upon the 'experience . . . of being alone, as an infant and small child, in the presence of mother'. The basis of the capacity to be alone, then, was also a paradox; Winnicott saw it as 'the experience of being alone while someone else is present':

'It is only when alone (that is to say, in the presence of someone) that the infant can discover his own personal life. The pathological alternative is a false life built on reactions to external stimuli. When alone in the sense that I am using the term, and only when alone, the infant is able to do the equivalent of what in an adult would be called relaxing. The infant is able to become unintegrated, to flounder, to be in a state in which there is no orientation, to be able to exist for a time without being either a reactor to an external impingement or an active person with a direction of interest or movement.'[47]

Much, in Winnicott's view, depended on this 'potential space between the subjective object and the object objectively perceived, between me-extensions and the not-me.' The earliest anxieties, or fears of the infant are associated with dread of an interruption in what Winnicott calls 'going on being'. The main danger the infant senses is that of a 'threat of annihilation' or fragmentation of the incipient ego, which Winnicott describes as 'a very real, primitive anxiety, long antedating any anxiety that includes the word death in its description.'

Winnicott held that this 'potential space' between the baby and the mother was the precursor of that between the child and the family, and eventually of that between the individual and society, or the world. In Winnicott's view, one development derived from the 'potential space' was thus, for the adult, the *location* of cultural experience itself. The 'potential space' could 'be looked upon as sacred 'to the individual in that it is here that the individual experiences creative living.'[48] Here—if he has sufficient trust in his environment—the individual can explore the interplay between himself and the world, and can create imaginative transformations of the world, not as mere fantasy, but as cultural products which can be seen and enjoyed by others.

If play is the paradigm of cultural activity, for Winnicott,

then the transitional object is that of the art work. As Khan
writes:

>'Winnicott was very well aware that his concept of the tran-
>sitional object had many close correspondences to some of the
>concepts in literature and art. For example, the Cubist collages of
>Braque and Picasso have distinctly the quality of the transitional
>object in so far as they assimilate the given to the created, the
>imagined to the concretely found in one space—that of the
>canvas—and there give it a new unity and reality . . . It is for this
>reason that Winnicott later on towards the end of his life was
>much more interested in how culture and all its vocabulary of
>symbols and symbolic activities help the individual to find as well
>as to realise himself. The concept of the transitional object has
>helped psychoanalytic thinking to re-evaluate the role of culture
>as a positive and constructive increment in human experience and
>not as a cause for discontent.'[49]

Winnicott's theory of 'potential space' is of the utmost
importance in understanding aesthetic experience. It explains, I
think, why it sometimes appears that there is an 'aesthetic
emotion' attaching to certain types of experience, and why this
seems relatively unrelated to most other kinds of adult emotions
about the world. For, if Winnicott is right, cultural activities are
those in which the experiences of the potential space are still
operative. I have often referred to two distinct kinds of aesthetic
experience which in the 18th century were identified as 'beauty'
on the one hand and the 'sublime' on the other. Each of these
can be seen as related to a cluster of concepts and categories
which, though taking different forms in different historical
moments, with one or other taking a temporary dominance,
persist. Beauty relates to 'classical', outline, 'order and inter-
relation', discrete form, 'carving modes', etc. Sublime relates to
'romantic', colour, 'the suffusion of the whole with an
emotional tone', engulfment, 'modelling modes', etc. I have
already suggested that the very category of the aesthetic only
came to be recognised as such, in history, as the emphasis came
to be placed on the latter type of experience *in a secular way*:
not only Fry, but also Burke, saw it as being *deeper* than the
pursuit of beauty (or its derivatives), as relatable to remote
kinds of emotion and experience before the differentiations and
specificities of a fully conscious relation to the world applied.
Indeed, I would go so far as to say that what historically was
affectively retrieved from mystifying religious ideologies by

romanticism and its derivatives became theoretically explicable (insofar as affects are ever explicable through theories) not in classical psycho-analysis, but through object relations theory.

Indeed, I would further suggest that there is a correlation between these two modes of the aesthetic and the distinction Winnicott draws between the 'object mother' and the 'environment mother.' Winnicott talks about a 'vast difference' for the infant between two aspects of infant-care, the mother as object, or owner of the part objects (especially the breast) that may satisfy the infant's urgent needs, and the mother as the person who wards off the unpredictable and who actively provides care in containing, handling, and general management. 'It is,' he writes, 'the environment-mother who receives all that can be called affection and sensuous co-existence; it is the object-mother who becomes the target for excited experience, backed by crude instinct-tension.'[50] The 'formal beauty' kind of aesthetic experience may be derived from feelings of separating out, whereas the sublime correlates with those of ecstatic fusion. Thus the two modes of aesthetic experience may correspond with the oscillating emotions of the potential space. Beyond that, the formal-beauty type of experience may relate to the excited responses to the object mother (and her part objects) and thus be more readily explicable in terms of classical psychoanalytic sublimation theory; one recalls that Burke held that formal beauty was characterised by smallness, smoothness and absence of angularity which, though it does not admit of a cut diamond, certainly evokes a breast. Whereas the sublime variety of experience may be derived from the relationship with the environment mother, hence perhaps the peculiar association between the sublime and landscape and not necessarily depicted landscape at that. Certainly, the enveloping and seemingly limitless phenomena of the sublime, and the depth of affect attributed to it (including the residual terror of the threat of complete self-annihilation) seem compatible with such a reading. It is, of course, upon the relationship with the environment mother that not just the sense of well-being, but of going-on being itself depends: hence perhaps the feeling of supreme significance, tinged with fear, which attaches to experiences such as that which Berenson described himself as undergoing on that summer day when he was about six years old. As Milner once put it, 'the problem of the relation between the painter and his world' is 'basically a problem of one's own need and the needs of the "other", a problem of reciprocity between "you" and "me"; with "you" and "me" meaning originally mother and child.' Different emphases within aesthetic experience, and demands that paintings in particular should confine themselves to one or other of its modes, involve, whatever their cultural mediations, emotions deriving from different aspects of this fundamental relationship.

Let us now return to the painting by Robert Natkin: I hope you will be able to see that my 'formal' description was as immediately explicable in Winnicottian terms as, say, Berenson's account of his aesthetic experience. Natkin often talks about the superficial 'seductiveness' of his paintings; the comparison between the immediate optical gratifications which the painting offers and the excited instinctual emotions evoked by the mother's breast is almost too evident to be worthy of comment. But the suffusing warmth of the painting, and its enveloping, recessive illusions of depth also seem to call forth 'very deep, very vague, and immensely generalized reminiscences,' which have to do with 'affection' and a 'sensuous co-existence' which at moments merges into a sense of fusion. Formally, this distinction relates to the contradiction between the skin of paint, as a limiting membrane, defining the extremities of self and of other, and that of a plummeting illusory space which does not allow you, the viewer, to remain on the outside but sucks you into itself. Indeed, the formal mechanics of this painting seem rooted in an immediate fashion in the emotions and paradoxes of 'the potential space'.

When I look back, I am sure that this feeling of goodness, this powerful aesthetic response which I felt when I first encountered Natkin's work in Bath had much to do with his ability to evoke such emotions and areas of experience in me. Let me give one illustration of what I mean by this. My description of the painting refers to the experience of it as 'tinged with an allusive unease, or even fear'. I found in my first attempts to write about Natkin that the description of this fear was always very difficult. Do you remember how Burke, in trying to describe the limitlessness of the sublime, had designated 'terror' as its ruling principle? This judgement earned him the derision of his contemporaries. There were those similarly who just could not see what I meant when I spoke of the anxiety, fear, terror, horror, or 'sense of tragedy' (I tried out all those terms) which a Natkin aroused in me. At one point, I believed that this elusive negative emotion could probably be explained in Oedipal terms: i.e. the intense pleasure in the intimate person of the mother involved in viewing the painting aroused fear of the wrath of the father. I now think that this was largely nonsense, or rather a projection backwards into much earlier fears which the paintings aroused of later and more 'manageable' ones. The unease, or anxiety, I am now convinced, relates to that earliest fear of the infant of an interruption in what Winnicott called, 'going on being,' the threat of annihilation of the ego. The Natkin certainly evokes intimate, sensuous and affectionate responses, but the way in which the painting seems to call into question the autonomy of the viewer as separate from itself, the way it sets him loose and drifting in a boundless, unstructured illusion of space, can touch upon such primitive anxieties.

Perhaps I should also say that when I saw Natkin's work I was in a potentially responsive phase: I encountered his painting for the first time when my own psychoanalysis was moving backwards, away from preoccupations surrounding my relationship with the father towards an analysis of feelings involved in the prior relationship with the mother. Within the terms of the psychoanalytic transference, the analyst was becoming the Mother for me. During the subsequent unravelling of my analysis, I frequently referred to Natkin's paintings.

Natkin is deeply acquainted with the conventions of his time; his style, or 'visual ideology', is indeed that of the colour field. But he tears through that ideology (as surely as Vermeer did through that of 17th century Holland) not by a flight into a supra-historical domain of 'timeless' spiritual essences, but rather by a penetration metaphorically downwards, into the region of psycho-biological being, into that great reservoir of *potentiality* upon which our hopes for a better personal and social future ultimately rest. In a 1967 interview, Natkin said:

> 'The word taste is often in bad repute, but I like to think of taste—of good taste, or of great taste—as an important factor. I use the word taste not in the sophist sense; but think about how we first learn of the outside world. The baby picks things up and puts them into his mouth. It is through the tongue, I believe that taste has to do with the "tongue of the eye", and it is through

the tongue of the eye that I make my judgements. If I didn't use that, then I would have to rely on style.'[51]

I think that 'aesthetic experience' as known through taste, or the tongue of one's eye, has much to do with an affective evocation of 'how we first learn of the outside world.' The seemingly immediate correspondence in aesthetic experience between sense perceptions, and affects, or feelings, is of course significant here. We often forget how close the language of sensory touch is to that of the emotions: feel (feeling), move (moving), touch (touching) refer to a world of physical sensation and emotional response which is, as it were, prior to the terrain of ideology and structure. The question of course arises as to whether the aesthetic is thus 'regressive' in character. I have already stressed the value of the primary processes in the realisation of the full potentialities of the individual. Here, I would refer again to Williams' observation on the aesthetic that it represented an attempt to express a human dimension which the dominant values of society appear to exclude. But these are points to which we will return.

I want to discuss one more example of Natkin's work, but before I do so, I wish to say something about his life. Natkin was born in Chicago in 1930, of a poor, Jewish-Russian immigrant family. From the beginning his childhood was marred by excessively erratic mothering: his memories are of intrusions, impingements, threats, violence, and fears of abandonment, played out against the grotesque panorama of a screaming, suspicious extended family. It was almost impossible for him to find himself. His only cultural experience until adolescence was movies and vaudeville. He began to paint in adolescence.

He went to the Chicago Institute as a painting student where he was influenced by a local school of grotesque painters, 'The Chicago Monster Roster'. Simultaneously, he was profoundly affected by the collection at the Chicago Institute, especially by the magnificent range of Post-Impressionist works which it contained. Indeed, Natkin's 'visual ideology' was as much inflected by that particular moment of French painting as it was by more contemporaneous stylistic influences. I now know (as I did not when I first saw his work) that there is a correspondence between Natkin's struggle to give his paintings form and aesthetic integrity, and his personal struggle to structure his chaotically disorganised psychological space. Indeed, Natkin's formal development can be seen as a vivid narrative of his psychological development. Immediately after leaving art school, he oscillated between portrait painting, and his own variety of abstract expressionism. Finally, he abandoned the portraits complaining about the limitations and fixity which the physiognomy of facial features imposed upon him. His abstract work in the 1950s is characterised by a search for a sense of a limiting membrane, a skin that can contain the fragmented elements out of which the painting was made. He often experimented with collage at this time. His gradual success in achieving order and coherence within his picture space paralleled his transformation of himself through psychoanalysis.

He began to make what I would regard as serious work after his move to New York in the early 1960s. Many of his paintings—he called them '*Apollos*'—were marked by a strong, vertical organisation; these continue to this day. In the 1970s, however, they have been supplemented by *Intimate Lighting* and *Colour Bath* works, using a more diffuse, softer, less strident form of pictorial organisation, and a more inclusive kind of space. I consider that there is a correlation between his resplendent, actively and vertically organised *Apollos* and a split-off male component within him; and, say, the enticing *Intimate Lighting* paintings and a split-off female component. These, he is constantly trying to re-integrate on the surface in new ways, as, for example, in his *Bath-Apollo* series. He frequently uses (and playfully improvises upon) an underlying grid which functions as an equivalent of ego-structure. The grid, or vestiges of the grid, bind in what would otherwise be the self-annihilating limitlessness of infinite internal space. In his best work of the 1970s, Natkin seems to me to have been constructing artificially, through visual forms, that potential space which was largely (though not entirely) denied him by the nature of his environment in infancy. Indeed, it was the space in Post-Impressionist painting, which he saw as an adolescent at the Chicago Institute, which first seemed to hold out to him the glimmering hope of becoming something other than that which he was—a fractured and dissociated individual, in his own self-estimation, monstrous.

Natkin often says that he feels that everything he has ever painted from the time of those early portraits onwards is a face. This even applies to the powerful *Redding View* paintings he made in the early 1970s after moving to the countryside: for the first time, there was some correlation between his work and observed natural phenomena, for example in his light and colours. Natkin now says that these paintings have about them a quality he can only define as expressing 'The Face of the Earth'. It was at about this time that he felt his personal and creative life was going well, better than ever before: he was aware of a feeling of having found his place, and of having made himself a better place to be. In 1975, after he had achieved complete mastery over the skin-depth illusion, Natkin burst into a series of works—his *Face* paintings—which I consider among his best hitherto. The face theme in Natkin can be related to another central idea of Winnicott's.

In Winnicott's view, in the infantile phase of the separating-off of the not-me from the me, a major task of the infant is the 'separating out of the mother as an objectively perceived environmental feature.' The baby at the breast, or in his mother's arms, gazes into the mother's face and, as Winnicott puts it:

> '. . . ordinarily what the baby sees is himself or herself. In other words the mother is looking at the baby and what she looks like is related to what she sees there.'[52]

The mother then, by responding to the baby, acts as a mirror through which the baby finds himself. But when the mother fails to respond, when she reflects 'her own mood . . . or the rigidity of her defences', the baby does not see himself. In this situation:

> '. . . perception takes the place of apperception, perception takes the place of that which might have been the beginning of a significant exchange with the world, a two-way process in which self-enrichment alternates with the discovery of meaning in the world of seen things.'[53]

Such a lack of predictability on the part of the mother leads to withdrawal, a sense of displacement, and a threat of chaos, or annihilation in the infant—a threat which can be exaggerated by congenital sight defects, such as the acute astigmatism (an optical defect which prevents the rays of light from being brought to a common focus) from which Natkin suffered.

I am suggesting that, for Natkin, the canvas surface became a surrogate for that reciprocal encounter which, biographically, he had lacked with the 'good' mother's face. (Photographs I have seen of his mother confirm a locked artificiality of expression.) In his early portraits, he begins by depicting the masked, maternal grimace, often accompanied by acute pictorial disorganisation, bordering on incompetence. Later, he

Robert Natkin, *Apollo*, 1979.

turned to 'expressive' portraits but found that he had to unlock
(and then abandon) the fixed facial features altogether in order
to discover his own identity, face, or style through a reciprocal
exchange with the paint sur-face itself, a surface which, though
it responds to every movement and gesture, allowing one to
constitute one's own reality, retains its autonomy, materiality
and separateness as well.

   At moments when Natkin's paintings did not go well, they
fell into the fixed, rigid grimace of an unresponsive mask: I
have in mind here certain unfortunate symmetrical paintings he
produced, and some over-ordered, atypical, 'hard-edged' or
architectural versions of the *Apollos*. Sometimes, he even
lapsed into the bland, dial-like roundness of tondi in which
psychological necessities triumphed over and debased aesthetic
or formal considerations. But the Face paintings of 1975 stand
at the opposite extreme in his project. They seem to touch
intimately, directly and convincingly upon, and also to *transform*, these earliest pre-verbal experiences. Here, one suspects,
is the mother's face into which Natkin (and not only he) would
have liked to have stared: this is the ideal of that which he was

denied, or which he perceived only in glimpses, a face suffused with subtle tenderness, apperceived more than it is perceived, a face whose features are, in one sense, bound, yet in another fluid and gently mobile, a face which can transform itself infinitely in response to our gaze, which certainly has a skin which separates it from us but which, in the next moment, can engulf and enfold us into itself.

Spitz has described how 'the mouth-hand labyrinth-skin "unified situational experience" is merged with the first visual image, the mother's face.'[54] This 'situational experience' is surely the *subject* of these paintings. Historically, the masked grimace was probably that which Natkin most frequently experienced affectively in infancy; that, at least occasionally, he encountered the 'good' mother's face must certainly be assumed. The severe intensity of astigmatic suffusion manifest in this painting suggests a reconstituted reminiscence rather than a hallucination or fantasy. Through painting, he transforms the face into what it might have been, for him, and through this process discovers *himself*. When I look at Natkin's work, I am suggesting, I experience what Bell would have called 'aesthetic emotion' because it arouses a similar nexus of affects in me.

There are, of course, many abstract paintings which are much emptier than Natkin's. Can psychoanalysis help us to understand them? The early psychoanalysts tended to follow Freud in characterising the primary processes as something to be opposed, to be overcome by the rationality of the ego. This inevitably affected their view of aesthetics, and especially their attitudes to modernism. Franz Alexander, a Hungarian, became an analyst in 1921. He wrote a rather perceptive essay, 'The Psychoanalyst Looks at Contemporary Art', in which he correctly designated 1914 as the moment when 'the fatal explosion took place and the bubble of this aesthetic culture burst.' Although Alexander has an unusually sound grasp of the historical process, he claims that in art this moment gave rise to an 'elemental break-through from the unconscious of the primitive disorganized impulses of the id.' The 'unorthodoxy of space relations in contemporary drawings and paintings', he argued, 'most appropriately expresses not the empirical space which is conveyed to us by our senses, but the type of space which appears in our dreams.'

Alexander could see no positive value in this:

'A white square on a black background exhibited by Malevitch in 1913 was the ultimate logical consequence of this defeatist trend to ignore the surrounding universe, which had become unpalatable. What a contrast between this geometric art . . . and the magnificent attempts of Cezanne or a Van Gogh to introduce into the real world new principles of visual organisation.'[55]

For Alexander, 'from the point of view of history, the last forty years of Western civilization may be considered as a brief episode of acting out.' He welcomed evidences in certain American pictures (he does not say which) of 'the effort to bring the unconscious under rational control'; 'the road,' he declared, 'must eventually lead back to reality and reason.'

Must it? There is, as it happens, much in Alexander's analysis with which I agree: but I would like to question his too simple polarity of 'bad' breakthroughs of 'disorganized impulses of the id' as against 'good' submission of visual art to 'reality and reason'. There are, as I have already emphasised, *valuable* elements in primary process functioning, of peculiar importance for visual creativity. Milner was aware of a correspondence between the trajectory of her personal pursuit (i.e. learning to draw and paint in a new way which involved the questioning of perspective and outline) and a broader, historical transformation:

'As for the validity of the ideas about what I was doing when painting, whether they held for other people in other times and places I did not know. Probably not . . . I had certainly had to eliminate certain ideas absorbed from the intellectual climate of the epoch I had grown up in. And it was not only 19th century ideas about painting as pure representation that had had to be shed, it was also 19th century (and earlier) ideas about the efficacy of thought by itself, as an omnipotent God.'[56]

Within the professional Fine Art tradition (rather than within Milner's personal development) the process of challenging the 19th century, bourgeois ideology of painting as 'pure representation' began with the romantics. In the European continent, it took a massive leap forward in the art of the Post-Impressionists. Despite the work of Turner, however, any such impetus had been crushed out in Britain. Effectively, 'modern art' did not arrive here until the Post-Impressionist exhibitions which Fry organised at the Grafton Gallery in 1910 and 1912. Culturally, we can agree with Alexander, the First World War was the moment of collapse of the 19th century world view. But, in painting, Cubism failed to provide a new system of representation that could supplant the old academic conventions. What happened at this moment was that process of *kenosis* or self-emptying within the Fine Art tradition that I have described elsewhere. I would like now to confront Modernism at its weakest point and to ask whether there is anything that we can retrieve as being of value in this self-reduction towards blankness, which was already suggested in Malevitch, and which has, haunted the history of Modernism since. (I should hasten to add that I have frequently polemicised against this process elsewhere, and I do not wish to be thought of as *prescribing* it now.)

I would like to say first that this notion of blankness was itself an *image* albeit a *negative* image: it recurs in cosmological, theological, mystical and psychological writing from around 1910 onwards. It cannot, therefore, be wholly ascribed to the immanent development of the Fine Art tradition in the way in which I have tended to describe it previously. We can say crudely that this blankness represented a literal wiping clean of the slate of consciousness given the realisation that the structuring of the 19th century world view was wrong.

It is well-known, for example, that the decade 1910–1920 saw an eruption of mysticism. I am no defender of this mode of thinking: nonetheless, I would maintain that this mystical revival was a mystified structuring of primary process functioning, and hence of a whole area of experience, which had been thoroughly repressed by 19th century rationalism. In this writing, we often find an emphasis placed upon the *value* of blankness.

We find it, for example, in Rudolf Otto's book, *The Idea of the Holy*. This was first published in 1917; Otto showed that, like Alexander, he was aware of 'the uneasy stress and universal fermentation of the time, with its groping after the thing never yet heard or seen in poetry or the plastic arts.'[57] Otto was intent upon establishing the reality and autonomy of a category he designated as the 'numinous', and hence upon validating religious experience. Evidently, this is a project with which I have not one iota of sympathy. But Otto's *arguments*, *images*, and descriptions of *affects* interest me greatly, not least because they throw considerable light on the nature of the *kenosis* of Modernism.

Otto describes the numinous as 'perfectly *sui generis*' and as 'irreducible' to any other category.[58] As a materialist, it is perfectly safe for me to assume that, Otto's protestations notwithstanding, the 'numinous' *is* reducible. But the interesting point is that the arguments Otto elaborates to convince us that it is not are identical to those which Bell put forward to defend the autonomy of 'aesthetic emotion' in his book, *Art*. Just as Bell frequently assimilated art to religion, Otto equally frequently assimilates religion to art. Indeed, he insists that there is a 'hidden kinship' between the 'numinous' and the aesthetic category of the sublime, 'which is something more than a merely accidental analogy and to which Kant's *Critique of Judgement* bears distant witness.'[59] (At one point, Otto even says, 'the idea of the sublime is closely similar to that of the numinous, and is well adapted to excite it and to be excited by it, while each tends to pass over into the other.')

Thus Otto maintains that in the arts 'nearly everywhere the most effective means of representing the numinous is "the sublime".'[60] Now of course I would argue that when Otto talks about the 'numinous' he is merely offering another structuring of those same emotions—suppressed by 'rationalism'—deriving from the primary processes which are elsewhere structured in a less mystifying way through the aesthetic category of the sublime. In either instance the materialist course cannot be to denounce those categories so much as to reveal that which informs and underlies them. Interestingly, Otto—do not forget he was writing in 1917—argues that Western art has only two methods of *directly* representing the numinous (beyond its peculiar affinity with the sublime). These he maintains are *darkness* (enhanced by 'some last vestige of brightness') and *silence*. Oriental painting, he maintains, manifests a third way: 'emptiness' and 'empty distances.' He argues that 'remote vacancy is, as it were, the sublime in the horizontal', pointing out that the 'wide-stretching desert, the boundless uniformity of the steppe, have a real sublimity.' He goes on to stress 'the part played by the factor of void or emptiness' in Chinese painting where, he claims, it has almost become a special art to paint empty space, to make it palpable, and to develop variations upon this singular theme:

> 'Not only are there pictures upon which "almost nothing" is painted, not only is it an essential feature of their style to make the strongest impression with the fewest strokes and the scantiest

means, but there are very many pictures—especially such as are
connected with contemplation—which impress the observer with
the feeling that the void itself is depicted as a subject, is indeed
the main subject of the picture. We can only understand this by
recalling . . . the "nothingness" and the "void" of the mystics
and . . . the enchantment and spell exercised by the "negative
hymns". For "void" is, like darkness and silence, a negation, but
a negation that does away with every "this" and "here", in order
that the "wholly other" may become actual.'[61]

Otto, evidently, is talking about religious experience. But can
psychoanalysis throw any light upon this significant sense of
blankness which, as a derivative of the 'sublime', seems to be
common to certain types of aesthetic and to what Otto chooses
to call 'numinous' experience?

Here, we may take as our model 'the state of satiation
that follows satisfaction and allows for quietude to be re-
established.' Thus, in his extraordinary book, *The Psychoanalysis of Elation*, Bertram D. Lewin describes the related
symbols of silence, calmness, lack of motion, *Gestaltlosichkeit*,
and nothingness. He elaborates these in relation to his concept
of 'the dream screen'. This may be understood as the screen on
to which the visual imagery of a dream can be imagined to be
projected. Lewin regarded the screen as a symbol of both sleep
itself and of the breast—sleep, of course, commonly follows
oral satisfaction in infancy. The screen might thus be said to
represent the wish to sleep, whereas visual imagery represented
those wishes disturbing sleep. Lewin also describes a 'blank
dream' in which the dreamer is convinced that he has had a
dream but that it had no visual content. Lewin, noting that
such dreams could be accompanied by orgasm, interpreted this
vision of uniform blankness as a persistent after-image of the
breast.[62]

According to a very early paper by Charles Rycroft, however,
the dream screen was not a component of all dreams, but only
of the dreams of those who are entering a manic phase: it
symbolises the manic sense of ecstatic fusion with the breast and
denial of hostility towards it. In a detailed analysis of one such
dream presented by a patient, however, Rycroft, though admitting its defensive function, also suggested that the fantasy of
having fulfilled the wish to sleep at the breast, which the dream
symbolised, also represented an attempt to re-establish an
object-relationship with the mother an attempt which, as it

happens, in this instance proved successful leading to an advance in object relations and ego development.[63] (One is reminded here of Otto's 'void' or 'negation that does away with every "this" and "here", in order that the "wholly other" may become actual.')

In her little book, *On Not Being Able to Paint*, Milner (who was Rycroft's analyst) goes even further than this, in her account of the positive aspects of such negative experiences. Discussing the whole range to which we have been referring—elation, blankness, oceanic feeling, emptiness, etc.—she writes:

'Analysts have related experiences of this kind to satisfied sleep of the infant at the mother's breast. Certainly such experiences, especially those to do with ecstasy and elation, can be fitted into a coherent scientific pattern by our so relating them. But may we not be missing something important if we look on them only as an end product, as a hallucinatory getting back to where we have never quite given up wanting to be? Is it not possible that blankness, lack of mindfulness, can also be the beginning of something, as the recognition of depression can be? Is it not possible that the blankness is a necessary prelude to a new integration? May not those moments be an essential recurring phase if there is to be a new psychic creation? May there not be moments in which there is a plunge into no-differentiation, which results (if all goes well) in a re-emerging into a new division of the me-not-me, one in which there is more of the "me" in the "not-me", and more of the "not-me" in the me?'[64]

Rycroft said something parallel to this in an important lecture he gave in 1975 in which he affirmed the significance of the primary processes for imaginative and creative activity and emphasised the importance in them of a capacity which he designated as 'negative capability'.

But perhaps one should not over-stress the potentially positive character of this primary blankness. Winnicott once described the way in which fantasies (or mental representations) could function as a compulsive activity intended to fill and obscure a void within which the ego feared engulfment and annihilation, a void which was thus more like an absence than a benificent state of succoured quiescence. What, in psychological terms was this void? Again, one might recall Winnicott's remarks, 'emptiness is a prerequisite to gather in' and again, 'It can be said that only out of non-existence can existence start.' Theologians once argued that, out of the void,

God created the world: more recently, they have tended to characterise God as 'the ground of our being.' (That sense of a *primary absence* in cosmology persists, and takes new forms. Arthur Eddington ended his book, *The Expanding Universe*, by comparing scientists to the voyager who sights a distant shore, and strains his eyes to catch a vision of it. 'It changes in the mist,' he writes. 'Sometimes we seem to focus the substance of it, sometimes it is rather a vista leading on and on till we wonder whether aught can be final.' This causes him to end his book with a quotation from Shakespeare's Bottom, the weaver:

> 'I have had a most rare vision. I have had a dream,—past the wit of man to say what dream it was: man is but an ass, if he go about to expound this dream . . . Methought I was, and methought I had,—but man is but a patched fool, if he will offer to say what methought I had . . .
>
> It shall be called Bottom's dream, because it hath no bottom.'[65]

Whether a blank dream is a suitable analogy for our knowledge of the origins of the cosmos, or whether it is simply a psychological projection of this author is not something upon which I feel qualified to pronounce.) Psychoanalysis enables us to produce a material explanation of the theologians symbolic talk—and of aesthetic blankness. Even within the 'object relations' tradition some psychoanalysts, André Green among them, are now beginning to posit 'a primary absolute narcissism',[66] but of a kind quite different from that derived from instinctual auto-erotism as Freud conceived it. This 'absolute narcissism' is if you will, the 'non-existence' out of which the existence of consciousness starts, it is that void or blankness which is the ground of our psychological being. Bion held that the analyst should endeavour to approach this by seeking to achieve a state without memory or desire, a state of the unknowable, but yet the starting point for all knowledge. (Remember Berenson's imagined life 'in God, without memory, without individuality, and without an identity of our own'?) The analysand, too, can encounter such experiences. I found that my feelings about them expressed themselves through a story I wrote at the nadir of my own analysis, 'Robinson's Triune Sin.'[67]

As Green has pointed out, there has been a certain reluctance to acknowledge the negative aspects of this 'primary absolute narcissism'. They manifest themselves, however, in borderline

Goya, *The Sleep of Reason.*

states and psychoses when, as Green puts it, subjects struggle not only against primitive persecutory fears and the associated threat of annihilation, but also 'against the confrontation with emptiness which is probably the most intolerable of states feared by patients and whose scars leave a state of eternal dissatisfaction.' Together with Donnet, Green has described the blank psychosis, or *psychose blanche*, which they consider to be 'the fundamental psychotic kernel' which is characterised, among other things, by 'blocking of thought processes' and 'the inhibition of the functions of representation'.[68]

I remember that as my own analysis reached a point at which I seemed to be stumbling into some very primitive psychotic mechanisms, I looked at Goya's well-known image, *The Sleep of Reason*, and I thought that the infinite blankness which constituted the background of that extraordinary image was far more terrifying than the homely cacophony of bats, cats, and owls immediately behind the sleeper. Better the monsters than that seducing emptiness! There is no better way of demonstrating the capacity of modernism to engage with this deep terrain of human experience than by considering the case of Mark Rothko, still, for me, among the most moving of all painters.

Rothko was born in 1903, in Dvinsk, Russia. When he was ten, his family emigrated to the U.S.A.: his father died within a few months of getting there. Rothko seems to have begun his training as an artist by taking anatomy classes at the Art Students League in 1924. As a student, he was an accomplished 'realist' painter. One of the earliest surviving paintings from this period, the first in the recent retrospective at the Guggenheim, was an undated portrait of the artist's mother. The painting focuses upon the woman's expression. She is depicted through clear, binding outlines of a kind Rothko was soon to abandon. There is sadness in her face, but domineering hardness, and more than a trace of cruelty too. This is the psysiognomy of someone who has steeled herself against her own tenderness.

In the late 1920s, and for much of the 1930s, Rothko was a 'realist' painter of an expressionist predilection. His favourite subject matters were nudes, city-scapes (especially sub-ways) and domestic scenes. The sort of drawing which characterised his portrait of his mother disappeared very quickly. Some watercolours from this time—see, for example, No. 5, *The Bathers*, in the Guggenheim catalogue—already show female figures dissolving into vibrating expanses of colour. In the late 1930s, like many other New York painters, Rothko became interested in Surrealism. Simultaneously, he abandoned his attempt to depict the external world. He developed an over-riding interest in myths, symbols, and archetypes, and was preoccupied by the Oedipus story. He began to use semi-abstracted shapes and forms to give expression to these concerns. Some of Rothko's paintings in the 1940s make use of a 'polymorphous fabulism', a seething evocation of teeming submarine life. Lawrence Alloway has convincingly observed, 'Proliferating biomorphism is the analogue of manic activity in the artist': manic activity is invariably a form of desperate defence against underlying depression.

In the late 1940s, Rothko began to lose interest in drawn imagery even of this sybmolic kind. Outline and figuration melted away: he became concerned exclusively with floating, translucent patches of colour drifting against the picture plane. In 1950, Rothko's mother died. In this year, according to Diane Waldman, his 'mature style crystallized'.[69] From that time until his own death, 20 years later, Rothko produced the canvases for which he is justly renown. These are paintings consisting of quivering fields of colour, within which enticing rectangles float and recede. Rothko's sensibility to nuances of colour was extraordinary. There are tenuously sensuous modulations in his best painting that seems to draw us through a nuanced range of affects. I can gaze and gaze at these paintings. Rothko himself once said, 'I'm not interested in the relationship of colour or form or anything else. I'm interested only in expressing basic human emotions—tragedy, ecstasy, doom and so on. And the fact that a lot of people break down and cry when confronted with my pictures shows that I can communicate those basic human emotions . . . And if you . . . are moved only by their colour relationships, then you miss the point.'[70]

Sensuous pleasure is not all there is to a Rothko. Soon there enters in to that subtle drama within the boundaries of his canvases deep black spaces of beckoning nothingness which seem to invite you, the viewer, to annihilate yourself in them. These sinister clouds of emptiness, undulate there, encroaching upon the hedonistic affirmation of their surrounding colours. If you follow Rothko's work through chronologically you can see this black space growing and receding, always threatening a vacuous menace. What you are witnessing, of course, is nothing less than Rothko's struggle against a state beyond even depression and despair, the attempt, if you will, by the artist to construct a viable ground to his being over the imminent terror of empty, black space, through a realisation of sensuous, affirmative planes of colour.

In the great paintings Rothko produced in the late 1950s (now in the Tate Gallery) in purples and blacks, night is clearly encroaching. In *Two Openings In Black over Wine* you cannot be certain whether the blackness or the 'wine' constitutes the ground or the figure. Although the title suggests that you are looking at two gateways or windows into a vanishing vista which is rapidly being dissolved into the void, you could also read the 'openings' as flimsy sentinels, or vestiges of the affirmatively real, holding you back from being swallowed up within that nothingness. But, either way, there is no escape.

In 1969, Rothko began a series of monochromatic paintings in browns, blacks and greys. None of the hedonism of the earlier colour combinations remain. This is the 'negative sublime' in its absolute manifestation. The picture space has flattened out into something shallow, empty, and murky.

There is nothing there. Nothing. Nothing. Nothing. On 25 February, 1970, Rothko was found dead in a pool of blood on his studio floor. He appears to have slashed his arms in the crooks of his elbows.

Before I comment on Rothko's life and work, I want to refer to a paper by Melanie Klein, which describes a trajectory almost directly the *opposite* of Rothko's. Klein turns her attention to an article called 'The Empty Space', by Kren Michaelis, which was concerned with the development of her friend, a painter, Ruth Kjar.[71] I must say that I know nothing of Kjar beyond what I have learned about her from Klein on Michaelis on her— which is, I agree, a rather mediated knowledge. But, apparently, before she became a painter, Kjar was a wealthy woman, generally happy in her private life, of no pronounced creative talent, but subject to severe, sporadic, depressions. When she tried to account for these, she would say something to the effect that: 'There is an empty space in me, which I can never fill.' There were many paintings in Kjar's house, including one which she had on loan from a distinguished artist who happened to be her husband's brother. One day this painting was taken away: it had been sold. Michaelis comments, 'This left an empty space on the wall, which in some inexplicable way seemed to coincide with the empty space within her. She sank into a state of the most profound sadness . . . The empty space grinned hideously down at her.' However, although she had never painted before, she bought brushes and pigments and filled the space with a representation of a life-sized, naked negress. This was the start of a successful and satisfying painting career. Kjar became a portrait artist. The article by Michaelis ended with descriptions of two then recent paintings of Kjar's, one of an old woman, the other of her mother:

> 'Slim, imperious, challenging, she stands there with a moon-light-coloured shawl draped over her shoulders: she has the effect of a magnificent woman of primitive times, who could any day engage in combat with the children of the desert with her naked hands. What a chin! What force there is in the haughty gaze!
>
> 'The blank space has been filled.'[72]

As I hope you will by now expect, Klein argues that Kjar's depression left an empty, hostile space inside her, a space she could only overcome through the symbolic re-creation of her mother in painting.

Kjar redeemed herself by moving from the blank space to the reconstitution of the mother through art; Rothko reaches his death by seemingly travelling in the reverse direction, from a portrait of his mother towards absolute emptiness. In a sense, of course, Rothko's trajectory reproduces within itself not only the development of modernism, but also that of psychoanalysis, and one which is consequently built in to this course. He moved from the 'objective' world of anatomical study (of, say, such works as Michelangelo's Moses) to the 'internal objects' of Surrealism, of Dali's (or Klein's) ravaged Venus, towards the positive, undifferentiated colour fields of the potential space, with all its promises realised through transforming colours: but he uncovered there the threat of annihilation, and then the blank psychosis itself which subsumed him. That is the *narrative* of his paintings.

Interestingly, the British painter, William Scott, who knew Rothko fairly well, told me about a trip the latter made to Europe towards the end of his life, in 1966. Rothko told Scott that he was visiting museums but was only interested in looking at paintings of nudes. Scott interpreted this as frustration about the limitations of his *pictorial* practice, imposed upon Rothko by his extraordinary commercial success. But I suspect that there were much deeper psychological reasons for Rothko's obsession with the painted nude at this time. Was he still desperately hoping to fill that hideous space in the way that Kjar did when she painted her life-size portrait of a naked negress on the wall?

Clement Greenberg, who of course knew Rothko, once told me a story about a day in the 1940s when Rosenberg, the art writer, Jackson Pollock, Rothko and another man took a skiff out on to a lake. Greenberg stayed on the shore with Lee Krasner, Pollock's wife. Apparently, the skiff took water and began to sink. Some of those on board were, as Greenberg put it, 'man enough' to get out and swim for safety. Others, including Rothko, clung to the sinking boat as long as they could. Greenberg was standing by Lee Krasner when, white-faced, the crew came ashore. He did not like to ask what had happened; Lee Krasner, however did. Greenberg recalled—not without contempt—that Rothko said that, as the boat went down, and he stayed there unable to plunge into the water and start swimming, he was thinking of his mother.

Natkin, one might say, travelled back into the 'potential space' and found a way, through recreating it on canvas, of

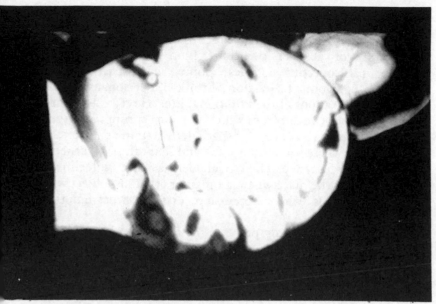

Rudolf Baranik, *Napalm Elegy*, 1974.

'going on being'. (Although I do not deny that in his sweeter works there is more than a little manic denial of that which Rothko dared frontally to confront.) Rothko encountered the 'absolute primary narcissism' of non-being. Natkin causes us to affirm our potentialities, our possibilities for transforming ourselves and the world. Rothko reveals to us the sombrest and blackest of human emotions. It is not just that, if we are receptive to him, he causes us to, as he put it, break-down and cry. He reveals a black hole at the base of consciousness, which is beyond even despair:

> O the mind, mind has mountains; cliff of fall
> Frightful, sheer, no-man-fathomed. Hold them cheap
> May who ne'er hung there.[73]

Much recent psychoanalytic work has been concerned with the nature of internal space in its positive and negative realisations. Traditional Kleinian formulations depended upon a visual image of a space containing all kinds of objects.[74] Into these objects and that space it was supposed that patients projected those parts of their personality that they had split off. The degree of fragmentation and disintegration of that which was thus projected could be correlated with the degree of the individual's disturbance. Bion has attempted a more precise elaboration of these concepts, which is of great significance for the study of abstract painting. Bion suggests that such geometrical concepts as lines, points, and space 'derived originally not from a realization of three-dimensional space but from the realizations of the emotional life.' He regards them as returnable to the realm from which they first sprung. He argues that the geometer's concept of space derives from an experience of 'the place where something was', and so it can be returned to make sense of such psychological ideas as that 'a feeling of depression' is 'the place where a breast or other lost object was', or that 'space' is 'where depression, or some other emotion, used to be.'[75]

I hope you will already perceive the relevance of this kind of work to an understanding of painting like Rothko's. But let us push on further into Bion. His work is, I know, difficult, at times even unnecessarily opaque. It is also rewarding. Bion points out that despite their intimate association, there is an essential difference between the geometer's space and that prevailing in the domain of mental images. In the latter, an infinite number of lines may pass through any one point, but if one attempts to represent such a visual image by points and lines on a piece of paper, then there would be a *finite* number of lines. Bion says that this 'limiting quality' inheres in all realisations of three-dimensional space that approximate to the points, lines and space of the geometer. Such limitation, however, does not inhere in mental space until the attempt is made to represent it through *verbal thought*.

Bion thus postulates mental space as 'a thing-in-itself' that is unknowable but which can be represented (subject to certain limitations) by thoughts. He goes on to refer to a certain category of patient who cannot tolerate the degree of frustrating limitation involved in this transition from mental space to thoughts—whether through the process of verbalisation or that of geometric realisation. Such patients might therefore be said to lack the equipment that would help them to map a realisation of their mental space. Bion likens their position to that of the geometer who had to 'await the invention of Cartesian co-ordinates before he could elaborate algebraic geometry.' In such cases, Bion suggests, the process of projection of parts of the self which Klein describes takes place in a mental space which has no visual images to fulfil the functions of a co-ordinate system; neither the 'faceted solid' nor the 'multi-dimensional, multi-linear figure of lines intersecting at a point' are possible. In such circumstances, Bion comments 'The mental realization of space is therefore felt as an immensity so great that it cannot be represented even by astronomical space because it cannot be represented at all.'[76]

Under these conditions, projection is necessarily explosive, violent, and disintegrative. It is accompanied by such immense fear that the patient may only be able to express it by a sudden and complete silence. Bion says that the ensuing state can most easily be expressed by using surgical shock as a model or metaphor. In this state the dilation of the capillaries throughout the body so increases the space in which blood can circulate that the patient may bleed to death in his own tissues. 'Mental space,' writes Bion, 'is so vast compared with any realization of three-dimensional space that the patient's capacity for emotion is felt to drain away and to be lost in the immensity.'[77]

This space is felt by the patient to be 'so vast that its confines, temporal as well as spatial, are without definition.' Interestingly, Bion goes on to argue that in such instances, although the patient cannot, the analyst can use Euclidean ideas of points, lines and space to investigate the patient's mental state. In effect, part of the therapeutic process becomes the patient's ability to make use of concepts of points, lines and space for the understanding of emotional space. The analyst effectively provides 'a container for the patient's content, and a content for his container.'

Bion further describes a condition in which certain patients achieve a momentary state to which, he says, he almost wishes to apply the term 'non-existence'. This moment is followed by an externalisation or evacuation of 'non-existence', which is then experienced as a negative object that is immensely hostile 'and filled with murderous envy towards the quality or function of existence wherever it is to be found.' Under these circumstances 'space' becomes terrifying, or terror itself. Bion quotes Pascal: *'Le silence de ces espaces infinies m'effraie.'* At such times, 'the space of the ordinary man, the astronomer or the physicist, becomes confounded with "mental space", and its objects with the objects of "mental space".'[78]

The path that Rothko followed was the inverse of the process of therapy which Bion describes. He destroyed his grasp upon

Euclidean perspective, lines and space in his work. He penetrated into experiences prior to either the verbal, or the geometric representation of the world as differentiated from the self. He endeavoured to represent that 'immensity so great that it cannot be represented at all'. But he encountered there the unfathomable expanse of a mental space that had no visual images to fulfil the functions of a co-ordinate system. As the black rectangle undulated towards him, we may imagine that psychotic fear, or panic, which Rothko struggled unsuccessfully to contain. The nothingness and 'non-existence' is externalised through the canvases of the last year of his life. That 'non-existence' must have gazed down at him with 'murderous envy towards the quality or function of existence wherever it is to be found'. Bion's analogy between such fears and 'surgical shock', or bleeding to death within one's own tissues seems all too tragically appropriate to Rothko's case.

However, I certainly do not wish to be thought to be implying that Rothko's superlative achievement as a painter can be reduced to a regression into psychosis. In their extremely interesting book, *The Painted Message*, Billig and Burton-Bradley correctly insist that 'creativity and mental illness are two entirely different facets of human functioning.' They draw a 'clear-cut distinction between the creative process, however radical and even bizarre it may be, and the emergence of inarticulate, incohesive pathological structures.'[79] They do point out however that:

> 'When the personality disintegrates, the boundaries differentiating the individual from his environment break up. He withdraws the emotional energy with which he has endowed reality. If the disintegration becomes severe, the cohesive order of reality has disintegrated; the world resembles the mythological state of dreamtime that supposedly existed prior to creation. Space appears empty at first; as the illness advances, it becomes limitless, infinite, flat, and without depth. Objects, including other people, existing in the environment lose their significance and their plasticity. Patients may become disturbed by the inability to relate to the receding and emptying world around them; they are frightened by their feelings of isolation and their inability to be a part of the world.'[80]

One of their most interesting findings is that graphics by disintegrated persons, are *not* greatly culturally (or 'ideologically') mediated. 'As with Western patients, the structure of space in New Guinean psychotics' graphics corresponds closely to the level of the patients' personality disorganization. The structuralization of space reflects the image of the individual's structure of reality.' This structure, they argue 'is built upon a universal base from which culture differentiation originates.' They recognise the 'three-dimensional perspective of Western art' as a historically specific elaboration, as against the 'common universal patterns' of disintegrated persons of any society. They insist that 'the main difference between artist and patient is this: the mentally-ill individual is solipsistic and expresses his own inner feelings; the artist's work has societal meaning that evokes significant reaction in his audience.' Although the viewer's response may be heightened by a painter who suffers from deep inner conflicts, his work will be ruined if his personality disintegrates beyond a certain point. They believe 'the great artist, involved in his own conflicts, can free himself from the immediacy of their personal significance and transform them into a format that evokes consonant feelings in the observer.'[81]

Rothko participated in the culture of his time, even though he was revulsed by it. He did not reject the 'visual ideology' of late Modernism. Indeed, his mature work is limited to one of its genres, the colour field. His art can easily be differentiated from that of the insane through his consummate sensibility as a colourist. Few men or women have had a better grasp of the material practice of painting than he. Rothko used these conventions (indeed he created many of them) and his skills to make manifest in a most literal way his struggle against space which 'appears empty at first' and then becomes 'limitless, infinite, flat and without depth.' When he loses that struggle, in the last year of his life, his work loses its capacity to move us. The very late works interest me as a coda or confirmation of the nature of the project in which he was engaged. But in themselves they are precisely—nothing. They speak only of the grey, monochromatic silence of an impending grave.

By implying that Rothko reached down with culturally specific pictorial conventions towards 'universal', underlying spatial structures pertaining to levels of experience prior to cultural differentiations, I am not attempting to situate his work outside of history. For we have to ask not only why it is that in our own time work of this kind came to be made, but also how it was possible for it to achieve the kind of cultural centrality realised by Rothko. To any socialist who has not rejected the concept of alienation the answer will be self-evident.

But I would go further than this. I consider that there is a specific connection between the abstract painting of America and the experience of *exile*. Both Natkin and Rothko came from Russian Jewish families which had emigrated to the United States; so did Baranik and Olitski, two 'field' painters whose work I will discuss in a moment. I suspect that for such artists the psychological longings surrounding the person of the mother, phase and merge into cultural longings. The life of an exile is dominated by the absent presence of the mother-land.

Mark Rothko, *Portrait of Rothko's Mother.*

This acute, private accentuation of cultural displacement paradoxically enables these painters to touch upon a widely experienced sense of alienation or dislocation. To use Bion's language once more, it need not surprise us if the exile or immigrant is acutely attuned to the inadequacies of the geometer's space and to the presence of the absence within him of a continent that is elsewhere.

Recently I have begun to get to know, and greatly to admire, the work of the painter Rudolf Baranik. Baranik is, in effect, a grey monochromist, the sort of painter for whom, elsewhere, I have reserved my most scathing polemic. Yet Baranik is no formalist—at least, not in the sense of someone who is producing paintings about paintings. He situates himself within a particular strand of that which I would designate as the 'negative sublime', tracing descent through Ryder's night skies, Pollock, Reinhardt, and the late Rothko. Baranik, too, paints the enticingly vacuous blankness of modulated grey, grey space. He produces images of absence of his own encounter with 'absolute narcissism', and with the negative pessimism of an emptiness beyond the ravages of despair. And yet, in Baranik's case, this extreme negativity is redeemed as an historical image: he plummets into the passive depths of his own consciousness, in order to speak of history. Perhaps his finest series of works to date has been his *Napalm Elegy* in which the white face of a napalmed figure, from Vietnam, glows like a moon in this night sky. For all the reticence, and extreme understatement—reaching almost the threshold of silence—of these works, it must be admitted that few American painters have succeeded in speaking more effectively of the horror of the U.S.A.'s imperialist and genocidal intervention in South East Asia.

There are, I know difficulties in what I have been arguing. (I hope you have not forgotten that it was my intention to open up areas for discussion rather than to provide definitive, totalising accounts of them.) I have here pursued one mode of 'aesthetic experience' towards what I consider to be its material origins in our psycho-biological being. Far be it from me to claim that I have thus indicated the material basis of aesthetics in general for, whatever the historical origins of the term, it is now a category embracing phenomena remote from those we have been considering. I am not, and I would emphasise this, claiming to have produced a theory of why paintings in general are to be valued, but only of why certain specific examples of a particular type of abstract painting can powerfully move us.

I want to stress, however, that the quality of a work cannot be said to reside simply in the fact of its relationship to a given area of experience, so much as in the way that that relationship is materially realised through painted forms, i.e. the extent to which content has become effective form. If one assumed otherwise, one would have no way of distinguishing between, say, Gombrich's 'Bonnencontre' viewed through wobbly glass and a great Bonnard. Both, I have argued, touch upon the same terrain of experience, but to equate one with the other would be absurd.

The key term here, I am convinced, is that of expression. Within the single material practices of painting there are varieties of expressive practice. For example, I have had reason to refer several times to the Renaissance theory of expression which was rooted in the discovery of new anatomical knowledge, in which painters played a vital part; a work derived its strength from the way in which an artist transformed his raw materials so that the expressiveness of his depicted subjects communicated itself to his viewers. Similarly, the sorts of painting that we have been discussing here seem to me to be rooted in new affective knowledge of our psycho-biological being. (Rothko reveals the subject matter of his painting more vividly than does say a Bion text, yet they touch upon the same area of experience.) The strength or otherwise of the paintings depends at least in large part upon the artist's transformation of his givens which include both his pictorial conventions (delivered to him through ideology) and his physical materials (paint, canvas, etc.): the means of transformation is itself a material, and highly bodily process. It may be because all forms of effective expressive practice are so intimately enmeshed with the body that a work of art can outlive the historical moment of its production.

Expression, as I conceive it, could not be more remote from Crocean idealist views which would detach it from the psycho-biological processes of the artists on the one hand, and the material potentialities of his medium on the other. But perhaps I can clarify the point I am making by comparing and contrasting Natkin with another 'post-painterly' American abstractionist, Jules Olitski. In the mid 1960s, Olitski began to make a number of spray paintings which as a matter of fact received a lot of acclaim and attention. In these works, we are confronted with the same kind of potentially 'sublime' recessive haze that can be read as a skin, or an illusory suffusing depth, of the sort that we see in a Natkin. Indeed these paintings could be subjected to a similar 'interpretation' to that which I proposed for the Natkins here. Olitski, however, does not move me at all. None of his paintings manifest that affective strength which I feel in front of the best Natkins. Indeed, I am overcome by a sense of *inauthenticity* when I looked at Olitski: of something like milk-shakes, of faked and plastic flavours. Someone once described his paintings to me as 'painted Musak'. The label has stuck in my mind: it seems accurate.

I formulate this as an *affective* distinction, a difference if you will, in aesthetic experience. But it is not difficult to indicate the material basis of my judgement. As I pointed out in my description, Natkin's picture space is, in general, carefully constituted. I have often watched him paint. In the *Intimate Lighting*, *Bath*, and *Colour Bath* works he dabs the pigment on in layer after layer using indented cloths wrapped around a sponge. He paints like a dancer. (In fact, as an adolescent, he trained as a tap dancer, and has often done set designs for dance companies since.) The rhythms of his body inform the way in which he gradually builds up the image. This is both controlled and seemingly instinctive: watching him, it is possible to observe both his informing *energy* and his technical mastery of his medium working together. There is thus a real sense in which every painting he makes is imprinted with his touch and movement: it cannot but stand in an intimate close relation to his body, and be expressive of the emotions and sensations which he experiences through that body. The affective qualities of a good Natkin painting have the intimacy and emotional strength of a caress: we feel, and are moved by, the artist's *touch* pervading every part of the surface. With Olitski, this just is not the case. The spray gun is mechanical: its cloudy hazes *evoke* but do not *constitute* a space. An area of experience can be alluded to through such a technique; but it cannot be materially expressed by it.

Natkin (who is aware of a tendency towards over-sweetness even within his own work) likes to quote James Joyce's phrase, 'Sentimentality is unearned emotion.' Olitski is the sentimental painter of the colour-field, *par excellence*. To switch to other expressive modes, he offers us a 'Captive Slave' rather than a Venus de Milo. He is a Bonnencontre, and not an Ingres.

I do not think it is an exaggeration to say that he has about as much in common with the terrain of experience of which Natkin, at his best, is expressive as a plastic Madonna from Lourdes has in common with a Piero della Francesca.

Indeed, there is an article to be written, and perhaps one day I will write it, upon the 'banalisation of the sublime' in post-war American painting.[82] Many of the first generation of Abstract Expressionists—including Barnet Newman, Franz Kline, perhaps even Ad Reinhardt, and, of course Rothko—were desperately seeking forms to express that terrain of experience we have been exploring here. In my view, only Rothko came close to succeeding. Nonetheless, the nature of their enterprise must be acknowledged and respected. It is evident to me that Newman's formal devices, his stark division of the picture surface into two, and his simultaneous pursuit of a sensation of 'onement'—not to mention his entire rhetoric on the nature of the sublime, beginning with his 1948 text, *The Sublime Is Now*—could be understood in the psychological terms that I have been putting forward.[83]

For these artists, the pursuit of these shadowy areas of experience had the character of a desperate search. But, in the hands of many of their second and third generation followers, that search had become transformed into a question of *style*, a mannerism, a matter of 'visual ideology' in which the original, informing content was present only as a debased residue. To perceive Olitski's sprayed paintings as sublime is rather like hearing a canned tape of *Die Meistersingers* playing as one walks through an airport lounge to catch a plane.

There remains the question as to whether the kind of aesthetic search I have described is not fundamentally 'regressive', capable only of illuminating areas of infantile experience. Milner, you may remember, considered this possibility as she abandoned perspective and looked for a way of 'mixing' herself up more in objects—but she firmly rejected it. She thought that what she was doing had more of the character of a 'search' than a 'retreat', 'a going backwards perhaps, but a going back to look for something which could have real value for adult life if only it could be recovered.'

In a lecture he gave in 1975, Rycroft emphasised more strongly than ever before the importance of rejecting the simple assumption that the primary and secondary processes were antagonistic and the former emanated from some maëlstrom domain of a destructive id. He criticised the classical association of the primary processes with illness and the secondary with health, attributing such views to Freud's 19th century 'rationalism'. (Freud, you will recall, knew nothing of 'oceanic feeling, or aesthetic experience. He could not abide music. He was, one might say, anaesthetised to such things, just as in theory he could not fathom the infant-mother relationship.) Rycroft also emphasised how Freud assumed that the verbal mode was identical with ego functioning. His distrust of the iconic character of the primary processes led him to assume that painters painted scenes that could just as well be displaced by a written account of them. This view led to a built-in problem in classical psychoanalytic theory, reflected, for example in Alexander, in which any imaginative, or anti-ideological activity on the part of the artist was immediately regarded with analytic suspicion, or equated with neurosis and dream.

Rycroft, however, assumes the co-existence from the beginning of life of imaginative and rational processes, emanating respectively from the primary and secondary processes, and complementing rather than opposing each other. Creative people, he suggests, seem to be those who hold on to the imaginative in the midst of the rational, ideas which parallel those of Hartmann, the American ego psychologist, who saw 'adaptive regression' as being healthy.

Soon after making his great, pulsating, grey Bath paintings, Natkin began creeping down at the dead of night into his studio and struggling, when no one was looking, to make a new kind of 'realist' painting. I have not seen any of these works, and I do not know if he can be said to be succeeding. But what is happening to Natkin, seems to me to be, in a certain sense, what may be happening within the modernist tradition as a whole. Many painters are, as it were, leaving the 'dream screen' of blankness to attempt to establish new kinds of relationship with objects and the world. It is as yet early days: much of the new work remains confused, contradictory, and ambivalent. Nonetheless, I feel sure of one thing: if the new realism is to be realised in anything other than name, it is more likely to be through those who have travelled towards 'the ground of their being'—with all the risks that this involves—than through those who persist in denying it altogether.

It is here, I think, that these psychoanalytic insights into art potentially connect with the socialist perspective from which, you may remember, we set out on this quest. Milner, for example, noted when painting from nature:

> '. . . there occurred, at least sometimes, a fusion into a never-before-known wholeness; not only were the object and oneself no longer felt to be separate but neither were thought and sensation and feeling and action.'[84]

This led her to comment:

> 'This sense of union achieved in attempts to create a work of art, this transcendence of separateness, might it not have its parallel in the union with other people that working together for a common purpose achieves? Thus the illusion of no-separateness between self and other, which is an illusion so far as bodily life was concerned is not necessarily an illusion in the social sphere . . . the demarcation of the boundaries of one's spiritual identity are not fixed, they do not have to remain identical with one's skin.'[85]

Milner's argument here relates to that of Herbert Marcuse. Although I cannot accept all his aesthetic or political theories, I have the greatest respect for this thinker. You may remember that one of his most consistent themes was the defence of the autonomy of the aesthetic, vis-a-vis social or political reductions. (Marcuse of course used the term 'aesthetic' in a broader sense than that of the sublime which we have been discussing here.) In contrast to orthodox Marxist views on art, Marcuse saw the political potential of art 'in art itself, in the aesthetic form as such'. Furthermore, he argued that 'by virtue of its aesthetic form, art is largely autonomous vis-a-vis the given social relations. In its autonomy art both protests these relations, and at the same time transcends them. Thereby art subverts the dominant consciousness, the ordinary experience.'[86] A work of art, he insists, is authentic or true not by virtue of its content or the 'correct' representations of social conditions, nor by its 'pure' form, but by the content having become form. 'Aesthetic form, autonomy, and truth,' he maintained, 'are inter-related.' The truth of art 'lies in its power to break the monopoly of established reality (i.e., of those who established it) to *define* what is *real*.'[87] Thus 'The autonomy of art contains the categorical imperative: "things must change".'[88] For Marcuse, 'renunciation of the aesthetic form is abdication of responsibility. It deprives art of the very form in which it can create that other reality within the established one—the cosmos of hope.'[89]

Marcuse argued that the fact that a work truly represents the interests or the outlook of the proletariat or of the bourgeoisie does not yet make it an authentic work of art:

> 'The universality of art cannot be grounded in the world and world outlook of a particular class, for art envisions a concrete universal humanity (*Menschlichkeit*), which no particular class can incorporate, not even the proletariat, Marx's "universal class". The inexorable entanglement of joy and sorrow, celebration and despair, Eros and Thanatos cannot be dissolved into problems of class struggle.'[90]

Like Timpanaro, Marcuse argued that 'history is also grounded in nature'. He stressed that Marxist theory has 'the least justification to ignore the metabolism between the human being and nature, and to denounce the insistence on this natural soil of society as a regressive ideological conception':

> 'The emergence of human beings as "species beings"—men and women capable of living in that community which is the potential of the species—this is the subjective basis of a classless society. Its realisation presupposes a radical transformation of the drives and needs of the individuals: an organic development within the socio-historical. Solidarity would be on weak grounds were it not rooted in the instinctual structure of individuals.'[91]

Marcuse, of course, was a Freudian (of sorts) to the end of his days. I would prefer to say that the 'solidarity' of which he speaks is not rooted so much in 'instinctual structure' (at least not in 'instinct' as Freud conceived of it) as in the necessity of infant-mother object relations, and the long period of attachment and dependency of the human infant.

There remains a real sense in which this infant-mother relationship is both a paradigm, and the remote biological root, of the continuing potential for socialism. Painters and sculptors have returned to this theme again and again. It speaks of the past of each of us, and the future of all of us. That is one reason why, as a socialist, I would defend the affective, iconic exploration of the potentialities of that relationship as something of far greater significance than an excursion into infantilism. I would like to end by quoting the words of an unsuccessful poet about his struggle to realise verses expressive of 'sublime' sentiments evoked by his adult love for a woman. After abandoning the struggle to become a poet, he looked back on these attempts and wrote of them:

> '. . . a remote beyond, such as my love, became my heaven, my art. Everything grew vague, and all that is vague lacks boundaries; onslaughts against the present, broad and shapeless expressions of unnatural feeling, constructed purely out of the blue, the complete opposition of what is and what ought to be, rhetorical reflections instead of poetic thoughts but perhaps also a certain warmth of sentiment and a struggle for movement characterises all the poems in the first three volumes I sent to Jenny. The whole horizon of a longing which sees no frontiers assumed many forms and frustrated my effort to write with poetic conciseness.'[92]

As a matter of fact, this writer sees clearly into himself: he could not find precise forms to realise or express these powerful 'boundless' sentiments of change and becoming to which he refers. Nonetheless, it should not surprise us to learn that this writer is Marx, nor that, when he tried to write poems, they were of this character.

NOTES

I

1   Timothy Hyman, 'Painting 1979' *London Magazine*, Vol. 19 Nos 1 and 2, p. 12

2   Raymond Williams, 'Problems of Materialism', *New Left Review*, No. 109, p. 10

3   Karl Marx, *Grundisse*, Harmondsworth: Penguin Books, 1973, p. 111

4   ibid., p. 111

5   Ernst Fischer, *The Necessity of Art*, Harmondsworth: Penguin Books, 1968, p. 11

6   Karl Marx, *Preface and Introduction to 'A Contribution to the Critique of Political Economy'*, Peking: Foreign Languages Press, Peking, 1976, p. 4.

7   Walter Copland Perry, *Greek and Roman Sculpture: A Popular Introduction to the History of Greek and Roman Sculpture*, London: Longmans, 1882, p. 334

8   John Berger, *A Painter of Our Time*, London, Writers & Readers, 1976, p. 63

9   Daniel Read, 'Oil Painting and its Class', *New Left Review*, No. 108, p. 111

10 'In Defence of Art', *New Society*, Vol. 45, No. 834, 28 September 1978, pp. 702–704.

11 Roger Fry, *The Artist and Psychoanalysis*, London: The Hogarth Press

12 Clive Bell, 'Dr. Freud on Art', *The Dial*, April 1925, p. 281

13 Sebastiano Timpanaro, *On Materialism*, London: New Left Books, p. 34

14 ibid., p. 50

15 Williams, op. cit., pp. 10–11

16 Sebastiano Timpanaro, *The Freudian Slip*, London: New Left Books, 1976

17 *On Materialism*, p. 54

18 Charles Rycroft, 'Introduction: Causes and Meaning' in *Psychoanalysis Observed*, Harmondsworth: Penguin Books, p. 20

19 Louis Althusser, *Lenin and Philosophy and Other Essays*, London: New Left Books, p. 191
20 *On Materialism*, p. 103
21 Jon Halliday and Peter Fuller (eds), *The Psychology of Gambling*, London: Allen Lane, 1974; and Peter Fuller, *The Champions*, London: Allen Lane, 1978
22 Hans Keller, 'Sick Sport', *The Spectator*, Vol. 241 No. 7830, 29 July 1978, p. 20
23 Rudolf Otto, *The Idea of the Holy*, Harmondsworth: Penguin Books, p. 32
24 Howard Hibbard, *Michelangelo*, London: Allen Lane Penguin Books, 1975, p. 160
25 Sigmund Freud, 'The Moses of Michelangelo', in *Standard Edition of The Complete Psychological Works of Sigmund Freud*, 24 vols., London: The Hogarth Press, Vol. XIII, p. 216. (Hereinafter referred to as S.E.)
26 ibid., p. 222
27 ibid., p. 224
28 ibid., pp. 229–230
29 ibid., p. 233
30 ibid., p. 211
31. Ernest Jones, *Sigmund Freud: Life and Works*, 3 vols., London: The Hogarth Press, 1953–7, Vol. III, p. 437. (Hereinafter referred to as S.F.L. & W.)
32 ibid., p. 437
33 For discussions of Freud's collecting habits, see Jack Spector, *The Aesthetics of Freud*, London: Allen Lane, 1972 and Suzanne Bernfeld, 'Freud and Archaeology', *American Imago*, Vol. 8 (1951): pp. 107–128
34 Anthony Storr, *The Dynamics of Creation*, London: Secker & Warburg, 1972, p. 3
35 S.E. Vol. XVI, p. 376
36 S.E. Vol. IX, p. 8
37 S.E. Vol. XX, p. 65
38 Jones, S.F.L. & W., Vol. III, p. 441
39 See for example, R. Waelder, 'Psychoanalytic Avenues to Art,' *Psychoanalytical Epitomes*, No. 6, London: Hogarth Press, pp. 16–60 and the writings of Gombrich, Kris, and Wollheim on Freud's aesthetics.
40 Sigmund Freud, *Leonardo da Vinci*, London: Routledge & Kegan Paul, p. 34
41 ibid., pp. 128–129
42 See K. R. Eissler, *Leonardo da Vinci: Psychoanalytic Notes on the Enigma*, London: Hogarth, 1962
43 Edmund Wilson, 'The Historical Interpretation of Literature', in D. A. Stauffer, ed., *The Intent of the Critic*, Princeton, 1941

44 Richard Wollheim, 'Freud and the Understanding of Art' *British Journal of Aesthetics*, Vol. X, 1970, p. 214
45 Michael Hibbard, op. cit., p. 43
46 ibid. p. 261
47 Ernst Gombrich, 'Freud's Aesthetics', *Encounter*, January 1966, p. 33
48 ibid., p. 33
49 Wollheim, op. cit., p. 216
50 Gombrich, op. cit., p. 34
51 ibid., p. 34
52 Wollheim, op. cit., p. 216
53 ibid., p. 218
54 Gombrich, op. cit., p. 30
55 ibid., p. 33
56 Wollheim, op. cit., p. 217
57 ibid., p. 217
58 Earl E. Rosenthal, quoted in Spector, op. cit., p. 131
59 Wollheim, op. cit., p. 218
60 Jones, S.F.L. & W., Vol. I, p. 44
61 Fielding H. Garrison, *An Introduction to the History of Medicine*, London: W. B. Saunders, 1917
62 Henry Sigerist, *Great Doctors: A Biographical History of Medicine*, London: George Allen & Unwin, 1933, p. 63
63 Jones, S.F.L. & W., Vol. I, pp. 45–46
64 Garrison, op. cit., p. 438
65 op. cit.
66 *Principes scientifiques des beaux-arts*, Paris, 1878
67 Spector, op. cit., p. 68
68 Cited in Spector, op. cit.
69 *The Human Figure: its beauties and defects*, London: H. Grevel & Co., 1891, p. 3
70 ibid., p. 7
71 In Britain this project persisted longer than elsewhere, for example in the Slade Tradition as manifest in Henry Tonks (1862–1937)
72 Ernest Jones, S.F.L. & W., Vol. I, p. 50
73 Sigmund Freud, *The Origins of Psycho-Analysis*, Eds Marie Bonaparte, Anna Freud, Ernst Kris, London: Imago, p. 355
74 ibid., p. 350
75 Karl Pribram and Merton Gill, *Freud's 'Project' Re-assessed*, London: Hutchinson, 1976
76 S.E. Vol. XX, p. 253
77 Jones, S.F.L. & W., Vol. II, p. 408
78 ibid., Vol. I, pp. 43–44
79 ibid., Vol. II, p. 408
80 ibid., Vol. I, p. 44

242   *Art and Psychoanalysis*

81 S.E. Vol. XIII, p. 213
82 Jones, S.F.L. & W., Vol. III, p. 411
83 ibid., p. 409
84 ibid., Vol. II, p. 339
85 S.E. Vol. XIV, p. 62
86 O. Mannoni, *Freud: The Theory of The Unconscious*, London: New Left Books, 1971, p. 134
87 Ernst Kris, *Psychoanalytic Explorations in Art*, New York: I.U.P., p. 300
88 Harry Guntrip, *Personality Structure and Human Interaction*, London: Hogarth Press and the Institute of Psycho-Analysis, 1961
89 Mannoni, op. cit., p. 135
90 Jones, S.F.L. & W., Vol. II, pp. 339–340
91 ibid.
92 S.E. Vol. XIV, p. 70
93 Paul Roazen, *Freud and His Followers*, Harmondsworth: Penguin Books, 1979, p. 196
94 Guntrip, op. cit.
95 op. cit., p. 239
96 Jones, S.F.L. & W., Vol. III, p. 402
97 ibid., Vol. I, p. 48
98 Roazen, op. cit., p. 257: my account of these events relies heavily on Roazen's—easily the fullest published version.
99 Quoted Roazen, op. cit., p. 257
100 ibid., pp. 266–267
101 ibid., p. 274
102 ibid.
103 ibid., p. 275
104 'Freud and Homeostasis', Brit. J. Phil. Science, Vol. 7, no. 25, p. 61
105 'The human brain: An introduction', *The Human Brain*, London: Paladin, 1972, p. 17
106 ibid., pp. 17–18
107 op. cit., p. 134
108 *The Boundaries of Science*, London: Faber, 1939, p. 19
109 op. cit., p. 46
110 See Guntrip, op. cit., p. 147
111 op. cit., p. 33
112 Spector, op. cit. pp. 64–65 and 128–133

II

1 Walter Copland Perry, op. cit., p. 335
2 Adolf Furtwängler, 'The Venus of Milo', in *Masterpieces of Greek Sculpture*, Vol. II, London: Heinemann, 1895

3 See Jean Aicard, *La Venus de Milo: Recherches sur l'Histoire de la Decouverte*, Paris: Sandoz et Fischbacher, 1874
4 Quoted Aicard, op. cit., p. 216
5 ibid., 210 ff
6 ibid.
7 op. cit., pp. 377–378
8 Quatre-mere de Quincy, *Sur La Statue Antique de Venus*, Paris, 1821
9 Charles Clarac, *Sur La Statue antique de Venus Victrix*, Paris, 1821
10 See Furtwängler, op. cit.
11 *The Newcombes*, London: Collins, n.d. pp. 236–237
12 Quoted in Gombrich, op. cit., p. 31
13 *Lord Leighton*, London, 1975, p. 88
14 'Albert Moore' in catalogue for *The Victorian High Renaissance* exhibition organised by Minneapolis Institute of Arts, 1978, p. 144
15 *Victorian Painters*, London: Barrie Cresset, 1974, pp. 202–203
16 *La Statue de Milo Dite Venus Victrix*, Stockholm: 1878 and *Ueber die Plinthe der Venus von Milo*, 1884
17 *Gazette des Beaux Arts*, 1890, No. i, p. 376
18 *Revue Archäologique*, 1890, Vol. 15, p. 145 *La Vénus de Milo*, Paris: 1871 and 1892
19 *Die hohe Frau von Milo*, Berlin: 1872
20 *Die Venus von Milo*, Hanover: 1882
21 *Geschichte der grieschischen Plastik*, Leipzig: 1893
22 *Spectator*, 5 October 1861, p. 1091
23 *A History of Greek Sculpture*, London: 1890, Vol. II, p. 285
24 op. cit.
25 op. cit.
26 op. cit., p. 383
27 ibid., p. 387
28 ibid., p. 401
29 *Histoire de la Sculpture Grecque*, Paris: 1892, Vol. II p. 468ff.
30 Venus de Milo, *The Spinner*, New York: Exposition Press, 1958
31 'The Beginnings of Greek Sculpture' in *Greek Studies*, London: 1922, p. 223
32 *The Nude*, Harmondsworth: Penguin Books, p. 44
33 ibid., p. 45
34 *Collected Poems*, Edinburgh and London: William Blackwood, Vol. I, pp. 286–287
35 'The Venus pin-up', *New Society*, 23 October 1975, p. 222
36 ibid., p. 222
37 ibid., p. 222
38 Clark, op. cit., p. 84
39 op. cit., p. 222

40   ibid., p. 222
41   Isaac Asimov, *A Short History of Biology*, London: The Scientific Book Club, p. 41
42   ibid., p. 41
43   *A Marxist Looks at Jesus*, London: Darton, Longman & Todd, pp. 45–46
44   For a discussion of Plekhanov's views on art see, Mark Rosenthal, 'Relative VS. Absolute Criteria in Art', re-printed in *Artery*, No. 10, Summer 1976, pp. 14–17
45   *Plekhanov's Literary Heritage*, Vol. III, p. 214
46   Rosenthal, op. cit.
47   *Art and Social Life*, Moscow: Progress Publishers, pp. 24–25
48   ibid., pp. 25–26
49   ibid., p. 27
50   op. cit., p. 334
51   *Critique of Taste*, London: New Left Books, p. 212
52   op. cit., p. 83
53   op. cit., pp. 138–139
54   op. cit., p. 219
55   'Art and the Inner World', *Times Literary Supplement*, No. 3,827, 18 July 1975, pp. 800–801
56   *Introduction to the work of Melanie Klein*, rev. ed., London: Hogarth Press, and *Klein*, London: Fontana, 1979
57   'Life without father', *Times Literary Supplement*, No. 3,827, 18 July 1975, p. 798
58   'An Examination of the Klein System of Child Psychology,' in *The Psychoanalytic Study of the Child*, No. 1, London: Imago, 1945
59   op. cit., p. 207
60   op. cit., p. 477
61   *The Psycho-Analysis of Children*, London: The Hogarth Press and the Institute of Psycho-Analysis, 1975
62   Segal, 1973, p. 5
63   'The Nature and Function of Phantasy', in *Developments in Psycho-Analysis*, ed. Joan Riviere, London: The Hogarth Press and the Institute of Psycho-Analysis, 1952
64   *A Critical Dictionary of Psychoanalysis*, Harmondsworth: Penguin Books, 1972, p. 77
65   Guntrip, op. cit., p. 226
66   'Theoretical and Experimental Aspects of Psycho-Analysis', *British Journal of Medical Psychology*, Vol. 25, pts. 2 and 3, p. 124
67   'Art and the inner world,' p. 800
68   'A Psycho-Analytical Approach to Aesthetics', *International Journal of Psychoanalysis*, Vol. 33, 1952, p. 197
69   'Art and the inner world,' p. 800

70   ibid., p. 800
71   *The Image in Form*, Harmondsworth: Penguin Books, 1972, p. 120
72   ibid., p. 100
73   'Form in Art', in *New Directions in Psycho-Analysis*, ed. Klein, Heimann, and Money-Kyrle, London: Tavistock, 1955, pp. 406–420
74   'Art and the Inner World,' p. 801
75   ibid., p. 801
76   ibid., p. 801
77   Robert Descharnes, *The World of Salvador Dali*, London: 1962, p. 164
78   John Rickman, 'The Nature of Ugliness and the Creative Impulse', *International Journal of Psycho-Analysis*, Vol. 21, 1940, pp. 297–298
79   ibid., p. 298
80   See Linda Hyman, 'The Greek Slave by Hiram Powers: High Art as Popular Culture', *Art Journal*, Vol. 35, No. 3, pp. 216–223
81   Quoted ibid., pp. 222–223
82   'Introduction to the work of Melanie Klein', p. 92
83   *The Philosophy of Art History*, Cleveland, Ohio: Meridian Books, 112–113
84   *Introduction to the work of Melanie Klein*, p. 92
85   'Prolegomena to a Psychology of Art' *British Journal of Psychology*, Vol. 28, 1938, p. 297
86   'The Ultimate Basis of Aesthetic experience' *British Journal of Psychology*, Vol. 29, 1939 p. 180

III

1   *On Not Being Able to Paint*, London: Heinemann Educational, p. xvii (First published in 1950, under pseudonym, 'Joanna Field'.)
2   ibid., p. xvii
3   ibid., p. 9
4   ibid., p. 10
5   ibid., p. 10
6   ibid., pp. 11–12
7   ibid., p. 12
8   ibid., p. 15
9   ibid., p. 15
10   ibid., p. 16
11   ibid., p. 16
12   ibid., p. 17
13   ibid., p. 17
14   ibid., p. 17
15   *On Modern Art*. London: Faber, 1966, p. 53

16   'Bonnard', in *The Moment of Cubism and Other Essays*, London: Weidenfeld and Nicolson, 1969, p. 121
17   ibid., p. 119
18   Harold Rosenberg, *De Kooning*, New York: Abrams Books
19   A selection of my articles and lectures is to be published by Writers and Readers Publishing Cooperative in the autumn of 1980
20   John Berger, *Success and Failure of Picasso*, London: Writers and Readers, 1980
21   When Leonard Woolf put Bell in his novel, he described him as 'A fat round body, and his little round fat mind . . . one of those men so small mentally and morally that anything which took place in his little mind or little soul naturally seemed to him to be one of the great convulsions of nature.'
22   *Art*, London: Grey Arrow Edition, p. 22
23   ibid., p. 23
24   ibid., p. 133
25   ibid., p. 180
26   ibid., p. 26
27   ibid., p. 140
28   ibid., p. 147
29   ibid., p. 91
30   ibid., p. 42
31   *History of Thought in the Eighteenth Century*, London: Harbinger Books, 1962, Vol. I, p. 69
32   ibid., p. 3
33   'Painting and Perspective', in *Origins of the Scientific Revolution*, ed. Hugh Kearney, London: Longmans, p. 20
34   ibid., p. 26
35   *Art and Culture*, Boston: Beacon Books, 1965, p. 41
36   'Dr. Freud on Art', *The Dial*, April 1925, p. 282
37   'Problems connected with the Work of Melanie Klein', in *Trends in Psycho-Analysis*, London: The Hogarth Press, pp. 57–89
38   op. cit.
39   'The Position of Psycho-Analysis in Great Britain', in *On the Early Development of Mind*, London: Imago, 1956, p. 359
40   *The Origins of Love and Hate*, Harmondsworth: Penguin Books, p. 29
41   ibid., p. 29
42   *Attachment and Loss*, Harmondsworth: Penguin Books, p. 39
43   ibid., pp. 12–13
44   op. cit., p. 389
45   *Primary Love and Psycho-analytic Technique*, London: Tavistock, 1964

46 Re-printed in *Psychoanalytic Studies of the Personality*, London: Tavistock, 1952
47 op. cit., p. 284
48 *Playing and Reality*, Harmondsworth: Penguin Books, 1974, p. 177
49 *New Left Review*, No. 50, July-August 1968, pp. 3–57
50 ibid., p. 42
51 *Through Paediatrics to Psycho-Analysis*, London: Hogarth, p. xiv
52 See A. Ehrenzweig, *The Psycho-Analysis of Artistic Vision and Hearing*, London: Routledge & Kegan Paul, 1953; 'A new psychoanalytical approach to aesthetics', *British Journal of Aesthetics*, Vol. 2 (1962), pp. 301–317; and *The Hidden Order of Art*, London: Weidenfeld & Nicolson, 1967
53 In *Meditations on a Hobby Horse*, London: Phaidon, 1963, pp. 30–44
54 In Glover, op. cit., pp. 1–24. (Interestingly, in re-printing this text in 1956, Glover prefaced it with remarks indicating that in his view it was even at that time 'a museum piece'.)
55 op. cit., p. 40
56 ibid., p. 40
57 ibid., pp. 40–41
58 ibid., p. 41
59 *The Hidden Order of Art*, p. 272 Andor Ehrenzweig
60 'Psycho-analysis and Art', in *Psycho-analysis and Contemporary Thought*, London: Hogarth Press, p. 96
61 'Beyond the Reality Principle', *Imagination and Reality*, London: Hogarth, p. 106
62 'Psycho-analysis and Art', p. 99
63 *On Not Being Able to Paint*, pp. 115–116
64 In *Problems of Human Pleasure and Behaviour*, London: Hogarth, p. 123
65 ibid., pp. 123–124

IV
1 I have recently completed a monograph on Robert Natkin for Abrams Books in New York. The following description constitutes the opening section of that book. Further material and information on many of the themes concerning Natkin's painting touched upon here can be found in the monograph.
2 *New York Times*, 1 December 1978, p. 17
3 Robert Natkin, Andre Emmerich Downtown Gallery Catalogue, 1974, pp. 3–5
4 Nicos Hadjinicolau, *Art History and Class Struggle*, London, Pluto Press, 1978, p. 6
5 ibid., pp. 179–180

6   ibid., p. 182
7   'American painting since the last war,' *Art Monthly*, No. 27, June 1979, pp. 6–12 and No. 28, July/August 1979, pp. 6–12
8   'Introduction', *Aesthetics*, Oxford: Oxford University Press, 1978, p. 12
9   See Lionello Venturi, *History of Art Criticism*, New York: Dutton, p. 114
10 ibid., p. 161
11 *Philosophical Enquiry into the Origin of our Ideas of the Sublime and Beautiful*, London: 1756
12 Venturi, op. cit., pp. 190–191
13 *Kant*, Harmondsworth: Penguin Books, 1955, p. 193
14 *The Future of Painting*: The Bodley Head, 1923, pp. 24–25
15 ibid., p. 31
16 Quoted, Milner, *On Not Being Able to Paint*, pp. 24–25
17 ibid., p. 25
18 op.cit., p. 53
19 *Keywords*, London: Fontana/Croom Helm, 1976, p. 27
20 Quoted in Benedetto Croce, *Aesthetic*, New York: The Noonday Press, 1963, p. 391
21 ibid., pp. 390–391
22 *Politics and Letters: Interviews with New Left Review*, London: New Left Books, 1979, pp. 340–341
23 Bell, op. cit., pp. 21–22
24 ibid., p. 23
25 Hauser, op. cit., p. 113
26 *Sketch for a Self Portrait*, New York: Pantheon, 1949, p. 9
27 ibid., pp. 17–18
28 ibid., p. 18
29 ibid., p. 19
30 ibid., p. 19
31 ibid., pp. 19–20
32 ibid., p. 20
33 ibid., p. 21
34 Quoted in Studio International, October 1971, Vol. 183, No. 937, p. 134
35 *The Florentine Painters of the Renaissance*, London: Putnam, 1898, p. 4
36 ibid., p. 5
37 Fry, op. cit., p. 7
38 ibid., p. 19
39 ibid., pp. 19–20
40 *Playing and Reality*, Harmondsworth: Penguin Books, p. 131
41 *Through Paediatrics to Psycho-Analysis*, London: Hogarth, 1977, p. xxxvii

42 ibid., p. xxvii
43 *Playing and Reality*, p. 108
44 ibid., p. 118
45 *Through Paediatrics*, p. xx
46 *Playing and Reality*, p. 116
47 *The Maturational Processes and the Facilitating Environment*, London: Hogarth Press, 1965, p. 34
48 *Playing and Reality*, p. 121
49 *Through Paediatrics*, p. xx
50 ibid.
51 'Maximum Not Minimum: An Interview with Robert Natkin', by Harold J. McWhinnie, *Per/Se*, Spring 1968, p. 40
52 *Playing and Reality*, p. 131
53 ibid., p. 132
54 R. A. Spitz, *The First Year of Life: A Psychoanalytic Study of Normal and Deviant Development of Object Relations*, New York: I.U.P. 1965
55 'The Psychoanalyst Looks at Contemporary Art' in William Phillips, ed., *Art and Psychoanalysis*, New York: Peter Smith, 1953
56 Milner, op. cit., p. 141
57 *The Idea of the Holy*, Harmondsworth: Penguin Books, 1959, pp. 73–74
58 ibid., p. 21
59 ibid., p. 78
60 ibid., p. 81
61 ibid., p. 85
62 *The Psychoanalysis of Elation*, London: Hogarth, 1951
63 'A Contribution to the Study of the Dream Screen', in *Imagination and Reality*, London: Hogarth, 1968, pp. 1–13
64 Milner, op. cit., pp. 154–155
65 *The Expanding Universe*, Cambridge: Cambridge University Press, 1933, p. 126
66 'The Analyst, Symbolization and Absence in the Analytic Setting (On Changes in Analytic Practice and Analytic Experience)', *International Journal of Psycho-Analysis*, Vol. 56, 1975, pp. 1–22
67 In *New Stories Two*, London: The Arts Council of Great Britain, 1977
68 J.-L. Donnet and André Green, *L'enfant de ca. La Psychose blanche*, Paris: Editions de Minuit, 1973
69 *Mark Rothko*, New York: Guggenheim Museum and Abrams Books, 1978, p. 273
70 Quoted in Lee Seldes, *The Legacy of Mark Rothko*, New York: Dutton, 1973, p. 74
71 'Infantile Anxiety-Situations Reflected in a Work of Art and in

the Creative Impulse', in *Contributions to Psycho-Analysis, 1921–45*, London: Hogarth, 1948, pp. 227–235

72 ibid., p. 235
73 Gerard Manley Hopkins, 'Carrion Comfort', in *Gerard Manley Hopkins*, Harmondsworth: Penguin Books, 1953, p. 61
74 *Attention and Interpretation*, London: Tavistock, 1970, p. 8
75 ibid., p. 10
76 ibid., p. 12
77 ibid., p. 12
78 ibid., p. 20
79 *The Painted Message*, Cambridge, Massachusetts: Schenkmen, 1978, p. 82
80 ibid., p. 83
81 ibid., p. 20
82 For discussions of the revival of American sublime (but not for its banalisation) see Robert Rosenblum, 'The Abstract Sublime', *Art News*, 1959, November 1961: and Lawrence Alloway, 'The American Sublime', *Topics in American Art Since 1945*, New York: Norton, pp. 31–41
83 *The Tiger's Eye*, 15 December, 1948, pp. 51–53
84 op. cit., p. 142
85 ibid., p. 143
86 Marcuse, op. cit., p. ix
87 ibid., p. 9
88 ibid., p. 13
89 ibid., p. 52
90 ibid., p. 17
91 ibid., p. 17
92 Quoted in David McLellan, *Marx Before Marxism*, Harmondsworth: Penguin Books, 1970, p. 63

CREDITS

We gratefully acknowledge the following sources:
Heinemann Educational Books Ltd., 22 Bedford Square, London
W.C.1, for all quotations from Marion Milner, *On Not Being Able to
Paint*, 1950 and the drawing *Two Jugs*. Sigmund Freud Copyrights
Ltd: *Drawings after Michelangelo's Moses*. Ernst Gombrich and
Phaidon Press, Ltd: *The Three Graces seen through rolled glass*.
Marcel Duchamp, *Nude Descending a Staircase* and Paul Cézanne,
Grandes Baigneuses, Philadelphia Museum of Art. Pierre Bonnard,
The Open Window, The Phillips Collection, Washington. John de
Andrea, *Untitled*, Courtesy of the Artist. Clive Barker, *Chained
Venus*, Courtesy of the Artist. Peter Fuller, *Untitled Painting* and
Adam and Eve, Courtesy of the Artist. Mark Rothko, *Portrait of
Rothko's Mother*, Estate of Mark Rothko. Rudolf Baranik, *Napalm
Elegy*, Courtesy of the Artist. Robert Natkin, *Apollo Series*, Courtesy
of the Artist.

BEYOND THE CRISIS IN ART *PETER FULLER*

Has post-modernist art reached an impasse? This is the question underlying this provocative collection of essays and interviews with some of the leading artists of our time. Peter Fuller looks critically at recent art from pop to conceptualism and examines the impact of new visual media on conventional fine art. He reassesses the work of major contemporary figures and conducts probing interviews with Hockney, Carl Andre and Caro.

0 906495 33 4 H/B **£5.95**   0 906495 34 2 P/B **£2.95**

THE NAKED ARTIST   *PETER FULLER*

A pioneering study which draws extensively on recent findings in zoology, paleontology, biology and psychoanalysis to reach new and startling conclusions which throw new light on the origins of art and cultural activity in our species.

The book also contains studies of Hopper, Landseer, Poussin, Spender, Wyeth, Hamilton and the war photographer Donald McCullin.

0 863160 45 X H/B **£8.95**   0 863160 46 8 P/B **£4.95**

AESTHETICS AFTER MODERNISM
PETER FULLER

In this important new lecture, Fuller argues that a change of sensibility is sweeping through the Western world. He traces the origins of the present cultural crisis back into the decay of religious belief and the change in the nature of work that took place with the Industrial Revolution. Fuller claims that we may now be facing an imminent General Anaesthesia – which may engulf us all.

0 896160 44 1 P/B **£1.50**

PERMANENT RED — *JOHN BERGER*

This first collection of John Berger's writings on art is both an historical and personal document. The young Berger here discusses such subjects as twentieth century masters, the difficulty of being an artist today and the lessons learned from the past.

0 906495 07 5 H/B **£4.95**   0 904613 92 5 P/B **£2.50**

SUCCESS AND FAILURE OF PICASSO
JOHN BERGER

Picasso died the wealthiest and most famous artist of our century. His prodigious talent, the enigmatic nature of his unceasing artistic vitality, made him into a legendary figure in his own lifetime. In this brilliant critical reassessment, John Berger traces Picasso's life and work from his childhood in Spain to his last drawings, and not only penetrates the aura around Picasso, but illuminates the position of art in our society.

0 906495 10 5 H/B **£7.95**   0 904613 77 1 P/B **£2.95**

A PAINTER OF OUR TIME — *JOHN BERGER*

What is the artist's place in Western Society?
What relationship can there be between his art and politics?
Such are the problems which Berger explores in this illuminating and provocative first novel.

0 904613 12 7 H/B **£4.95**   0 904613 13 5 P/B **£2.95**

ABOUT LOOKING   *JOHN BERGER*

This collection of essays and articles, written over the last ten years, is a fascinating record of a search for meaning within and behind what is looked at.

Why do zoos disappoint children?

When an animal looks us in the eyes, what does that look mean today?

Why do we take snaps of those we love?

How do the media use photographs of far-away events?

These are some of the questions which John Berger suggests answers to in this new book, which follows the widely-acclaimed *Ways of Seeing*.

He describes how a masterpiece he saw in the late 1960s looked quite different a decade later. He discusses how a forest looks to a woodcutter; how fields look to a peasant; how the world looked to a 19th century barber's son. Each painting he considers, whether it be by Grünewald, Millet, Courbet, Magritte or Francis Bacon, is evidence for him of an experience which belongs as much to life as to art.

This is a book for those who wish to look.

0 906495 25 3 H/B **£5.95**   0 906495 30 X P/B **£3.95**